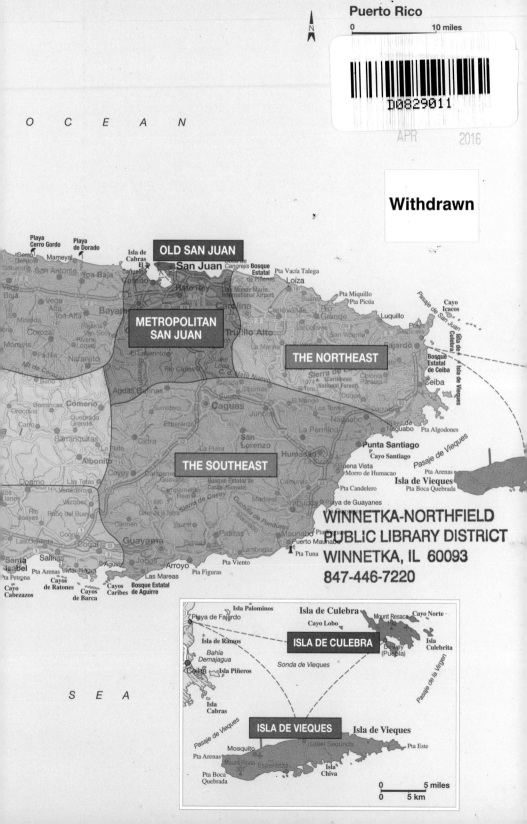

Puerto Rico

0   10 miles

N

O C E A N

Playa
Cerro Gordo
Playa
de Dorado
Mameyal
Cerro
Gordo
Sabana
San Antonio
Toa Baja
Vega
Baja
Vega
Alta
Toa Alta
Miranda
Corozal
Morovis
Padilla
Naranjito
Mt de Corozal
Beno
Orocovis
Barrancas
Comerío
Quebrada
Grande
Carro
Barranquitas
La Plata
Cidra
Aibonito
Coamo
Las Tetas
Vázquez
Río
Jueyes
Rabo del Buey
Las Ochenta
Cayo
Santa
Isabel
Salinas
Pta Petrona
Pta Arenas
Mar Negro
Cayos
de Ratones
Cayos
de Barca
Cayos
Caribes
Bosque Estatal
de Aguirre
Cayo
Cabezazos

Isla de
Cabras
El
Cañuelo
Cataño
OLD SAN JUAN
San Juan
Boca de
Cangrejos
Bosque
Estatal
de Piñones
Pta Vacía Talega
Loíza
Hato Rey
Luis Muñoz Marín
International Airport
Carolina
Canóvanas
Pta Miquillo
Pta Picúa
Suárez
Río
Grande
Luquillo
Pasaje de San Juan
Cayo
Icacos
Pta Y
Saldinera
Bayamón
**METROPOLITAN
SAN JUAN**
Trujillo Alto
La Dolores
San Vicente
La Marina
Fajardo
Bosque
Estatal
de Ceiba
Pajaros
Van Scoy
Rivers
Lomas
El Laberinto
Río Cañas
Lake
Loíza
C. d. Hato Nuevo
THE NORTHEAST
Sierra de
(Caribbean
National Forest)
1074
El Toro
Colonia
Paraíso
Ceiba
Aguas Buenas
Sumidero
Celada
Lomas
Guaraba
El Mango
Los Torres
Duque
Naguabo
Playa de
Naguabo
Pta Algodones
Comerío
Esperanza
Caguas
Juncos
San
Lorenzo
La Permina
Punta Santiago
Cayo Santiago
Pasaje de Vieques
Humacao
La Suiza
Buena Vista
Morro de Humacao
Pta Arenas
Isla de Vieques
Pta Boca Quebrada
THE SOUTHEAST
Cayey
Campanero
Guavate
Comunas
Pta Candelero
Playa de Guayanes
Campamento
Real
Bosque Estatal de
Carite (Guavate)
Sierra de Cayey
Cerro de la Tabla
Madroal
Yabucoa
Guayamilla
Cuchilla de Panduras
Vázquez
890
Carmen
Yaguel
Cayo Lobo
Maunabo
Patillas
Lambogla
Pta Tuna
Maunabo
Puerto Maunabo
Pta Seguras
Guayama
Cogot
Pulmar
Pta Viento
Jobos
Arroyo
Pta Figuras
Aguint
Las Mareas

S E A

Isla de Culebra

Isla Palominos
Playa de Fajardo
ISLA DE CULEBRA
Mount Resaca
189
Cayo Norte
Cayo Lobo
Isla de Ramos
Bahía
Demajagua
Ceiba
Isla Piñeros
Sonda de Vieques
Dewey
(Pueblo)
Isla
Culebrita
Pasaje de la Virgen
Isla
Cabras
ISLA DE VIEQUES
Mosquito
Isabel Segunda
Isla de Vieques
Pta Este
Pta Arenas
Mount Pirata
Esperanza
Isla
Chiva
Pta Boca
Quebrada

0   5 miles
0   5 km

INSIGHT GUIDES
PUERTO RICO

Contents

THE BEST OF PUERTO RICO: TOP ATTRACTIONS

From Indian heritage sites to colonial gems, and sandy beaches to extraordinary ecological sites, here is a rundown of Puerto Rico's most spectacular attractions.

△ **Old San Juan**. On a spit of land jutting out into the sea is this beautifully preserved Spanish colonial city, colorfully decorated in pastel shades with cobbled streets, enticing bars and restaurants, quirky shops and atmospheric hotels. It is guarded by fortresses built to protect this jewel in the Spanish Empire. See page 103.

▽ **Museo de Arte de Puerto Rico, San Juan**. This converted hospital in Santurce houses works by well-known Puerto Rican artists dating back to the 17th century, as well as regional and international works. See page 128.

△ **Río Camuy Cave Park.** One of the most dramatic subterranean cave systems yet discovered lies in this park. Trains take passengers between caves and sinkholes that have taken the Camuy River millions of years to erode. See page 171.

△ **El Yunque.** More than 100 billion gallons of rain falls here every year, making it the perfect habitat for 26 endemic animal species. See page 142.

△ **Playa Flamenco, Culebra**. This is a perfect, uncrowded, half-moon beach of white sand and translucent turquoise water, totally unspoilt by tourism after decades of occupation by the US Navy. See page 235.

△ **The Carnival at Ponce**. Carnival usually falls in February, is a riotous affair, with lots of dressing up, dancing, and (of course) rum. See page 204.

▽ **Phosphorescent Bay, Vieques**. Known for its glowing waters, the high concentration of bioluminescence is generated by microscopic organisms in the water. Take a boat trip out into the bay to agitate the trillions of dinoflagellates, and watch them light up. See page 232.

△ **Las Cabezas de San Juan**. On the far northeastern tip of the island, this nature reserve comprises an incredible diversity of landscapes, with beaches, lagoons, mangrove forest, and coral reefs among them. See page 146

△ **Arecibo Observatory**. Sitting in the heart of the karst country, a region of archetypal limestone erosion, Arecibo has the largest single-dish radio telescope in the world. It has been silently scanning the universe, making maps of distant solar systems, and listening for messages from other planets since 1960. See page 175.

▷ **Tibes Indian Ceremonial Park**. One of the Caribbean's most important Amerindian archeological sites. Visit the museum to find out more about the Amerindian peoples. See page 205.

THE BEST OF PUERTO RICO: EDITOR'S CHOICE

Dazzling beaches fringed by coral reef, steamy rainforests harboring unique flora and fauna, and elegant architecture are all waiting to be experienced in Puerto Rico. Here, at a glance, are the editor's top tips for making the most of your visit.

BEST FESTIVALS

Carnival in Ponce. A colorful, exuberant and noisy fiesta, with *vejigantes*, parades, music, food and drink, and fun for all the family. See page 204.
Loíza's Saint James festival. This blends African and Christian traditions, with masqueraders, ghouls, and terrifying *vejigantes*, wearing masks made of coconuts or gourds. See page 141.
Fiesta de San Sebastián. In Old San Juan, St Sebastian is a four-day street party with a carnival atmosphere attracting thousands of revelers. See page 113.
Aibonito Flower Festival. Growers and artisans come together in June to compete, display, and sell plants and crafts in a riot of color. See page 220.
Día de las Máscaras, Hatillo. A boisterous December festival when men dress up with colorful masks enacting the murder of boys by King Herod. See page 174.

The Río Abajo Forest Reserve plays host to the endangered wild parrots of Puerto Rico.

A group of vejigantes parading in Ponce.

FOREST AND NATURE RESERVES

Río Abajo Forest Reserve. In the karst country is subtropical wet forest with limestone caves, streams, and the endangered Puerto Rican parrot. See page 168.
The peaks of El Yunque National Forest. Looming above mangroves, beaches and lagoons, this is a playground for hiking, cycling, swimming, and kayaking. See page 142.
Guánica. The best example of a subtropical dry forest in the Caribbean, with some 700 plant species and half the island's birds. See page 208.
Boquerón Nature Reserve. A fabulous mangrove forest and noted bird refuge, with migratory nesting waterfowl as well as resident species. See page 187.
Jobos Bay Estuarine Reserve. This reserve protects mangrove forest, cays, and salt flats, and is home to large numbers of fish and rare birds. See page 210.

Exploring Puerto Rico's amazing underwater world.

ADVENTURE SPORTS

Caving. Keen spelunkers will find the karst country in the northwest riddled with limestone sinkholes, caves, and underground rivers to explore. See page 170.

Mountain biking. Get muddy in the forest, try the steep hills of Domes, Rincón, or ride to the beach in Guánica State Forest. See pages 183 and 208.

Ziplining. Whiz through the canopy of El Yunque forest or fly a mile across a valley at Toro Verde in the Cordillera Central. See pages 142 and 223.

Canyoning/Rappeling. Cañon San Cristóbal is a prime site for river adventures, with tiered waterfalls, sheer rock faces and boulders galore. See page 223.

Hiking. State forests have well-maintained trails for a gentle walk in the park or a hike up a mountain for a 360-degree view. See Forest and Nature Reserves.

WATERSPORTS

Diving. If you can't get out to Desecheo or Mona Island (the Puerto Rican Galapagos), The Wall off the south coast is more accessible. See pages 236 and 237.

Kayaking. Paddle along a channel through the mangroves to reach Laguna Grande, Fajardo – fantastic at night for its bioluminescence. See page 146.

Surfing Rincón. On the west coast is the Caribbean's stellar surf strip, where you find huge waves, particularly in the winter months. See page 182.

Kiteboarding. The cays off La Parguera offer the best flat water kiting on the island, with consistent wind December to August. See page 149.

Sailing. A variety of craft can be rented from the marinas at Fajardo for picturesque boating around the cays or trips to Vieques and Culebra. See pages 145, 229, and 233.

Kayaking is a wonderful way to explore the island.

BEST BEACHES

Playa Luquillo, east of San Juan. This is a popular beach with families and a safe spot for swimming. Kiosks sell fried snack food, busy at weekends. See page 145.

Playa Resaca, Culebra. A challenging hike through forest is rewarded with an arc of empty white sand, just what leatherback turtles like. See page 236.

Sun Bay, Vieques. A crescent of white sand backed by palm trees, sea grape, almond, and *quenepa*. An easily accessible paradise. See page 232.

Playa Boquerón. One of the loveliest beaches in the country, with a wide, curving bay backed by a palm grove and calm waters. See page 187.

Isla Verde. Only a minute from all the main resort hotels in San Juan, this white sand beach is one of the most popular on the island. See page 128.

The ever-popular Luquillo Beach.

Dance rehearsal at the Escuela de Bomba y Plena Doña Caridad Brenes de Cepeda, San Juan.

Café Lanassa, Vieques.

Carnival dancer in Ponce.

A HEADY MIX

Multi-faceted history, colorful culture, breathtaking scenery, and distinctive rhythms make Puerto Rico a truly "rich port."

Cheerful schoolgirls.

The pulse of Puerto Rico beats to a Latin rhythm, quickened by African drumming. Music is the life-blood of the people, whether it is the folk music of the countryside, sexy salsa or the latest urban trend from New York, brought back by Nuyoricans – Puerto Ricans who have migrated to the Big Apple for work.

This is a modern country, heavily industrialized and American-influenced in parts, yet with a strong sense of its Spanish colonial history and Amerindian heritage linked to an agricultural way of life. Boys ride horses bareback while their parents drive the latest SUVs; families celebrate special days with a feast of traditional food, yet burgers and pizza are equally popular for a treat.

Columbus christened the island *San Juan Bautista* (St John the Baptist) in 1493 but Juan Ponce de León switched its name with that of the capital, Puerto Rico (Rich Port). The original settlers – the Taínos – knew it as **Borikén**, the great land of the valiant and noble Lord. Once Spain's most important military outpost in the Caribbean, it has blossomed into a highly suc-cessful vacation destination.

Beach near Luquillo.

Located in the northeastern Caribbean, east of the Dominican Republic and west of the Virgin Islands, Puerto Rico is the smallest of the four Greater Antilles (Cuba, Hispaniola, Jamaica, and Puerto Rico): 100 miles (160km) long and 35 miles (56km) from north to south. It is blessed with glorious beaches, spectacular mountain ranges, the greenest of green rainforest and dry, tropical forest, giving it a range of climates, natural attractions, and outdoor activities.

The past is always present: in Taíno carvings, colonial architecture, first-class cuisine, and even in farming techniques. Yet the island has kept pace with the rest of the world – as its various designer stores, museums and art galleries, symphony halls, communications technol-ogy, and championship golf courses all attest. Puerto Rico is enigmatic: the modern and familiar mix naturally with the historic and exotic, whether you are choked by traffic fumes in the metropolis, singed by the sun's rays on the beaches or cleansed by the rain and fresh air of the mountainous rainforest.

Mother and daughter, Hatillo.

THE PEOPLE OF PUERTO RICO

Many centuries of immigration and a wide
range of ethnic types have merged into a
proud and dynamic Hispanic culture.

Puerto Rico is a vibrant, modern, bilingual, multiracial, and multicultural society, with a keen sense of its history. Once Spain's most important military outpost in the Caribbean, it has blossomed into a highly successful vacation destination.

Since the first inhabitants arrived thousands of years ago, this beautiful island has been home to Indigenous people, Spaniards, Africans, and more. There are the traces of Taíno blood left in the fine, high cheekbones of many, while evidence of the island's slave-trading days is impossible to ignore. There are women with skin the color of *café con leche*, who have tightly curled hair that is naturally auburn, and children with liquid-blue eyes and blond hair whose faces are exotically beautiful, thanks to any number of forebears – including traders, pirates, artisans, slaves, and colonists.

A typical smiling Puerto Rican welcome.

Data from a University of Puerto Rico study for 2005–09 reveals that 95 percent of Puerto Ricans speak a language other than English at home (Spanish) and 85 percent admit to not speaking English very well.

Over four centuries the Spanish laid the foundations of the island's culture. They constructed towns, roads, fortresses, and churches. Although the Taíno population was once thought to have been all but wiped out within a few years of Spanish colonization, 61 percent of the population carry Taíno DNA. Poor Spanish farmers married Taíno women and although few of these, known as *jíbaros*, remain today, their cultural imprint survives. Others hid out in the Cordillera Central, forming alliances with groups of runaway slaves. Farming methods, tools, food, and vocabulary survive from the Taínos.

African slaves were brought in to work the plantations, and they in turn contributed to the island's language, customs, music, and culinary traditions. Later, other Caribbean islanders arrived seeking jobs. Spanish loyalists sought refuge here, fleeing Simón Bolívar's independence movement in South America. In the late 18th and early 19th centuries many French settlers migrated to Puerto Rico, leaving behind upheavals in Louisiana and Haiti. Even farmers from Scotland and Ireland ended up on the island, hoping to benefit from its rich sugar cane economy. Chinese workers came to build roads; they were followed by Italians, Germans, and Lebanese. After 1898, US expatriates sought the island as a home and more recently Cubans, Dominicans, and Argentinians have settled here.

Hispanic America

After the struggles for independence, and power tussles with the Dutch and English, Puerto Rico eventually arrived at a strangely fruitful relationship with the United States and is essentially a crossroads of Hispanic and Anglo cultures. The island has been a part of the United States since 1898, and Puerto Ricans have been US citizens since 1917.

Many US corporations have bases on the island, and millions of Puerto Ricans spend their working lives on the mainland. Nevertheless, the island likes to keep its distance: in repeated referenda (plebiscites) Puerto Ricans have voted against becoming America's 51st state. They are happy to adopt the parts of a first-world, American lifestyle that suit them: living in gated communities, driving SUVs, sending their children to US schools, at the same time as preserving their Hispanic, Taíno

Puerto Rico is a multiracial country.

SANTERÍA

Puerto Rico is mainly Roman Catholic, with some Taíno and African traditions blended in. *Santería* and its Puerto Rican variant, *espiritismo*, descend from religious practices brought over by West African slaves during colonial times. Although many aspects of the source religion are preserved in *Santería*, it has developed into its own unique tradition heavily influenced by Catholicism. In this practice, *santeros* conflated the traditional gods, the Orishas, with the Catholic saints. Some Puerto Ricans believe that *jípia*, or spirits of the dead, sleep by day and roam the island at night, searching for wild fruit to eat.

or African customs which are more rural and Catholic in outlook.

Although English is spoken, Spanish is predominant – but it, too, is a mix. There is a heavy influence from the Spanish spoken in the Canary Islands, with words borrowed from the pre-Columbian Amerindian tongue and modern-day English. Both Spanish and English have official status. Despite a couple of years in the early 1990s when English was abolished as an official language for political reasons, it was soon restored. However, regardless of the law, fewer than a quarter of Puerto Ricans are completely bilingual; outside the big cities you will find it useful to know at least a few basic Spanish words and phrases to help you get around.

Even the island's weights and measures are split between the US and Hispanic methods. Confusingly, the island adheres half-heartedly to the metric system, which means that all distances are posted in kilometers, and gasoline is sold by the liter. Nevertheless, temperatures are still given in Fahrenheit, and speed-limit signs are still in miles per hour.

Pleasure and leisure

Puerto Rican people are a friendly and passionate lot, vivacious and expressive in their conversations – and their dancing. Even the youngest

shacks, but offer cold beer, snacks or a full meal, often with music on weekend evenings. Many have been run by the same family for decades.

In the United States, Christmas lasts perhaps a week; on the island the celebrations begin in late November and don't completely stop until mid-January. In addition to Christmas Day, Puerto Ricans celebrate Three Kings Day, or Epiphany, on January 6. Local children cut grass (to feed the Wise Men's camels), put it in boxes and place these under their beds on January 5, just before they go to sleep. The next morning, the grass is gone and gifts have been left mys-

A typical Friday night in Plaza Mercado, Old San Juan.

children have salsa in their blood and it is no accident that the world's best Latin singers, musicians and dancers have their roots in the island. Music and food are two elements which the people use to help them celebrate life to the fullest.

In Puerto Rico, work is seen not as an end in itself, but merely as a means to fund subsequent enjoyment. Weekends are taken very seriously, while fiestas and saints' days are also widely observed and celebrated. Eating local food, *comida criolla*, is a social occasion and Puerto Ricans especially like trawling roadside snack bars – kioscos – at weekends. Luquillo is famous for a string of some 60 kioskos along the beach road. These are often no more than

teriously in its place – much to the innocent delight of the youngsters throughout the island.

During this extended holiday period, it's presumed by residents that there will be company, people coming from far away to visit or just neighbors stopping by from roughly December 15 (also the official start of the Puerto Rican tourist season, which ends on April 15 of the following year) until the last *pasteles* are eaten and the last glasses of *coquito* (a delicious mixture of milk, rum, vanilla, cream of coconut and cinnamon) consumed.

Nuyoricans

Puerto Rico is one of the world's most densely populated countries. High birth rates and medical advances caused the death rate to plummet shortly after the Spanish-American War. Puerto Rico's population jumped to about a million by 1900, and 3.8 million by 2000, although according to a 2014 estimate it has fallen to 3.54 million. This gives a population density of nearly 1,080 per sq mile (418 per sq km), which is among the world's highest. Part of the reason for the decline in the population is a falling birth rate which, together with an aging population, is expected to see the demographic trend continue. Emigration is also a contributing factor and waves of migrations since World War II mean that there are now more people (4.9 million in 2012) in US cities such as Chicago, Miami, Los Angeles, Philadelphia and east coast cities, particularly New York, than there are on the island. The number of Puerto Ricans living in New York is believed to be twice the number living in metropolitan San Juan (395,000 in 2010). Puerto Ricans who have migrated to the mainland have usually moved there for economic reasons, taking advantage of their US citizenship to improve their employment prospects. They, and their descendants, are known as Stateside Puerto Ricans or Nuyoricans, and form the second largest Hispanic group in the US after the Mexicans. Community spirit and identity is strong among the diaspora, culminating in the annual Puerto Rican Day Parade in New York City as well as in many other cities. Even second generation Stateside Puerto Ricans have strong ties to the island, where they still have family. They send home remittances to their relatives and are important contributors to tourism revenues when they return home for visits. However, the disparity in income is not as great as in other Latino communities in the US and it is not unknown for Puerto Ricans living there to be supported by remittances from their families on the island.

Patriotism

Despite all varieties of political difference, pride is universal and strong. Though US flags fly alongside all Puerto Rican flags in public places (by law), and schoolchildren sing *The Star Spangled Banner* before *La Borinqueña*, the island's own beautiful anthem, being Puerto Rican always comes first. This isn't without its paradoxical side. The people who've chosen to live here,

> Although officially adopted in 1952, Puerto Rico's flag was first used in 1895; its "lone star" was the "guide of the patriots."

Puerto Ricans and Continentals alike, love the island intensely yet know that things are far from perfect – which is where patience and common sense come into play. *Así es la vida*. That's life.

Along with the islanders' resilient humor, there is also an ongoing sense of rebellious resentment in the face of authority, especially

Nuyorican showing his colors at the Puerto Rican Day Parade in New York City.

towards the US Navy. This became acute in 1970, when Culebrans were kept off Flamenco Beach – as they had been for decades – during practice bombing runs. "Enough," said 2,000 people all at once. The red flag went up to keep people off the beach; the majority of the population headed straight for it, loaded with picnic coolers. They were going to picnic until the US Navy stopped its target runs so close to their beach. Three years later, the Navy finally agreed to leave Flamenco Beach alone.

In 1999, the controversy of the naval presence in Vieques blew up as David Sanes, a civilian worker for the Navy, was accidentally killed by naval ordnance. Protesters stormed the island, including independence advocate Rubén Berríos, along with a group of his cohorts, who camped out on the island for almost a year. It seems that the protests succeeded. The Navy finally left the island in May 2003.

Poetry, poverty, and politics

Puerto Rico is a place where politics and poetry often merge; a place where its most celebrated leaders, among them Luis Llorens Torres and Luis Muñoz Marín, were also poets.

The island's residents cherish the things that have no price tags: family, friends, and the pleasure, challenging as it can be, of living here. There is poverty, certainly, a chronic ache to those who love their island, but art flourishes here too, with the craftworkers, musicians, painters, and sculptors. It gives Puerto Rico's beauty a face which is proud yet edged in sadness, exotic yet utterly recognizable.

The country's national anthem, *La Borinqueña*, which, unlike other nations' songs that speak of military might and triumph over adversaries, sums up the flavor. It celebrates a reality which is at the same time an ideal, *"a flowering garden of exquisite magic. A sky, always clear…"*

Playing Ball on Luquillo Beach.

PUERTO RICAN CELEBRITIES

For a small island, Puerto Rico has produced an astonishing number of celebrities in the world of entertainment.

One of the first to achieve international acclaim was **José Ferrer**, the first Puerto Rican to win an Oscar, for his performance in *Cyrano de Bergerac* in 1950. Singer, dancer and actress **Rita Moreno** shot to fame in 1961 in the film of *West Side Story*, for which she won the Best Supporting Actress Academy Award. She is the only Hispanic and only woman to have won an Emmy, a Grammy, an Oscar, and a Tony award. **Jennifer López** was born in New York to Puerto Rican parents. She is the highest-paid Latin actress in Hollywood. **Marc Anthony**, to whom López was married 2004–11, was also born in New York to Puerto Rican parents. He is the top selling salsa artist of all time, having sold over 30 million albums and won two Grammies and three Latin Grammies. The award-winning singer **Ricky Martin** was born in Puerto Rico where he was a member of the Latin boy band *Menudo*, but later moved to the US. However, in 2011 he became a Spanish citizen. The Puerto Rican actor and film producer, **Benicio del Toro**, also took Spanish citizenship in 2011, both men having ancestors from Spain.

Mural honoring the Muñoz Rivera
political dynasty inside the
Mausoleo Familia Muñoz Rivera,
Barranquitas.

DECISIVE DATES

Ancient times

5100 BC
The earliest known settlement on Puerto Rico of pre-ceramic (Archaic), hunter-gather people known as Ortoiroid.

AD 0–600
Saladoid people arrive from the Orinoco delta bringing horticulture (cassava, yucca, maize) and pottery.

600–800
The more sophisticated Ostionoid people bring more elaborate ceramics and built ceremonial centers and ball courts.

800–1500
Phases of Ostionoid people from Elenoid to Chicoid are the civilization the Spanish encountered and named Taínos.

Age of explorers

1493
Columbus lands and claims the island for Spain.

1508
Juan Ponce de León establishes settlement at Caparra.

1510
King of Spain appoints Ponce de León governor of San Juan Bautista, as Puerto Rico is then known.

1516
Entrepreneurs construct the island's first sugar factory.

1520s
The island is officially called Puerto Rico.

1521
Caparra settlement is officially named San Juan Bautista de Puerto Rico.

1531
Puerto Rico sends its first sugar exports to Spain.

1532
The army begins building La Fortaleza.

1539
The Spaniards begin building El Morro fortress.

1598
Ginger replaces sugar as main cash crop; influenza epidemic wipes out most of the able-bodied population of San Juan.

1625
The Dutch lay siege to San Juan, but soon retreat.

1797
British forces try to take San Juan; they retreat only a few weeks later.

1812
Spain grants conditional citizenship to island residents.

1813–18
Trade grows to eight times its previous level.

1887
Luis Muñoz Rivera becomes one of the founders of the Autonomist Party.

1897
Spain declares Puerto Rico an autonomous territory.

Juan Ponce de León.

Enter the US

1898
Spanish-American War; US troops bring the island under American jurisdiction.

1899
Hurricane San Ciriaco devastates the island's sugar and coffee industries.

1910
Muñoz Rivera elected Resident Commissioner to US House of Representatives.

1917
Jones Act extends US citizenship to Puerto Ricans.

1922
Nationalist Party is founded.

1936
Two Nationalist gunmen kill San Juan's police chief.

1937
Nationalist protesters killed in "Ponce Massacre".

1938
Luis Muñoz Marín, son of Luis Muñoz Rivera, forms Popular Democratic Party.

1942
Puerto Rico Industrial Development Company established.

Post-World War II

1946
Jesús Piñero is the first native governor in the island's history.

1948
Muñoz Marín takes office as first freely elected governor.

1950
Nationalists try to kill President Truman in Washington, and stir up revolt at home.

1952
Puerto Rico made a US Commonwealth (July 25).

Modern times

1964
Muñoz Marín resigns from political office.

1978
Police kill two young *independentistas*, sparking the Cerro Maravilla scandal.

1991
Hernández Colón abolishes English as one of Puerto Rico's two official languages.

1992
Governor Pedro Rosselló restores English as an official language.

1993
Voters elect to retain commonwealth status.

1998
Hurricane Georges wreaks havoc on the island. Voters reject statehood after a third national plebiscite.

1999
A civilian is killed on Vieques during bombing practice by the US Navy.

2000
Sila María Calderón, of the anti-statehood PDP, elected as first female governor.

2003
US Navy pulls out of Vieques after more than six decades of military exercises.

2004
A re-count of votes gives electoral victory to the PDP, led by Aníbal Acevedo Velá.

Alejandro García Padilla's inaugural address.

2006
Budget crisis and fiscal reform.

2007
Archeologists working on a dam project outside Ponce find important pre-Columbian Taíno site containing unprecedented petroglyphs, as well as hundreds of graves.

2009
The UN Special Committee on Decolonization passes a draft resolution calling on the US government to allow the Puerto Rican people to exercise their right to self-determination and independence.

2010
The US House of Representatives votes in favour of another referendum on Puerto Rico's status.

2012
In November, a slim majority of Puerto Ricans vote to change their ties with the US and become the 51st US state in a non-binding referendum.

2013
Alejandro García Padilla (PPD) is elected governor of the island.

2014
$2.5 million is set aside in the US spending bill for Puerto Rico to hold another referendum to determine its "future political status."

2014
President Barack Obama decorates the 65th Infantry Regiment, a Puerto Rican Regiment of the US Army, with a Congressional Gold Medal for its heroism during the Korean War.

BEGINNINGS

By the time the Spanish came, the indigenous peoples had created a sophisticated culture with ingenious farming techniques adapted to the terrain, and fine handicrafts.

The first people identified as living on Puerto Rico were a pre-ceramic, hunter-gatherer group named by archeologists as Ortoiroid. They depended heavily on shellfish and have left significant shell middens. The earliest evidence of these Archaic people dates from around 7,000 years ago, at Angostura, while further signs of human presence have been found at Hato Viejo dating from 5,200 years ago. It has been generally assumed that these early people inhabiting the Greater Antilles migrated from the Orinoco basin region of South America via Trinidad, but this has not been proved definitively.

> Archeologist Dr Ricardo Alegría (1921–2011) was responsible for the restoration of Old San Juan, Caparra, and Fort Jerónimo. He also excavated a large limestone cave near Loíza, known as Cueva María de la Cruz. Artefacts found were carbon dated to a pre-ceramic culture of the 1st century AD.

After the Ortoiroid came the Saladoid, 2,000 to 1,400 years ago, who brought pottery and horticulture so that they grew their own maize, yucca and cassava. Some 1,400 to 1,200 years ago came the Ostionoid, who were more sophisticated and constructed ceremonial centers, ball courts and made more elaborate ceramics. Later phases of the Ostionoid were named Elenoid (1,200–850 years ago) and Chicoid (850–500 years ago), and it was these people that Columbus encountered, calling them Taínos.

The Taíno were by then the dominant culture in the region and lived on the large islands of

Taíno drawings in the Cueva del Indio.

the Greater Antilles: Cuba, Hispaniola (Haiti and the Dominican Republic), Jamaica, Puerto Rico, and also the Bahamas. Their ancestors had migrated from South America and there was still trade, communication and war between different groups, all of whom were adept at making dugout canoes from huge trees. Their lands were under threat from invading Caribs, part of a new wave of migration and expansion, so their seafaring skills were important.

In his journal, Columbus describes a Taíno canoe which seated three men abreast and 70 to 80 in all. "A barge could not keep up with them in rowing," he wrote, "because they go with incredible speed, and with these canoes they navigate among these islands."

A stratified society

The Taínos in Puerto Rico lived in a rigidly stratified society under the control of the cacique (chief), Agüeybaná, at the time of Columbus's arrival. Up to 60,000 people lived on the island, which they called *Borikén* – "Island of the Brave Lord." They lived in villages called *yucayeques* of some 100 to 1,000 people under the control of a district *cacique*. Caciques could be men or women and were advised by shaman priests called *bohiques*. Beneath them were nobles (*nitaínos*) and commoners (*naborías*).

The Taínos spent the great majority of their time out of doors, yet they built large bell-shaped thatched houses in which as many as 40 family members slept. These were built around a large open space reserved for public ceremonies and for *batey*, which the Spanish referred to as *pelota* – a ball game. The house of the *cacique* was the largest in town and always fronted on this public square. At Tibes, in Ponce, an Indian village has been reconstructed from ancient ruins.

The Taínos believed in a polytheistic order of creation. Yocahú, the Supreme Creator,

Traditional Taíno dwelling.

Taíno carving.

PUERTO RICAN IDENTITY

The concept of Puerto Rican identity has been defined and redefined time and time again. Who is Puerto Rican? What is a Puerto Rican? Where do *boricuas* come from? Since 1998, professor of genetics Juan Carlos Martínez Cruzado and his team from the University of Puerto Rico in Mayagüez have conducted DNA studies on Puerto Ricans in search of their Indian heritage.Using a strand of hair and its root, they zero in on mitochondrial DNA, passed down intact from generation to generation. Initially, the study began in Maricao's Indieras area, where many people have specific Taíno-like traits, but further studies revealed that the Indian heritage is more prevalent in other areas than had been expected.

In 2008, after taking random samples from people across the island and from all walks of life, Cruzado's team found that 61 percent of the population, had, in effect, Taíno DNA. That suggests that Puerto Rico's Taínos may have survived much longer than previously thought, either holed up in the Cordillera Central hiding out with runaway slaves, or the women living with Spanish men as wives. The inhospitality of the mountains and the forest are probably what saved the bloodlines, as the Spanish rulers were reluctant to leave the relative comfort of the coast. However, it is said that the hospitality of the people of the cordillera now is due to the friendly nature of the Taínos who hid out there.

commanded all the gods, the earth and its myriad creatures. The angry god of the winds, Juracán, invoked the eponymous hurricanes. In the central square, the Indians observed religious worship and participated in ceremonial tribal dances.

Ceramic icons and clay idols displayed in anthropological museums are evidence of the religious past. South of Arecibo, at the 13-acre (5-hectare) Caguana Indian Ceremonial Park, used for religious purposes eight centuries ago, there are stone monoliths, 10 *batey* ball courts, and other artifacts.

Using *macanas* – stout double broadswords still used by Puerto Rican farmers – and pointed sticks, the Taínos cleared the thick woods and sowed their fields. Various sources of animal protein supplemented the starchy diet: fish and sometimes pigeon or parrot.

Handicrafts

In the time left over from farming, fishing, and hunting, the Taínos developed various handicrafts. Early Spanish settlers in the region greatly admired the Indian

This clearing in Caguana Taíno Ceremonial Park was used by the Taínos as a ball court.

Taíno agriculture

Traces of Taíno agriculture remain in Puerto Rico. Their ingenious method of sowing a variety of plants in earthen mounds called *conducos* is still employed by some farmers. The *conduco* system mitigated the problems of water distribution: water-intensive crops were placed at the bottom of the mounds and those requiring good drainage at the top.

Cassava bread, the staple of the Taíno diet, was made by grating and draining the root, which was then formed into loaves and baked. They also relied heavily upon yams, and among the plants the early settlers sent back to Spain were maize, beans, squash, and peanuts.

woodwork, in particular the dishes, basins, bowls, and boxes. Most prized of all were the ornate *duhos*, carved wooden thrones used by the *caciques*. Indian weavers used cotton and other fibrous plants to make colorfully dyed clothing, belts, and hammocks. But the handicraft that aroused greatest excitement among the Spanish was the gold jewelry that the Indians wore as rings in their ears and noses. They neither mined nor panned for gold and did not value it especially. When the Spaniards, smitten with desire for the precious metal, coaxed the natives into leading them to their sources, they were taken to beaches where gold nuggets from the ocean floor occasionally washed ashore.

Ponce de León, Puerto Rico's first governor.

THE SPANISH SETTLERS

At first the Spanish treated the Taíno population well, but soon the natives were enslaved as their invaders lusted for gold. Then came the trade wars.

Fifteen years passed between Columbus's discovery of the island of Borikén on November 19, 1493, and serious attempts to settle it. He came across the island by chance during his second voyage while he was trying to reach Hispaniola. Naming it San Juan Bautista, Columbus claimed it for the Spanish Crown and promptly departed. From 1493 until 1508, the Taínos living on the island enjoyed a period of benevolent neglect: from time to time, Spaniards sailed to San Juan from Hispaniola seeking to barter with locals for food. These encounters were always friendly.

Enticing gold

One Spaniard who visited the island was Juan Ponce de León. The natives' ornaments and gold trinkets caught Ponce de León's eye. He felt sure that the area was rich in gold, and he secretly scouted the southern coast for mining sites. In the early summer of 1508 Ponce de León and the Spanish governor of the Caribbean, Nicolás de Ovando, signed a clandestine agreement which granted Ponce de León rights to mine the island on condition that he would yield two-thirds to the king. Secrecy was of the utmost importance: Christopher Columbus's son, Diego Colón, had inherited the rights to exploit the island, but his family's desire for wealth had proved dangerous in the past. Physical abuse, dissolution of tribes, and starvation of the inhabitants of Hispaniola had been followed by rebellion and bloodshed.

In July 1508, Ponce de León and a band of 50 men – among them Luis de Añasco, the namesake of the river and village – set off for the island of San Juan Bautista. As they sailed

Christopher Columbus and his sons Diego and Ferdinand.

eastward along the northern coast, they made friendly contact with the Taíno, and Agüey-baná, the head *cacique* of the island, provided Ponce de León with an entry which ensured safe passage for him and his crew. Finally, after six long weeks of searching, the intrepid explorers found a suitable site for settlement. In a valley several miles inland on an arm of the Bayamón River, Ponce de León founded the island's first European town, *Caparra*. In official documents, it was referred to as *Ciudad de Puerto Rico*.

Relations between the Taínos and the Europeans proceeded well. Panning the riverbeds produced enough gold to persuade Ponce de León that the island merited permanent

Columbus and his crew were the first Europeans to encounter the Taínos. It was Columbus who called them "Indians," an identification that now encompasses all the indigenous peoples of the Western Hemisphere.

settlement. He had hoped for a small, strictly controlled group of Spaniards to live and work among the natives without committing abuses or arousing hostility. However, as soon as King Ferdinand caught wind of Puerto Rico's

excellent prospects he directed a number of family friends there. Meanwhile, Diego Colón also entered the scene. Incensed that Ponce de León had grabbed the island for himself, he granted titles to two of his father's supporters – Cristóbal Sotomayor and Miguel Díaz – and subsidized their establishment on the island.

San Juan Bautista was now destined to suffer what Ponce de León had tried to avoid. By a colonial ordinance called a *repartimiento*, one of Colón's men enslaved 5,500 Taínos, ostensibly to convert them to Christianity but in reality to press them into labor.

Engraving of Ponce de León mortally wounded while exploring Florida.

THE SETTLEMENT OF CAPARRA

The Caparra ruins, located in the eponymous sector in the municipality of Guaynabo, consist of the remains of the first permanent settlement established on the island by Juan Ponce de León in 1508. He called it Caparra, or Ciudad de (city of) Puerto Rico, although nowadays the area is known as Pueblo Viejo, or Old Town.

Although it had good breezes, the site lacked an important element: easy and direct access to the bay, which was vital for its subsistence. The most direct access was through a nearly impenetrable barrier of mangrove swamps – Caparra was not destined to become the most important city on the island.

The town was built around a public plaza, which was

the site of business and gatherings. The most important buildings, such as the fort incorporating a church, had stone foundations, still visible today. The residences were huts or small houses built of perishable materials. There were also corrals, stables, and warehouses.

In 1509, the settlement of Caparra was moved to the islet of San Juan, at the entrance of the bay, a site that was less vulnerable to attacks from the Taíno and with better access for transporting merchandise. The few remaining stone walls and surrounding area are now incorporated into the Museo y Parque Histórico Ruinas de Caparro, Guaynabo. The museum contains discoveries from here and other archeological sites on the island.

The slaves were divided and placed "under the protection" of 48 *hidalgos* (minor aristocracy, from *hijo de algo*, meaning "son of a somebody"). A combination of feudalism and capitalism, this was the *encomienda* system, and it was employed throughout Spain's 16th-century New World empire.

Across the northern coast the Spanish opened mines and panning operations, all supported by the free labor of the enslaved Taínos.

The king appointed Ponce de León governor in 1510 but did not empower him to relinquish the *repartimiento*. The mining business prolifer-

branding them on the face with the king's first initial. By June, peace once again reigned.

For a few years, the search for Puerto Rican gold continued at the expense of the Taínos' freedom, and until 1540, when the sources dried up, San Juan Bautista remained one of the New World's foremost suppliers of gold to Spain. To assuage the wounded sensibilities of Juan Ponce de León for stripping his office down to little more than a title, King Ferdinand gave him permission to explore the virgin peninsula northwest of the Antilles that the Spanish called *La Florida*.

Slave labor created the plantations.

ated, though there was so much competition for gold that the few who profited were men like Ponce de León, who made their fortunes selling food and supplies to the miners.

Moreover, not even Ponce de León himself could check the Spanish settlers' abuse of the local people, especially in the more remote western end of the island.

Indigenous resistance

During the winter of 1511, violence erupted, and guerrilla warfare soon spread through the island. Ponce de León responded immediately. Within a few days of the initial outburst he and his captains had captured nearly 200 Taínos, whom they subsequently sold into slavery,

An epidemic of smallpox which started in the silver mines of Hispaniola in 1518, spread to Cuba and then to Puerto Rico, where it is believed to have killed over half the Taíno population in 1519.

As people continued to migrate to the island of San Juan Bautista they brought new commercial enterprises with them. The days were gone when *hidalgos* left their homeland to strike it rich in New World gold mines. Gradually, the settlers turned their energies to agriculture. Land was plentiful and easy to come by, water was abundant and the climate mild.

Labor posed a problem at first, for the Taínos had disappeared quickly following the institution of the *repartimiento*. Epidemics of European diseases had quickly swept through the communities of enslaved natives, devastating the population.

Those Indians who escaped fled into the mountainous interior or across the sea to join the tribes of coastal South America, although many women were taken as wives by farmers and other Spanish men. Spanish women rarely ventured to the New World. However, West Africans, imported by Portuguese slavers and supplied by the Spanish Crown, provided an affordable labor replacement.

Peasant roots

Two sorts of farm developed. Some islanders, denied political and social status because they were *mestizos* (the progeny of a white and an Indian or black), were unable to obtain large land grants and credit. They resorted to subsistence farming and on their tiny plots raised cassava, corn, vegetables, fruit, rice, and a few cattle. Generally, *mestizos* cleared fields in inland regions that would not compete with the large coastal plantations. Puerto Rico's sizeable peasant class blossomed from the seeds of these 16th-century subsistence farmers.

In addition there were, of course, owners of large plantations. Usually of purely European ancestry, these immigrants and Creoles (born on the island) were chiefly interested in profit. After experimenting with a variety of crops, including ginger and tobacco, they finally settled on sugar as being the most dependable and profitable cash crop. It was relatively new to Europeans, but their sweet tooth appeared to be insatiable.

In 1516, entrepreneurs constructed the island's first *ingenio* – a factory in which raw cane is ground, boiled, and reduced to sugar crystals. A decade and a half later, Puerto Rico sent its first sugar exports to Spain. Ferdinand's successor, Holy Roman Emperor Charles V, was so encouraged by it that he provided a number of technicians and loans for the industry's growth. Peripheral industries burgeoned as well: demand for timber to fuel the *ingenios* and food to fuel the laborers soared, and where sugar is processed, so inevitably rum is produced. Determined to squeeze all the profit out of their sugar cane, the Spanish settlers built distilleries soon after harvesting the first sugar crop.

By 1550, there were 10 active *ingenios* on the island, but the restrictive policies of the mercantilist King Philip II led to a major crash in the industry during the 1580s. Eventually it recovered its pre-eminence, but throughout Puerto Rico's history sugar was one of its most troubled industries.

Horses and husbandry

After the collapse of the sugar trade, ginger emerged as the most successful product, and despite edicts from the monarch – who

The El Morro fortress, finished in the 1540s.

THE MIGHTY LION

Born around 1460 in San Servos, Spain, Don Juan Ponce de León is known essentially for three things: the discovery of what is now Florida, the conquering and governing of Puerto Rico, and his never-ending search for the mythical Fountain of Youth. Historians believe he sought not only the age-restorative waters but also gold and silver thought to be at the site of the fountain. He explored many regions in his quest, but a poisoned arrow shot into his stomach brought his explorations to an abrupt halt. His epitaph, by poet and historian Juan de Castellanos, reads "Here lie the bones of a Lion/mightier in deeds than in name."

preferred the cultivation of sugar – it flourished until the market bottomed out through a surplus. Animal husbandry was another lucrative industry. The armies that conquered Peru, Central America, and Florida rode Puerto Rican horses, and island *hatos* (cattle ranches) supplied the local garrisons with meat.

The possibility of foreign aggression remained a constant threat. By the 1520s, the economic and strategic promise of the island – now officially called Puerto Rico – had become apparent. Moreover, the individual with the clearest sense of Puerto Rico's potential and

foreign invaders. In the 16th and 17th centuries the French, English, and Dutch dedicated themselves to unseating the powerful Habsburg monarchs both at home and abroad. As part of this campaign, they launched attack after attack on Spaniards in the New World. Many of these attacks were carried out by privateers.

Fortifications

Encouraged by rumors of impending assault by French war vessels, San Juan officials in 1522 initiated the construction of the port's

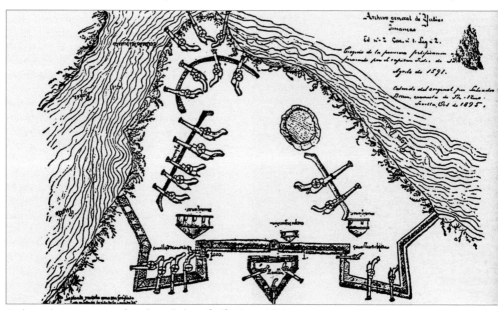

Foreign navies were a constant threat, hence the heavy fortifications at El Morro.

importance was gone. Juan Ponce de León had been fatally wounded in an encounter with Florida Indians in 1521; his remains are interred in the Cathedral of San Juan. Without a leader close to the Spanish king, defensive measures were hard to obtain.

In the year of Ponce de León's burial, the colonialists transferred the capital city from the site chosen by him to a large natural bay to the north, renaming it San Juan. Mosquitoes had plagued settlers incessantly in the old river-bank town, and the site proved too small to support increased river traffic as agriculture and industry developed.

Advantageous as the new location was for shipping, it left the people vulnerable to

first garrison. The wooden structure had not been completed before they realized it would be insufficient in the face of an attack. The island's first real defensive edifice was not completed until 1530, when descendants of Ponce de León built a house of stone, Casa Blanca, designed to provide a refuge for colonialists in the face of foreign aggression. The house still stands in Old San Juan. But not even Casa Blanca fulfilled the defensive needs of the settlement, particularly given the expected large-scale population growth. Two years later, the army began building La Fortaleza, sometimes known as Santa Catalina. Today it houses the offices of the governor of Puerto Rico, and it holds the distinction of being the oldest executive mansion in the Western Hemisphere.

La Fortaleza did little to supplement the defenses already provided by Casa Blanca. Before it had been completed, army officers informed the crown that it had been built in "a poor place" and begged the appropriation of funds for another fortress. El Castillo de San Felipe del Morro (or, simply, El Morro) was the product of their entreaties. Placed on the rocky tip of the San Juan Peninsula, the fortification, which was finished in the 1540s, did much to assuage the fears of the northern capital's residents.

Bartolomé de las Casas was a fierce defendant of Taíno rights.

But Puerto Ricans had more to be concerned with than the French alone. The celebrated "sea dogs" of the English Queen Elizabeth I, Francis Drake and Captain John Hawkins, forcibly seized dozens of Spanish cargo ships traveling between the Antilles and Spain. In 1585, open war broke out between the two nations. England's well-known defeat of the Spanish Armada in 1588 left Spain permanently disabled as a naval power.

More defenses

The Council of the Indies, the bureaucracy that oversaw the enforcement and administration of Spanish colonial policy in the Western Hemisphere, conferred upon the governor the title of Captain-General and directed him to improve the island's military preparedness. Governor Diego Menéndez de Valdés exercised tremendous initiative during the 1580s. A number of fortresses were constructed during his tenure, including El Boquerón and Santa Elena in San Juan. Menéndez ordered the refurbishing of the land bridge La Puente de San Antonio – now La Puente de San Gerónimo – and the strengthening of La Fortaleza. He also requisitioned artillery and ammunition, expanding the troop count from 50 to 209 men.

Menéndez stepped in just in the nick of time. A string of English assaults, launched with the intention of capturing Puerto Rico, was thwarted thanks to sturdy defenses. A historic confrontation in the autumn of 1594 resulted in an English defeat. During one of these battles a cannonball shot through the side of Francis Drake's ship and mortally wounded John Hawkins, who was with Drake in his cabin. Drake was forced to retreat.

Yet the English would not give up. While the Spanish king nearly doubled – to 409 – the number of troops at the San Juan garrison of El Morro, the veteran sea warrior George Clifford, third Earl of Cumberland, secretly planned an assault. He was aided by an influenza epidemic in 1598, which wiped out most of the able-bodied population of San Juan. As a result, the city was seriously unprepared for the imminent attack.

Influenza's revenge

From a point 80 miles (129km) east of the capital, Cumberland's troops marched toward San Juan in June, easily taking fortifications as they proceeded. On July 1, the defenders who had been forced to hole up in El Morro surrendered the town. But the same scourge which had weakened the Puerto Ricans now struck the English conquerors. More than 400 English soldiers died of influenza within six weeks. The Puerto Ricans promptly availed themselves of the British state of weakness. Refusing to acknowledge Cumberland's authority, they engaged relentlessly in skirmishes on the outskirts of the town. On August 27, Cumberland withdrew from the island, destroying two plantations in his wake.

Next, the Dutch entered the picture. Determined to bring Spanish dominance of the Caribbean to an end, they commissioned Boudewijn Hendrikszoon to take over the island. Hendrikszoon's fleet of eight vessels arrived in San Juan harbor on September 24, 1625. In the course of the next three days the Dutch slowly advanced, forcing a Spanish retreat into El Morro.

The siege of San Juan lasted a month. Finally, the courageous captains Juan de Amezquita and Andrés Botello led surprise attacks on the Dutch trenches on October 22. The next 10 days of battle left the Dutch fleet severely damaged – one ship destroyed and the troops depleted. The island was confirmed as a Spanish domain.

In the 1630s and 1640s, King Philip IV of Spain realized his plan to fortify the entire city of San Juan: seven fortresses were linked by a line of stone walls.

In control

Having seen off the English and the Dutch, the island was now relatively safe from invaders, and attention was turned to the problem of establishing a strong economic base. But, as a Spanish colony, Puerto Rico was allowed to keep open only one port – San Juan – and was barred from trading with non-Spanish powers. These strictures seriously limited the chances for economic growth.

In the mid-16th century, when the influx of African slaves diminished, Britain threatened Spain on the high seas, and when non-Spanish producers in the West Indies developed more efficient sugar production, the sugar industry collapsed. Virtually nothing was exported in the 1560s and 1570s.

Contraband trade

Ironically, what turned the flagging island economy around was the circumvention of the Spanish mercantilist policies that had been the cause of Puerto Rico's problems to begin with. Refused permanent concessions by the crown, the planters and merchants on Puerto Rico engaged increasingly in illicit foreign trade. Local produce – sugar, livestock,

The patron saint of sailors.

BARTOLOMÉ DE LAS CASAS

Bartolomé de las Casas (1484–1566) was a colonist and slave owner on Santo Domingo, who became the first priest to be ordained in the Americas, in 1510. He participated in the Spanish conquest of Cuba in 1513 and witnessed the torture and genocide of the Native Americans by his fellow colonists. In 1514 he became convinced that he should give up his slaves and returned to Spain to argue against slavery. He became famous for his advocacy of the rights of Native Americans, whose cultures he described with care and attention. It was he who described the Taínos' social structure, divided into *caciques* (chiefs), *bohiques* (shamans or priests), *nitaínos* (noblemen), and *naborías* (common folk). He initiated what became known as the Black Legend, which formed images of the Spaniards as predatory colonists and the Indians as innocent victims.

Bartolomé de las Casas's book *A Short Account of the Destruction of the Indies*, published in 1552, gives a vivid description of the atrocities committed by the *conquistadores* in the Americas – most particularly, the Caribbean, Central America, and modern-day Mexico – including several events he witnessed, having traveled widely in the region and being appointed the first resident Bishop of Chiapas. His work resulted in several improvements in the legal status of the indigenous peoples of the Americas.

tobacco – was exchanged for slaves, staples, tools, and other manufactured goods. By the mid-17th century almost everyone, from clerical authorities to soldiers, from friars to peasants, was involved in smuggling. The coastal towns of Aguada, Arecibo, Cabo Rojo and Fajardo grew into busy centers of illicit international trade.

Word of the proliferation of contraband activity and privateering in Puerto Rico eventually got back to Spain. Recognizing that the island's problems were critical, the king sent a commissioner, Alejandro O'Reilly, to evaluate

Slave market in Puerto Rico.

the state of Puerto Rico. O'Reilly's report of 1765 was remarkably comprehensive and perspicacious. He reckoned the island's population had reached about 45,000: 40,000 free men and 5,000 slaves. Most of the urban inhabitants lived in northeastern coastal towns and earned their livelihood through smuggling and the black market. Smuggling was so prevalent that O'Reilly could report extensively on prices, supply, demand, and distribution.

In 1765, a Spanish council met to review O'Reilly's report and to formulate a solution to the Puerto Rican problem. Recognizing the need for a stronger enforcement agent to curb contraband trade, Spain more than doubled the *situado* and installed Don Miguel de

Muesas as governor. He was instructed to create a sturdy domestic economy. By building bridges and roads, by strengthening defenses, and by improving public education, he hoped to promote agricultural prosperity and domestic self-sufficiency.

Despite the ability with which O'Reilly pleaded Puerto Rico's case, Spain continued to see the development of the island's economy as secondary to its importance as the first naval fortification in the New World empire. Further, a population boom – largely attributable to immigration – had more than tripled the number of residents on the island by the turn of the century.

Meanwhile, Great Britain had its eye on Puerto Rico and was showing a readiness to acquire it. In 1797, after Napoleonic France and Spain had declared war on Britain, a British fleet of 60 vessels manned by 9,000 troops under the command of General Abercrombie landed at Boca de Cangrejos. On April 17, they took Santurce and quickly laid siege to the walled capital. Militia detachments from around the island arrived and launched a counterattack. Abercrombie ordered a retreat on May 1.

Shifting control

In 1807, the US president, Thomas Jefferson, placed an embargo on all trade with the Spanish West Indies, which as a result cut exports by more than half. Napoleon's invasion of Spain in 1808 sent shock waves through the empire and Puerto Rico's economy suffered. Although the US embargo was soon lifted, trying to respond to the threat Napoleon's armies posed on Spain's borders, the colonies were required to ship an extraordinary supply of resources which could be used to outfit and maintain Spanish troops.

The Napoleonic Wars led to a complete reorganization of colonial rule. As control over the transatlantic territories became weakened, several countries in the Americas won independence from Spain. A provisional assembly called the *Cortés* was convened in Spain to rule in the name of the deposed King Ferdinand VII. Fearing that Puerto Rican separatists who sympathized with the rebellious colonialists in South and Central America – Mexico and Venezuela particularly – would instigate revolutions at home, Puerto Rico was recognized as an overseas province of Spain with the right to send a parliamentary representative to the *Cortés* in Cádiz.

An island Creole by the name of Ramón Power Giralt went as the colony's emissary in 1809 and was elected vice president of the assembly until his death three years later. He pushed for reforms designed to ameliorate the social and economic ills of the island. Puerto Ricans gained status as Spanish citizens; tariffs on machinery and tools were dropped; a university was founded; and measures were taken to improve the island's industry. The significantly. The *cédula de gracias* declared by Ferdinand VII in 1815 ended the Spanish trade monopoly in Puerto Rico by permitting trade with other countries. However, according to the dictates of the king, only Spanish vessels were allowed to carry on the exports.

Once again, the colonial governors took exception to Spanish policy. Disobeying the king's orders, they gave right of entry to ships regardless of their origins. Also, under a civil intendancy plan instituted by Power Giralt, an independent official was appointed to oversee financial affairs, rather than their being left in

The US flag flies prominently outside the University of Puerto Rico.

Cortés disbanded in 1814 when Napoleon retreated and King Ferdinand VII returned to the throne. But the king, wary of the independence fever pervading the colonies, left in place a fair number of Power Giralt's reforms in a *cédula de gracias* (royal decree) that was granted in 1815.

Increasing independence

The recovery following this tumultuous period included tremendous growth in the island economy. Power Giralt's economic reforms remained in place and, for the first time since their institution, began to have a real effect. Not only was trade with the wealthy United States permitted, but the tariffs were also decreased the hands of the governor. Alejandro Ramírez Blanco filled the post first. During his tenure he opened several ports, abolished superfluous taxes, and increased the export of cattle.

Between 1813 and 1818 Puerto Rican trade expanded to approximately eight times its previous level, and in 1824 the king finally relinquished the last vestiges of mercantilism, conceding the right of Puerto Rican ports to harbor non-Spanish merchant ships. The future of the Puerto Rican economy became clear to many. Spain was neither a reliable nor a tremendously profitable trading partner, and the more Puerto Rico moved away from its dependence on the mother country, the faster its economy would develop.

Battling in the Spanish-American War.

SELF RULE AND THE UNITED STATES

"It wasn't much of a war, but it was all the war there was," said Teddy Roosevelt. Even so, the Spanish-American War marked a turning point for Puerto Rico.

Puerto Rico was not immune to the independence movements and events in other Spanish colonies. The influence of Simón Bolívar was felt on the island as one after another of Spain's former South and Central American colonies achieved their independence. For the first time, agitators for Puerto Rican autonomy were vocal and posed a serious threat to the Spanish government. At the beginning of the 19th century there were several plots, but conspirators were invariably discovered by the army and either executed or exiled.

After the restoration of Ferdinand to the throne in 1814, a series of governors with absolute power ruled Puerto Rico. On the first day of 1820, an army commander declared the liberal reformist constitution of 1812 to be still in effect. One by one officials of various districts joined him. The already weak king, hoping to avoid an all-out revolution, had to concede, and decided to resurrect the *Cortés*, disbanded in 1814. José María Quiñones went to Spain as the representative from Puerto Rico in 1823. He submitted a plan to introduce more autonomy to the island colonies, particularly in the administration of domestic affairs.

Reign of oppression

The *Cortés* approved Quiñones' proposal, but its intentions fell to pieces before it could see them through. In 1823 the constitutional government of Spain collapsed. The king returned to absolute power and appointed the first of 14 governors of Puerto Rico who exercised total authority over the colony, collectively staging a 42-year reign of oppression and virtual martial law.

The first of these dictators was Miguel de la Torre. Hanging on to the governorship for 15 years, Torre imposed a 10pm curfew and

Dr Ramón Emeterio Betances.

established the *visita* – an island-wide inspection network that allowed him to keep abreast of activity in the colony and maintain tight security. Although Torre's reign was oppressive, it had some benefits. He took control of the country's development, built roads and bridges and brought in huge numbers of slaves to foster sugar production, contributing significantly to the development of the local economy.

Separatist action

In 1837, deputies from Puerto Rico and Cuba, the two remaining colonies, were excluded from the Cortés. The deputy returned to Puerto Rico and constitutional town councils were disbanded. In January 1838 the new Governor,

Field Marshal Miguel López de Baños published a repressive edict banning a range of activities including the flying of kites. His aim, however, was to regulate the supply of labor

> During 1858 and 1859, Samuel Morse set up a two-mile telegraph line, the first in Latin America, between two haciendas in Puerto Rico belonging to his relatives. Spanish and US flags flew side by side at the inauguration ceremony.

US and Puerto Rican flags fly harmoniously over El Morro.

and prevent vagrancy, forcing those who did not own property to seek employment. If they remained unemployed for a month they had to work for the state on half pay or even face imprisonment. This naturally created resentment among workers, the jornaleros, as they were known.

Later in 1838 a group of separatists plotted another putsch, but word of the conspiracy leaked out and several of the participants were executed; others were exiled. Subsequent governors instituted the *libreta* laws which required all inhabitants of Puerto Rico to carry passbooks detailing their work history and restricted unauthorized movement. It was a troubled time for the island. To add to the

colony's misery, in the 1850s a cholera epidemic swept across the island, claiming the lives of 30,000. Ramón Emeterio Betances, a doctor renowned for his efforts against the epidemic, was exiled in 1856 for his separatist activities.

Intimidated by the growing separatist fervor, the Spanish Crown invited Puerto Rico and Cuba in 1865 to draft a colonial constitution in the form of a "Special Law of the Indies." The documents which emerged called for the abolition of slavery, freedom of the press and speech, and independence on a commonwealth basis. While the crown dragged its feet in granting these concessions, in Puerto Rico the angry governor, José María Marchessi, exiled several leading reformists, including the recently returned Betances. Fleeing to New York, they joined with other separatist Puerto Ricans and Cubans.

From New York the autonomists directed the independence movement during the 1860s and 1870s under the aegis of the Puerto Rican Revolutionary Committee. Covert satellite organizations formed in villages and towns across Puerto Rico, particularly around Mayagüez. On September 23, 1868, several hundred men congregated at a farm outside the northwestern mountain town of Lares. Marching under a banner that read *Libertad o Muerte. Viva Puerto Rico Libre. Año 1868* ("Liberty or Death. Long Live Free Puerto Rico. Year 1868"), they took the town and arrested its officials. They elected a provisional president and proclaimed the Republic of Puerto Rico. The republic would be short-lived. Troops sent by the governor met the rebel front at San Sebastián and won an easy victory. Within six weeks the echoes of the "Grito de Lares" (Shout of Lares) had died completely, although it has retained lasting symbolic importance in the Puerto Rican independence movement (see page 172).

Brief independence

Puerto Rico did enjoy a brief flash of autonomy in 1897. The Autonomist Party voted to fuse with the monarchist Liberal Party of Spain after forming a pact with its leader, Mateo Sagasta, which guaranteed Puerto Rican autonomy if the Liberals came to power. On the assassination of the Spanish prime minister, Sagasta became Spain's leader; he immediately declared Puerto Rico an autonomous state.

Adopting a two-chamber constitutional republican form of government, as agreed with Sagasta, the Puerto Ricans elected a lower house of assembly and half of the delegates to the upper house. The governor was still appointed by Spain, but his power was restricted. The new government assumed power in July 1898. Later that month General Nelson A. Miles of the United States landed on the southern coast with an army of 16,000 men. It was the beginning of the Spanish-American War and the end of short-lived Puerto Rican autonomy.

Miles tried to assuage the inhabitants' anxiety about annexation as a United States protectorate, however, telling them: "We have come … to promote your prosperity and to bestow upon you the immunities and blessing of the liberal institutions of our government." His assurances did not pacify everyone. Emeterio Betances, now aging, issued a warning to his fellow people: "If Puerto Rico does not act fast, it will be an American colony forever."

On December 10, 1898, the Treaty of Paris, which settled the final terms of Spain's surrender, was signed. In addition to a large

19th-century Spanish currency.

The US Navy had advocated buying Puerto Rico and Cuba ten years before the Spanish-American War in 1898, to provide coaling and repair stations to give their ships greater range and a strategic military base if a trans-Isthmus canal were built.

reparations payment, the United States won Puerto Rico and the Philippines from Spain, but Puerto Rico wasn't exactly a grand prize at the time. Two percent of the population owned more than two-thirds of the agricultural land, yet 60 percent of the land owned was mortgaged at high interest rates.

The US steps in

"It wasn't much of a war, but it was all the war there was," Teddy Roosevelt reflected on the Spanish-American War. On August 31, 1898, Spain surrendered. The Puerto Rico campaign had lasted only two weeks, the whole war less than four months. General

Political turmoil and natural disaster

The United States set up a military government, and Puerto Rico was placed under the charge of the War Department. Assuming a hard-headed approach to underdevelopment and a lagging economy, the first three governors-general enjoyed almost dictatorial power. They introduced American currency, suspended defaulted mortgages, and promoted trade with the United States. They improved public health, reformed tax laws, and overhauled local government.

But to many Puerto Ricans, autonomy was still vital. A leading autonomist leader, Luis Muñoz Rivera, organized a new party in an attempt to reach a compromise between the separatists and the US government. The Federal Party and its ally, the new Republican Party, advocated cooperation with the United States, especially in commercial matters, full civil rights

Puerto Rico faced an unhappy future. The economy was on the brink of collapse, the hostilities with inept American administrators continued, and there were the apparently insurmountable difficulties of widespread illiteracy and poverty.

Test case for US colonial policy

For the next 48 years, Puerto Rico and the US had a strange colonial-protectorate relationship. While it was widely acknowledged that the latter possessed enormous wealth from which the former stood to benefit, Puerto Ricans also

American medical officers at Coamo Springs.

and an autonomous civilian government. But not even the conciliatory approach that Muñoz Rivera endorsed satisfied the McKinley administration. The colonial governor-general, George W. Davis, reported to the president that "the people generally have no conception of political rights combined with political responsibilities."

As if political turmoil were not enough, Mother Nature interfered in the form of Hurricane San Ciriaco in 1899. Three thousand people died, and the damage to property was immense. The hurricane devastated the vital sugar and coffee crops and left a quarter of the island's inhabitants without homes. The US Congress awarded only $200,000 to the island in relief payments.

feared that Betances's prediction would come true – that Puerto Rico would be swallowed up culturally and economically if its bonds with the US were to strengthen.

Puerto Rico looms large in recent American history. It was the first non-Continental US territory and served as the test case for the formation and implementation of colonial policy.

Special interest groups in the United States polarized into two lobbies. The agricultural contingent, fearing competition from Puerto Rican producers whose labor costs were lower, allied with racists who dreaded the influx of the "Latin race" which would result from granting US citizenship to Puerto Ricans. And as proof of Benjamin Franklin's observation that politics makes strange bedfellows, these opponents of the administration's Puerto Rican colonial plan found themselves under the blankets with liberal Democrats who opposed all imperialism.

The burgeoning of a colony

With the passing in 1900 of the Foraker Act, Puerto Rico took on a brand new colonial status, but reception of the Act could have been better. An immediate challenge to its constitutional legality brought it before the US Supreme Court, where the majority declared that constitutionality was not applicable in an "unincorporated entity" like Puerto Rico. Dissenting Chief Justice Fuller wrote that it left Puerto Rico "a disembodied shade in an intermediate state of ambiguous existence."

Reluctant US citizens

On the eve of the United States' entry into World War I in 1917, President Wilson approved the Jones-Shafroth Act granting US citizenship to all Puerto Ricans. This Act affronted many Puerto Rican statesmen. For years they had pressed for a break from the US and now, in blatant contradiction of their demands, Congress was drawing them in even more. Muñoz Rivera, the Resident Commissioner, had beseeched Congress to hold a plebiscite – but to no avail.

The "Catch-22" of Puerto Rico's relationship with the US had emerged full-blown. The more political maturity the colony showed, the more fervently Nationalists agitated for independence. The more hostile to the US the colony seemed to American lawmakers, the more reluctant they were to give any ground.

During this period of strong antagonism between Puerto Rico and the United States, the island's economy and population actually grew rapidly. Improved health care resulted in a significant drop in the death rate. Meanwhile, employment and production increased, and government revenues rose. Big American corporations pocketed most of the profits from this growth, and Congress assured them of continued wealth.

The Puerto Rican national crest.

EXODUS TO HAWAII

The 1899 floods caused by 28 days of continuous hurricane rain damaged the agricultural industry and left 3,400 dead and thousands of people without shelter, food, or work. As a result, there was a shortage of sugar from the Caribbean in the world market and a huge demand for the product from Hawaii and other sugar-producing countries. To meet the demand, plantation owners began a campaign to recruit laborers in Puerto Rico.

On November 22, 1900, a first group of 56 Puerto Rican men began their long journey to Maui, Hawaii. The trip was long and harsh. They first set sail from San Juan harbor to New Orleans, Louisiana. Once in New Orleans, they were boarded on a railroad train and sent to Los Angeles, California. From there they set sail to Hawaii. According to the *Los Angeles Times*, dated December 26, 1901, the Puerto Rican workers were mistreated and starved by the shippers and the railroad company. They arrived in Honolulu, on December 23, 1900, and were sent to work in different plantations on Hawaii's four islands. By October 17, 1901, 5,000 Puerto Rican men, women, and children had made their new homes on the four islands. Records show that, in 1902, 34 plantations had 1,773 Puerto Ricans on their payrolls.

Today there are almost 30,000 Puerto Ricans or Hawaiian-Puerto Ricans living in Hawaii.

In contrast, the average Puerto Rican family earned between just $150 and $200 a year; many *jíbaros* had sold their own little farms to work for farm estates and factories.

The Labor movement

Pablo Iglesias, a disciple of Samuel Gompers, one of the great fathers of American trade unions, led the move to organize Puerto Rican laborers. By 1909 the labor movement, organized under Iglesias's leadership as the Free Federation, identified itself with the labor union movement in the US. It even assumed the task

Rise of the Nationalist Party

Two hurricanes accompanied the collapse of the economy – San Felipe in 1928 and San Cipriano in 1932 – destroying millions of dollars' worth of property and crops. Starvation and disease took a heavy toll on the population during the Depres-

> *Puerto Rico lies between the Caribbean and North American plates and experiences frequent tremors, although the most recent major earthquake and tsunami was in 1918.*

Dissident Pedro Albizu Campos arrested in Puerto Rico.

of Americanizing Puerto Rico.

"The labor movement in Porto [sic] Rico," Iglesias wrote, "has no doubt been, and is, the most efficient and safest way of conveying the sentiments and feelings of the American people to the hearts of the people of Porto Rico."

A 1914 cigar strike and then a 1915 sugar cane strike brought useful publicity. Iglesias was subsequently elected to the new Senate of Puerto Rico in 1917.

The Great Depression nearly undid Puerto Rico. The desperation of the 1930s caused sugar cane workers to go on strike nationally in 1934 – an unsuccessful strike that would eventually lead to the formation of the Puerto Rican Communist Party.

sion. Across the island, haggard, demoralized people waited in long queues for inadequate government food handouts. But out of the poverty and deprivation, a new voice emerged.

It belonged to Pedro Albizu Campos, a former US Army officer and a graduate of Harvard Law School. He was of a generation of Puerto Ricans who were children at the time of the United States' takeover. Equipped with a great understanding of the American system, he used it to become a leader of militant revolutionaries. Albizu Campos's accusation was that (according to both American foreign policy and international law) the United States' claims on Puerto Rico were in fact illegal, since Puerto Rico was already autonomous at the time of occupation.

The strength and seriousness of Albizu Campos's Nationalist organization were made abundantly clear on February 23, 1936. Two of his followers, Hiram Rosado and Elías Beauchamp, shot and killed the chief of police of San Juan. The assassins were arrested and summarily beaten to death, and Albizu Campos and seven key party members were imprisoned in the Federal Prison in Georgia.

A year later, however, the party was still strong. Denied a permit to hold a demonstration in the town of Ponce, a group of Albizu Campos's followers dressed in black shirts assembled to march on March 21, 1937. As the procession moved forward to the tune of *La Borinqueña* – the Puerto Rican anthem – a shot rang out. The origin of the gunfire has never been determined, but within moments police and marchers were exchanging bullets. Twenty people were killed and another 100 wounded in the panic-stricken crossfire that ensued. The governor called the affair "a riot"; the American Civil Liberties Union labeled it "a massacre." The event is still remembered today as *La Masacre de Ponce*.

Pedro Albizu Camposwaves from his prison cell after talking to reporters.

THE FORAKER ACT

On April 2, 1900, US President McKinley signed a civil law that established a civilian government in Puerto Rico. Although officially known as the Organic Act of 1900, it was more commonly referred to as the Foraker Act for its sponsor, Charles Benson Foraker.

The new government had a presidentially appointed governor, an Executive Council comprising both Americans and Puerto Ricans, and a House of Delegates with 35 elected members. There was also a judicial system with a Supreme Court. All federal laws of the United States were to be in effect on the island. In addition, a Resident Commissioner chosen by the Puerto Rican people would speak for the colony in the House of Representatives, but have no vote. The first civil governor of the island under the Act was Charles H. Allen, inaugurated on May 1, 1900, in San Juan.

An initial 15 percent tariff was imposed on all imports to, and exports from, the United States, and the revenues would be used to benefit Puerto Rico. Free trade was promised after two years. The colonial government would determine its own taxation programs and oversee the insular treasury. Ownership of large estates by American corporations was discouraged by prohibiting businesses to carry on agriculture on more than 500

San Juan old and new: the San Geronimo fort and the high-rises of Condado.

MODERN TIMES

Colony or commonwealth? Or independent state? The innovative "Operation Bootstrap" helped to decide the issue in the 20th century but the debate rumbles on today with referenda planned as Puerto Rico contemplates its future with or without the US.

The United States began to export Puerto Rico's share of the New Deal in 1933, but it was not a winning hand. President Franklin Roosevelt sent a string of appointees to the Governor's Mansion in San Juan, but their efforts proved inadequate and aggravating to many Puerto Ricans. Then, from amidst the crumbling political parties, a brilliant star in Puerto Rico's history appeared.

Luis Muñoz Marín, son of the celebrated statesman Luis Muñoz Rivera, had served in government since 1932 and had used his charm and connections with the American political elite to bring attention to the plight of the colony. In 1938, young Muñoz Marín founded the Partido Democrático Popular (PDP), running on the slogan "Bread, Land and Liberty," and adopting the *pava* – the broad-brimmed straw hat worn by *jíbaros* – as the party symbol. In 1940, the *populares* took over half the total seats in the upper and lower Houses.

Agricultural laborers at work on a sugar plantation in 1946

A people's governor

Muñoz Marín, elected leader of the Senate, decided to try to work with the new governor to achieve recovery. The appointee, Rexford Guy Tugwell, was refreshingly different from his predecessors. Able to speak Spanish and evincing a genuine compassion for the Puerto Ricans, he seemed promising. Muñoz Marín's good faith paid off. By improving the distribution of relief resources and by proposing a plan for long-term economic development, contingent upon continued union with the United States, Muñoz Marín convinced Tugwell that Puerto Rico was finally ready to assume the responsibility of electing its own governor.

As a first step, the United States appointed Puerto Rico's Resident Commissioner, Jesús Piñero, to the post. In 1946, Piñero became the first native governor in the island's history. Simultaneously, the US unveiled plans for the popular election of Puerto Rico's governor, demonstrating new confidence in the colony.

The people elected Muñoz Marín, of course. In 1948 he took office as the first popularly elected governor and put forward his proposal for turning Puerto Rico into an associated free state. Learning from the newly independent Philippines, where instant autonomy had crippled economic and social progress, the US delayed endorsing Muñoz Marín's plan.

However, in 1950, President Truman approved Public Law 600, the Puerto Rican Commonwealth Bill. It provided for a plebiscite in which voters would decide whether to remain a colony or assume status as a commonwealth. As the latter, Puerto Rico would draft its own constitution, though the US Congress would retain "paramount power." In June 1951, Puerto Ricans voted three to one in favor of the commonwealth.

Two disturbing events punctuated the otherwise smooth transition to commonwealth status. On the very day that President Tru-

Luis Muñoz Marín, Puerto Rico's brilliant political star and the first popularly elected governor.

man signed Public Law 600, a group of armed Nationalists marched on the Governor's Mansion, La Fortaleza. In a brief skirmish a policeman and four Nationalists were gunned down. Simultaneously, outbursts in five other towns left over 100 casualties, including 27 dead. The violence extended beyond Puerto Rican shores. Two Puerto Ricans from New York traveled to Washington and made an attempt on the president's life a month later. In March 1954, four Puerto Rican Nationalists fired into the House of Representatives from the visitors' gallery, wounding five Congressmen.

Muñoz Marín resigned from political office in 1964 but his party remained in power. In

> *The Puerto Rico Convention Center in San Juan is a beacon of modern architecture and has won accolades for its waved roof and liberal use of glass. It is the largest in the Caribbean, accommodating groups of up to 10,000 people.*

1966, a commission determined that commonwealth, statehood, and independence all deserved consideration. Seven months later the PDP, pushing for a decision, passed a bill mandating a plebiscite. Muñoz Marín re-entered the fray in support of continuing as a commonwealth. He argued that Puerto Rico had been placed fourth in the worldwide rate of economic progress only due to its relationship with the US. Further, he claimed, statehood could easily bring an end to the independent culture of Puerto Rico. His arguments held sway; two-thirds of the ballots in 1967 were cast for commonwealth status.

Operation Bootstrap

Muñoz Marín had long ago recognized that the key to averting future economic catastrophe lay in avoiding a dependence on agriculture. Relying heavily on one or two crops left Puerto Rico subject to too many risks: weather, foreign production, and interest rates. The government established the Puerto Rico Industrial Development Company in 1942 to oversee the development of government-sponsored manufacturing. When the state plans floundered, the administration canceled the program and initiated a brand new plan, known as Operation Bootstrap. Aimed at developing an economy based on rum, tourism, and industry, the program sent dozens of PR agents to the mainland on promotional tours extolling the Puerto Rican climate, geography, economy, and people.

During the early years of Operation Bootstrap, manufacturing jobs quadrupled to over 20,000, but between 1950 and 1954 over 100,000 Puerto Ricans moved to the mainland to take advantage of the post-war labor market. In New York, Puerto Ricans became the archetypal Latinos, later celebrated in *West Side Story*. A slowdown followed the resumption of peace, but in 1955 manufacturing contributed more to the economy than agriculture for the first time ever.

Operation Serenity

As a complement to Operation Bootstrap, the government instituted a program entitled Operation Serenity, which had the uplifting of the arts as its objective. Programs to promote both music and art were administered by the Institute of Puerto Rican Culture. The thinking at the time was that "man cannot live by bread alone." Poster-making got its debut at the Department of Community Education, where serigraph and lithograph techniques were developed with a certain success. Puerto Rico's new-found skill of poster-making promoted government instructional films and art exhibits, and also portrayed local history. A large group of artists and filmmakers were thus able to develop their skills through the Community Education programs.

Today, the production of Puerto Rico's imaginative posters goes back to those days in the 1950s when the islanders began to pick themselves up from their meager conditions.

Tax holiday

Operation Bootstrap later evolved into Section 936, a clause in the US Internal Revenue Code that partially exempted manufacturers from having to pay federal income tax on profits earned by their subsidiaries in Puerto Rico. Although 936 was phased out in 2005, some 2,000 factories still operate throughout the island, churning out everything from Microsoft software to Bumble Bee tuna, all for the huge American market.

In 1985, when Section 936 was first threatened by congressional budget-cutters, former governor Rafael Hernández Colón came up with a novel approach to save it: he offered to link 936 to President Reagan's Caribbean Basin Initiative (CBI), a trade program designed to help the struggling economies of Central America and the Caribbean. As a result of the deal, Section 936 was extended for 20 more years, and Puerto Rico ended up funding at least $100 million worth of development projects per year in selected beneficiary nations.

The island's heavy dependence on US federal aid programs and local government jobs have led some to call Puerto Rico a "welfare state." Critics of the island's political system say the same Operation Bootstrap that created jobs for island residents also contributed to the system's current bloated payroll and Puerto Ricans' belief that the government must provide for them.

In 2006, Governor Aníbal Acevedo Vilá, faced with a $738 million fiscal year-end shortfall, ordered a two-week partial government shutdown that put 100,000 people out of work.

While it was hoped that the budgetary woes would eventually be resolved by the implementation of the island's first-ever sales tax on consumer goods and services – set at 7 percent – the work stoppage actually sparked an economic slump.

Economic woes

Although manufacturing still accounts for 42 percent of economic output, the island's low-

Poster for the Works Progress Administration (WPA) promoting tourism for Puerto Rico, c.1940.

cost lure has disappeared. The government is having to restructure the economy, reducing the public sector payroll and forcing the island to compete in the global economy. The tax system is to be reformed over six years with reduced tax rates for individuals and corporations. Greater emphasis is being placed on luxury tourism, with the construction of five-star resorts and vacation homes. Tourism currently accounts for just 7 percent of the island's GNP.

Despite economic troubles, residents, even the poorest, enjoy a relatively high standard of living; Puerto Rico had a per capita income of around $28,500 in 2013, although this could be grossly underestimated, owing to the

Treasury department's inability to capture, via income tax, a thriving underground economy of cash and bartering.

The belief in an underground economy is fueled by visible prosperity. Virtually every Puerto Rican owns a TV and telephone; there are 1.5 million cars on the island, almost one for every two inhabitants; and fuel consumption is half of the Caribbean total.

On the other hand, Puerto Rico is plagued with serious problems such as overpopulation, high unemployment (14 percent in 2014), water contamination, deforestation, a high incidence of HIV/Aids, and a high crime rate. Sociologists and economists blame many of the island's problems on the identity crisis caused by uncertainty over Puerto Rico's unusual political status.

Federal tax and voting rights

Under commonwealth status, Puerto Ricans are exempt from US federal income tax, though they do pay personal income taxes to their own government. Although island residents cannot actually vote in American presidential elections, they can vote in the Democratic and Republican primaries. They also elect a Resident Commissioner

The aftermath of Hurricane Georges, Canovanas.

THE BORINQUENEERS

In 1908, the Puerto Rico Regiment was created within the US military, later to become the 65th Infantry Regiment, also known as the Borinqueneers. Some 18,000 Puerto Ricans served in World War I, mainly guarding strategic installations on the island and the Panama Canal Zone. In World War II, 65,000 Puerto Ricans were called up. Most of these served in segregated units such as the 65th Infantry Regiment in Puerto Rico, Panama, other Caribbean islands, Hawaii, North Africa, Italy, France, and Germany.

In 1950, there were some 20,000 Puerto Ricans in the US Armed Forces, of whom over 4,000 were in the 65th Infantry Regiment, made up of Puerto Rican soldiers and sergeants under mostly continental officers. They fought in every major campaign of the Korean War and were highly decorated for bravery. A total of some 61,000 Puerto Ricans served in Korea and more than 3,000 were killed or wounded.

Puerto Ricans continue to serve in US military campaigns, from Vietnam to Iraq and Afghanistan. Thousands of young men and women are recruited on the island, often joining up to escape poverty as well as for patriotic reasons. At home the war against terror is not universally popular, with many criticizing the system under which Puerto Ricans can die for the US but not vote for their Commander in Chief, the President.

to the US House of Representatives who has a voice – but no vote – on legislative matters.

Puerto Rican politics

Contrary to popular belief, Puerto Rico's No. 1 pastime isn't baseball – it's politics. Everywhere you'll find people enthusiastically discussing and arguing about the political situation. The pros and cons of statehood, commonwealth, and independence – as well as the activities of politicians – dominate most conversations.

There are three main political "players": the Partido Popular Democrático – PPD (Popular Demo-

In 2011, it was ruled out that decades of US Naval exercises had been harmful to the health of Vieques residents, and assured that heavy metals and explosive compounds in the soil, groundwater, air, and fish posed no health hazards.

The year 1998 marked the 100th anniversary of the US presence in Puerto Rico, and a December plebiscite saw about 51 percent voting for the fifth alternative on the ballot –

Patriotic graffiti.

cratic Party), the Partido Nuevo Progresista – PNP (New Progressive Party), and the Partido Independentista Puertorriqueño – PIP (Puerto Rican Independence Party). There are other, smaller, non-registered parties, such as the Puerto Ricans for Puerto Rico Party (registered in 2007 but failed to get enough votes in the 2008 elections to remain registered), the Puerto Rican Nationalist Party and the Socialist Workers Movement.

The PIP pushes for complete independence. Though highly visible, it garners few votes. The PNP and the PPD dominate the political landscape. Like the PIP, the PNP and PPD platforms are status-driven. PNP supporters seek statehood while PPD members favor the current commonwealth status.

"None of the Above" – narrowly defeating the 46 percent who opted for statehood. Less than 3 percent favored independence. The status controversy continues, with reports issued in 2005 and 2007 by the President's Task Force on Puerto Rico's Status.

Self-determination

In 2009, the UN Special Committee on Decolonization approved a draft resolution calling on the US government to allow the Puerto Rican people to exercise their inalienable right to self-determination. In 2010 the US Congress voted in favor of a process to determine Puerto Rico's status, setting the wheels in motion for a new referendum. In November 2012, for the first time in its history, more Puerto Ricans favored becoming a state than maintaining the island's status quo as a US Commonwealth.

Just over half of those who voted (54 percent) said that they would like to change their Commonwealth status. In a second question, 61 percent said they would support statehood, 33 percent said they'd like a new pact with the United States, and just 5 percent said they'd like to become independent. The last time Puerto Ricans were asked about their feelings on statehood, in 1998, a majority opposed becoming a state.

Although relatively safe for tourists, Puerto Rico's homicide rate has soared to 26.5 per 100,000 in 2012, more than five times that of the US. Most murders involve drugs' turf wars in public housing projects.

In 2013 the White House announced that another plebiscite would be held in Puerto Rico to determine its future political status and in the 2014 spending bill, $2.5 million was set aside for this purpose.

Alejandro García Padilla on the campaign trail.

HURRICANES

Puerto Rico is no stranger to hurricanes. Indeed, the word hurricane comes from the Taíno language and their god, Hurakán. Periodically, the Spanish colonists would have their lives and livelihoods blown away by hurricanes, which they named after the saint's day on which they arrived. One of the worst recorded storms was the 1899 San Ciriaco hurricane, which lasted 28 days, killed 3,369 people and caused incredible damage. The ferocity of this storm was exceeded in 1928 when San Felipe II struck, with wind speeds of 200mph (320kmh). Nearly 30ins (76cm) of rain fell in 48 hours and 312 people lost their lives. No building survived untouched and the economy was left in ruins with sugar mills and factories reduced to matchsticks. In 1932, Puerto Rico was hit by San Ciprián, which killed 225 people. The next serious hurricane was Donna (San Lorenzo) in 1960, when some 15–20ins (38–50cm) of rain fell in 6–10 hours, causing rivers to overflow. Flash flooding killed 137. In 1998, Puerto Rico sustained losses of $2 billion as Hurricane Georges wreaked its havoc just as the island was recovering from four other hurricanes. The death toll was 12, and about 80,000 homes were destroyed. Many storms have hit the island since then, most recently Irene in 2011, but most of the damage has been caused by flash flooding and mudslides rather than by winds, and Gonzalo in 2014, with no major damage.

Paso Fino Horses

With a history as long as Spanish colonial rule, Paso Fino horses are an amalgam of races producing a proud and elegant demeanour.

The noble Paso Fino horse has been on Puerto Rico as long as the Spanish and is now a symbol of Puerto Rican culture for its feisty spirit (*brío*), elegant movement, and stamina. When Columbus embarked on his second voyage in 1493 he took with him 25 saddle horses, which had been suspended in slings during the voyage with very little to eat or drink. Nevertheless, they were expected to carry the conquistadores as they landed on Hispaniola. In 1509, Juan Ponce de León brought some of their offspring with him when he moved to Puerto Rico including mares for breeding. These hardy little horses were Andalucians, Barbs, Zapateros, Valenzuelas, Cartujanos, and Spanish Jennets, bred by Spanish monks. Subsequent voyages brought more horses from the same breeds, which soon mixed to become a distinct Puerto Rican race.

The Jennet has now died out but it is this breed that gave the Paso Fino its identifying four-beat, lateral gait. Even when crossed with the other breeds, the resulting offspring all inherited the lateral movement, giving the smooth ride and endurance that was so prized by the gentry, while proving to be valuable workhorses for estate managers. Selective breeding on the island preserved this trait, which occurs naturally in Puerto Rico Paso Fino horses, even as foals, unlike others that have developed from different strains of Spanish horses in Colombia or Peru, which often have to be trained.

Characteristics

The lateral gait of a Paso Fino horse is low and smooth, typically described as a *taca, taca, taca, taca* sound, while the horse's demeanour is poised, proud and elegant. Puerto Rico Paso Fino horses have three paces: fino is fully collected with a fast footfall; corto is a faster pace similar to a trot with medium collection and extension; largo is more extended and faster, with horses travelling up to 25 mph. Horses were raced in the 18th and 19th centuries, with a racetrack built in 1882. Puerto Rico Paso Fino horses are noted for their fine and light-footed step, whereas the Colombian Paso has a rapid, piston action. Colombian paces are trote,

trocha and galope, which are diagonal, rather than lateral paces. At the turn of the 20th century a magnificent Andalucian stallion called Faraon was put to a Paso Fino mare to give greater nobility to the bloodstock. His great grandson, Dulce Sueño, became the archetypal Paso Fino horse and all Pure Puerto Rican Paso Fino horses can trace their lineage back to him. Horses come in a variety of colors and range in size from 13hh to 15hh, usually with long flowing manes and tails. They are intelligent, strong and kind and can be used for endurance, gymkhana, barrel racing or showing, but are naturals at working cattle on the ranch.

Paso Fino horse, Andalusian Stallion with traditional Spanish bridle.

Preserving the breed

With the invasion of US forces during the Spanish-American War, came greater awareness of the breed. Many servicemen were impressed with what they saw and took horses back to the US with them. These were subsequently interbred with other American breeds. More recently, however, breeders have realised the value of the Pure Puerto Rico Paso Fino and have started a breeding program to prevent them dying out. The Pure Puerto Rico Paso Fino Federation of America Inc. has registered fewer than 500 horses, while the Puerto Rican Department of Agriculture's Commissioner of Paso Fino believes that there are only about 2,500 worldwide and is working with the Federation to ensure their preservation.

Coconut is a key ingredient in Puerto Rican cuisine.

Chicharrónes, a specialty of Bayamón, are not for the diet conscious.

PUERTO RICAN CUISINE

Food is the centerpiece for family gatherings or social events in Puerto Rico. Traditional recipes with Spanish, Taíno, and African influences are still everyone's favorites.

Carib and Spanish destruction of Puerto Rico's native Taíno tribes, for all its ruthlessness, was far from complete. It has been said that Puerto Rican society today reflects its African and Indian origins more than its Spanish ones, and there is much truth in that. Non-Spanish ways live on in customs, rituals, language, and all aspects of life, and one can see in many facial features the unfamiliar expression of the Taínos, a race otherwise lost to us forever. But nowhere is the Taíno influence more visible, or more welcome, than in Puerto Rican cuisine, one of the great culinary amalgams of our hemisphere.

Imagine a Taíno man – call him Otoao and set his caste at *naboria*, one of the higher agricultural castes in the Taíno hierarchy – rising one sunny morning after having won a glorious victory the previous day over the invading Caribs. This victory was cause for an *areyto*, the Taíno ritual that either preceded or followed any happening of even the remotest importance. Births, deaths, victories, defeats... it's *areyto* time. Like other socio-religious Taíno festivals, *areytos* required intricate preparations for whatever food and drink was to be served, and, as a *naboria*, Otoao was in charge of hunting and fishing for the tribe.

Not that Otoao's wife Tai had it terribly easy. As a *naboria* woman (a woman's caste was determined by that of her husband), Tai was responsible for the cultivation and harvesting of the fields *(conucos)*, as well as the preparation of the meals. These were elaborate, and the Taínos managed to get an astounding range of food on the banquet table.

The menu that evening included roast *jutías* (or hutia, a rodent), seasoned with sweet red chili peppers, fried fish in corn oil, fresh

Fresh local produce.

shellfish, and a variety of freshly harvested vegetables. Among the vegetables were *yautías* (starchy tubers similar to potatoes and yams), corn, yams, cassava, and the same small red chili peppers used to season the *jutías*. Bread was *casabe*, a mixture of pureed cassava and water cooked between two hot rocks. For dessert, the Taínos had fresh fruit picked from the extensive variety available on the island. The culmination of the celebration was the drinking of an alcoholic beverage made from fermented corn juice.

This activity was accompanied by the ceremonial inhalation of hallucinogenic fumes thought to make the warriors fitter for battle. The Taínos made hallucinogens of many sorts, the most common of which used the hanging, bell-shaped flowers of the *campana* tree to make a potent and mind-bending tea.

Most of the dietary staples of the Taínos survive in the Puerto Rican cuisine of today, albeit some in altered form. Puerto Rican cooking is now an amalgam of Taíno, Spanish, and Afri-

In Puerto Rico, adobo is a seasoned salt that is generously sprinkled on meats and seafood prior to grilling or frying.

Influences from around the world

As different ingredients and cooking techniques were introduced to the island by its early settlers, a local culinary tradition began to take shape. Most important of the early imports were the Spanish cattle, sheep, pigs, goats, and other grillable creatures. Along with the animals came an almost infinite number of vegetables, fruits, and spices from the farthest reaches of Spain's vast colonial empire. A subtler, but no less important, influence on the food supply was the introduction of European farming methods and agricultural equipment.

Tostones (fried plantains) are a popular accompaniment.

can traditions. Much of this intermingling took place early in the island's history, with Spanish colonists incorporating a variety of their own ingredients and techniques into the native cuisine, most of which were found to blend surprisingly well. A tremendous addition to this culinary mélange was made by the Africans brought as slaves shortly thereafter.

African tradition is responsible for what is perhaps the greatest achievement in Caribbean cooking – the combination of strikingly contrasting flavors which in other culinary traditions would be considered unblendable. One of these savory concoctions is *pastelón*: ripe plantains layered between well-seasoned ground beef and usually served with rice.

Surprisingly, many of the agricultural staples that look indigenous to the island were in fact brought to Puerto Rico from elsewhere. Among the great variety of crops imported were coffee, sugar cane, coconuts, bananas, plantains, oranges, ginger, onions, potatoes, tomatoes, garlic, and much more. These products, along with those already present, were to mold what was to become the Puerto Rican culinary tradition.

It is ironic that included in these imports are several for which Puerto Rico was to become renowned. Puerto Rican coffee was long considered the best in the world by Europeans. And the plantain, arguably the most popular staple in Puerto Rican cuisine, is something of a national symbol. A man who is admired for honesty and lack of pretension is said to have on him the *mancha del plátano*, or "stain of the plantain."

Traditional dishes and drinks

Puerto Ricans tend to season their food in a subtle manner. The base of a majority of native dishes is the *sofrito*, an aromatic sauce made from pureed tomatoes, onions, garlic, green peppers, sweet red chili peppers, coriander, anatto seeds, and a handful of other spices. This *sofrito* adds a zesty taste to stews, rice, beans, and

a variety of other dishes, but only the blandest of palates would consider it to be piquant.

The most popular dinner dishes are stewed meats, rice, and beans, and a huge selection of fritters. Rice dominates many local main courses; expect a big heap with *arroz con pollo* (chicken served with rice sometimes cooked in coconut milk). *Asopao* is probably Puerto Rico's most widely loved dish. This soupy stew thickened with rice can be made with chicken, pork, or seafood and is the Puerto Rican equivalent of an Italian risotto or a Spanish paella, served as a hearty meal or a gourmet creation.

Street-corner temptations.

A FEAST OF FOOD FESTIVALS

Puerto Ricans are passionate about their food and have several festivals devoted entirely to the celebration of local produce or culinary creations. The largest is Saborea Puerto Rico, at Escambrón Beach in April (www. saboreapuertorico.com). Restaurants set out their wares and celebrity chefs give demonstrations. Everybody who's anybody in the industry is there, local or international. You can get a ticket to a single event up to a pass for the whole weekend show, with tastings and samples of gourmet food, rum, and wine on offer.

SoFo Culinary Fest is a more romantic event, held on Fortaleza Street in Old San Juan usually in August and December. SoFo is an abbreviation of South

Fortaleza, and the street is closed to traffic for the event. Local restaurants set up outdoor bars and stalls showcasing their specialties and you can find everything from street food to sit down gourmet bistros offering nouvelle cuisine with a local twist. This is the place to find Puerto Rican food, from fritters to suckling pig, with any number of variations on *mofongo* to delight a discerning palate.

There are also smaller, regional festivals, such as the Mango Festival in Santa Isabel, the Sugar Festival in Yabucoa, the Shrimp Festival in Moca or the Coconut Festival in Rincón, all held in May, as well as the Coffee Festival in Maricao in February.

As in the rest of the Hispanic Caribbean, the traditional cuisine is heavy food, rich with an invigorating assortment of beans, from *arroz con habichuelas* (rice with beans) and *arroz con gandules* (pigeon peas) to *lechón asado* (whole

> The quenepa (Melicoccus bijugatus) fruit's sweet/sour pulp, reminiscent of a lychee crossed with a lime, is a pale yellow or salmon color, but the juice stains things brown and was used by the Taíno to dye cloth.

A staple meal: guinea hen, rice, and beans, enjoyed with the local Medalla beer.

roast suckling pig) prepared almost exclusively for holidays and family gatherings, and its counterpart, *pernil* (roast pork shoulder, cooked the same way for fewer people). Both the suckling pig and pork shoulder are seasoned with *adobo mojado*, a thick, fragrant paste of garlic, oil, vinegar, salt, peppercorns, and herbs such as coriander and oregano. Christmas time on the island is not complete without *arroz con gandules*, *lechón asado*, *pasteles* (tamales made from plantains and *yucas* filled with a meat stuffing), and, as dessert, a *majarete* made with rice flour, coconut milk and pulp, sugar, and spices. During Lent, seafood dishes include the traditional *serenata*: codfish in a vinaigrette

sauce served with tomatoes, onions, avocados, and boiled tubers.

Strangely, for a place with so much marine life – grouper, yellowtail, spiny lobster, squid, sea snail, conch, and shark – Puerto Ricans (like Cubans and Dominicans) prefer chicken and pork. However, red snapper (*chillo*), shrimp (*camarones*), and lobster (*langosta*) are enjoyed by the locals, as is salt cod – known as *bacalao* – which is a staple. Seafood lovers will find plenty of good restaurants to choose from, as well as local *fondas*, where specialties such as *mofongo relleno* (fried mashed plantain) with *mariscos* (seafood) are firm favorites. The most popular local snacks include *alcapurrias*, meat or crab fritters.

Popular desserts include *flan* (crème caramel or custard), made of cheese, coconut, or vanilla; and *guayaba con queso* (candied guava fruit slices with cheese). Fruit is popular and plentiful, and includes mango, papaya, and passion fruit. Local fruits and vegetables can be found, often sold from roadside trucks, which are a good way of stocking up with items such as oranges – chinas – sold in large bags at good prices.

Rum is the traditional alcoholic drink, whether straight up or in cocktails, such as the ubiquitous *piña colada*. Local coffee has become something of a gourmet product, with several boutique coffee producers taking the bean more upmarket. The best can be found in the Cordillera Central, where it is grown on small farms around Maricao, Las Marías, Lares, Ciales, Jayuya, and Adjuntas. Buying direct from the farmers ensures that you are getting 100 percent Puerto Rican coffee, whereas coffee sold in supermarkets can contain beans from elsewhere to make up the difference if the local harvest has been insufficient for local consumption.

Modest, mouthwatering meals

The island offers a great variety of restaurants. Typical restaurants serving local food are only rarely luxurious or expensive. In fact, among Puerto Ricans, a rule of thumb applies that the shabbier the establishment, the better the food. The best native creations are found at modest little local *fondas*, where the prices are as reasonable as the food is distinguished. In a *fonda*, you can pick up a generous plate of rice and beans, *biftec criollo* (steak), *tostones* (fried plantains), salad, a can of beer, and dessert for about

$12–15. At the low end of the economic scale are delicious sandwiches made with a mixture of red meats, cheeses, tomatoes, and other ingredients. Among the most popular are *cubanos* and *media noches*. The *cubano* consists of pork loin, ham, and Swiss cheese on *pan de agua* (similar to French bread), while the *media noche* is smaller and uses egg bread.

International cuisine

Puerto Rico has become a proving ground for all sorts of global cuisine. Chinese food has become a staple, with fast-order restaurants

island ingredients, international flavors, and gourmet presentation. Chefs such as Pikayo's Wilo Benet and Roberto Treviño, co-owner of Budatai, are internationally renowned for their innovative cooking and they participate in TV shows and competitions.

If "gourmet" international food is not your style, the franchise fast-food boom has played a significant role in motivating local eateries to dispense wide varieties of food such as plantain fritters, stuffed potatoes, and seafood salad, while employing novel merchandising techniques to promote them.

Arroz con gandules is a Christmas specialty.

everywhere. Spanish restaurants, too, abound. The Spanish-style Puerto Rican *panadería* (bakery) has a wide assortment of delicacies. The famous Cuban sandwich is very popular, as are Spanish *tortillas*. Italian food is probably consumed more than any other type. Pizza parlors can be seen everywhere, and home delivery is common. Mexican eateries run hot and heavy in the San Juan area. Even Thai and Japanese restaurants can be found, and *sushi* is gaining in popularity.

While Puerto Ricans love to eat in *fondas*, it does not mean their palates are unsophisticated. Restaurants in Old San Juan, Isla Verde, and the Condado attract thousands of food lovers annually with their fusion of traditional

REGIONAL SPECIALTIES

Though Puerto Rico is too small to have regional cuisines, a number of dishes are limited to particular areas of the island. For example, seafood dishes tend to be accompanied by *sorrullos* (corn fritters) in most of the restaurants on the south coast. Guavate is known for its roadside stands selling *lechón asado*, Humacao is famous for its *frituras* called *granitas*, while Bayamón and its environs offer a truly unusual snack in *chicharrón*, a sort of massive pork crackling sold on the highways in and out of the city. It's an acquired taste, but once you've acquired it, you'll understand why there are so many hefty individuals wandering the streets.

Detail of the town square mosaic in
Loíza, a town known for its rich
African heritage.

ISLAND ART

Flamboyant modern painting and sculpture sit alongside remarkable folk art, colonial representative painting, and a vast Taíno legacy of ancient art. The surprising number of museums and galleries reflects Puerto Ricans' appreciation of beauty, color, and innovation.

Puerto Rico's art scene offers delights to the mind and senses as meaningful and alluring as those of its landscape. This may mean entering a room of serene carved religious figures *(santos)* in a busy family environment; or wandering into a museum or gallery in Old San Juan, only to find yourself as taken by a beautifully landscaped 17th-century courtyard as by what you see on the walls; or talking to a local artist or scholar and finding that his passion for the island and its craftsmen is yours.

Museum isle

The Institute of Puerto Rican Culture owns a vast amount of the island's cultural inheritance. It runs the Galería Nacional (National Gallery), located in the restored Antiguo Convento Dominicano (Old Dominican Convent) in Old San Juan, which contains many important Puerto Rican paintings and other art works from the 18th century to the 1960s, including several by José Campeche, Francisco Oller Ramón Frade, and Rafael Tufiño. The National Gallery is a must-see for anyone interested in the development of art on the island, although it lacks contemporary works from the last 50 years. The first exhibition room is devoted to colonial art, the second to works by Campeche and Oller, the third to arts, crafts and santos, and the fourth to modern art. Old San Juan itself is particularly fortunate as an artistic center; besides its museums, it has a dozen contemporary art galleries, a few co-operatives, and craft shops of all descriptions.

If buying art interests you as much as just looking at it, Old San Juan is certainly the spot to begin your shopping spree. You'll find fine *santos* and other crafts at Puerto Rican Art & Craft, and prints as well as paintings at Sin Título, Coabey, Atlas Art, and Botello (see page 254). You can also

The Porta Coeli Church in San Germán houses an important collection of religious art.

see the work of future arts luminaries at the exhibition hall of the School of Visual Arts (Escuela de Artes Plásticas) in front of El Morro fort.

Museum of Art

The Museo de Arte de Puerto Rico in Santurce (www.mapr.org) has given the island great prominence as the cultural leader in the region. This converted hospital, designed in the 1920s neoclassical style, is a masterpiece in itself. The building houses a 400-seat theater, upscale restaurant, meeting rooms, and a lavish garden. Works by well-known Puerto Rican artists date back to 1600, and the collection also includes regional and international works.

The museum of the University of Puerto Rico in Río Piedras, San Juan (Museo de Historia, Antropología y Arte), exhibits only a fifth of its collection, but that small proportion is of top quality, from pre-Columbian art to the strongest and most respected painters of the present day.

But the last word on international art must go to the Museo de Arte de Ponce (www. museoarteponce.org), envisioned by the late Governor Luis A. Ferré and executed by architect Edward Durrell Stone. Here, in a series of dramatically sunlit hexagonal rooms, art reflects the full range of the drama of human life, from the simplest of faces in Jan van Eyck's *Salvator Mundi* to an overpopulated *Fall of the Rebel Angels* to Rossetti's wonderfully confrontational *Daughters of King Lear*. *Flaming June*, the 1895 magnum opus of Lord Frederick Leighton, hangs here, having been bought by Ferré in the 1960s after it failed to sell at auction because it was considered old-fashioned.

Santos

Many of Puerto Rico's greatest achievements have been in the folk arts, and these retain a broad appeal, (see page 70). Most notable are

Religious art at the Museo de Arte de Puerto Rico in Santurce.

ART FOR THE PEOPLE

It's easy to display art in a museum. The challenge is to take it to the people, redefining it with a contemporary aesthetic. That was the challenge undertaken by the Puerto Rico Art Museum when it came up with Graphopoli, the first urban art biennial event, held in the summer of 2008, with simultaneous displays in San Juan, Ponce, Caguas, and Mayagüez. Urban artists from the island competed in a show integrating art and music, and clearly demonstrating that art is not found only in museums. They painted their creations on nine monumental structures before the public eye, changing the way art is conceptualized in Puerto Rico.

the Puerto Rican *santos*, arguably the island's greatest contribution to the plastic arts. These wooden religious idols, evoking an uncanny spiritual quiet, vary greatly in size and shape. The baroque detail of the earliest pieces reflects both their period origins and the tastes of a Spanish clientele. But as Puerto Rico began to develop a stronger sense of colonial identity, as well as an artisan tradition, *santeros* began to carve figures of a striking simplicity.

The proof of the healing powers of *santos* is said to be attested to by the presence of *milagros* (miracles), small silver appendages in shapes of parts of the body. These were donated by people who had prayed to particular saints for intercession in healing parts of the body. You can find such *santos* in the Cristo Chapel in Old San Juan. Though *santos* by the great masters are difficult to come by, there is hardly a home on the island where you won't find at least one *santo* of some sort, greatly revered and passed on from generation to generation.

Ancient heritage

Puerto Rico has inspired its residents to create art for thousands of years. The oldest signs of artistic expression are the petroglyphs found around the island, such as those at La Piedra Escrita near Jayuya, Caguana Indian Park near

In addition to drawings, there were also carvings of wood or stone in the shapes of people or animals, used as icons for ceremonial and religious purposes. The first people with knowledge of pottery arrived on the island about

Galería Botello (www.botello.com) is an oasis on busy Calle del Cristo in Old San Juan. Its cool, arched halls, refreshing patio, and collection make it a sanctuary. Check out Angel Botello's iconic sculptures and paintings.

Street mural in San Juan – proof that art isn't confined to museums.

The place to find experimental art and emerging artists is Santurce, where there are several contemporary art galleries and alternative spaces.

Utuado, Tibes Indian Park near Ponce, and La Cueva del Indio at Las Piedras (see page 167) near Arecibo. The standing stones of the *batey*, or ballpark, as well as the walls of the tunnels and passages through the boulders and rocks of the "cave" at Las Piedras are decorated with drawings of the sun, faces, animals, and geometric shapes, showing that their art was varied and not just figurative.

2,000 years ago. Ceramics were highly stylized and decorated, becoming progressively more so with time as techniques and skills improved.

Evidence of the vast Taíno legacy is found at the university museum in Río Piedras, which holds the cultural heritage of the island. Recent digs have been especially abundant in discoveries, some of them dazzling in quality. Amid the expected – amulets, potsherds, tools – are some baffling curiosities, like stone collars: great solid yokes at once regal and unwearable. In one intriguing case concerning Puerto Rico's early Taínos, men bend and sway together in entranced harmony. In another are two partially exposed skeletons, a few broken possessions at their sides.

José Campeche

For all the diversity of Puerto Rico's many cultural traditions, it was not until the 18th century that the island produced its first major artist in the Western tradition: José Campeche (1751–1809). In spite of never having left the island and having been exposed to European painting only through prints, Campeche still managed to create paintings of mastery. His religious works show a weakness for sentimentality, with their glut of *putti* and pastel clouds, but the inner peace which Campeche succeeds in displaying in his main holy figures dispels all

(1833–1917). His work is housed in all three main sources: the National Gallery and the museums at Ponce and Río Piedras. To this day, the extent of his influence on Puerto Rican painting is immeasurable.

Unlike Campeche, Oller lived and travelled abroad throughout his life. He studied under Courbet, was a friend of both Pissarro and Cézanne, painted European royalty, and yet remained loyal to – and fiercely proud of – his island homeland. He was a Realist with Impressionist ideas, able to paint gorgeously everything he saw. He was adept at all genres:

The stunning Museo de Arte de Puerto Rico is housed in a converted hospital.

possible doubt as to his stature as an inspired and talented artist.

There are two such masterpieces in the Ponce museum, but it is in a formal portrait which hangs in the National Gallery that one sees Campeche at the height of his powers. The eponymous *Governor Ustariz* stands in a magnificent room, with sunlight entering from behind. In his left hand are the first plans to pave the streets of San Juan; outside in the distance are men laboring busily to make his dream into a reality. It is truly a triumphant picture.

Francisco Oller

A more accessible painter, and something of a local hero in Puerto Rico, is Francisco Oller

ARTISANS AT THEIR BEST

Several Puerto Rican cities and towns play host to interesting artisan events, where visitors can see and buy art and souvenirs by local craftspeople. At San Juan the El Morro Annual Artisan Fair has been staged for over ten years. It usually takes place in July, with a wide variety of local handicrafts, including paintings, sculptures and woodcarving, presented at Castillo San Felipe El Morro. In the municipality of Aibonito, the first St. Joseph Carving Contest took place in March 2015, with woodcarving on display at the local Federico Degetau Museum on and a live woodcarving event held in the public Plaza in Aibonito.

portraits, still lifes, and landscapes – such as *Hacienda Aurora*, resonating with the vibrant colors of Puerto Rico, which are just as much in evidence today.

> Gallery nights, when many of Puerto Rico's talented young artists are discovered, are held in Old San Juan on the first Tuesday of each month from 7–10pm.

A piece of work which defies reproduction is Oller's *El Velorio* (The Wake, 1893). An enormous painting, it covers an entire wall in the university museum and illuminates the common man's universe in a fashion that recalls the work of Brueghel the Elder. Here people laugh, cry, drink, sing, and dance, while on a lace-covered table an almost forgotten, stone-white dead child lies strewn with flowers.

Oller's legacy to Puerto Rican painters has been one not only of technique but also of theme. Since his time, island painters have taken an overwhelming pride in Puerto Rico's diverse populace and landscape. Miguel Pou and Ramón Frade were among the earliest to follow Oller's lead, doing some spectacular genre work in the early part of the 20th century.

Frade's painting *El Pan Nuestro* (Our Bread, familiarly known as *The Jíbaro, 1905)* is a splendid homage to Puerto Rico's country farmers. Shyly surveying us with a bunch of plantains in his arms, this tiny old fellow appears to be a giant, with the land miniatured at his feet and his head haloed by a cloud.

The contemporary scene

The 1940s saw a rise in printmaking, which has left that medium one of the most vibrant in Puerto Rico to this day. Funded by the government, printmaking projects lured a slew of fine artists, many of whom are still active. Of particular note are Rafael Tufiño, Antonio Martorell, José Rosa, and Lorenzo Homar. Posters by Ramón Power illustrate some of the clarity and strength from which the best of Puerto Rican artists continue to draw.

Over the past 30 years, almost all Puerto Rican artists have studied abroad, and the consequence has been a broadening and an increasingly avant-garde range of attitudes. Some artists have remained abroad, like Rafael

Ferrer, whose work is as popular in New York as it is in San Juan, and Paris resident Ricardo Ramírez. Others have returned to work and teach, producing an art with a Puerto Rican flavor. Myrna Báez falls into this category, her canvases interweaving past and present, inner and outer space. Her *Homage to Vermeer* shows a lone figure in an interior surrealistically touched by landscape. Reflectively, she seems to have loosed a phantom of tropical hubris as she opens the drawer of a nearby table.

The large fraternity of Puerto Rico's artists show reverence for the island and its

Colorful mural in Ponce's Museo de la Historia.

people. Color plays an integral part. The art of Augusto Marín, Angel Botello, Francisco Rodón, and Mari Mater O'Neill can be bought in Puerto Rico and in New York auction houses for hefty prices.

The late Rafael Tufiño's woodcut ink prints tell the story of Puerto Rican life at mid-century. A group of Tufiño's pictures are often on display at the Tourism Company's headquarters in Old San Juan. Luis Cajiga paints dazzling flamboyant trees and humble *piragua* vendors. Jorge Zeno's and Sylvia Blanco's imaginative techniques are good examples of surrealistic art, while John Balosi's sculptures and paintings of horses are treasured for their originality.

FOLK ART WITH A FLAVOR ALL ITS OWN

Many of Puerto Rico's handicrafts have evolved out of necessity, and focus on function as well as form, but some of it is just plain fun...

Puerto Rico's most exquisite form of "folk art" actually borders on "fine art": *santos*, the carved religious figures that have been produced here since the 16th century. But over the centuries, the country's folk art has expanded into many other areas, with today's artisans producing a great variety of paintings, non-religious sculpture, jewelry and many other more quirky – and collectible – artifacts.

Usually bursting with bright colors, Puerto Rican folk art has an almost childlike quality. Many times folk artists base their themes on the nature around them: roosters, iguanas, and the tiny *coquís* (tree frogs) are frequently depicted.

Old San Juan is the best place to see – and purchase – local folk art, either in shops and galleries or at the weekend craft market at Plaza de la Dársena in front of Pier 1 (10am–8pm). Sometimes it is open on other days as well, depending on cruise ship arrivals. In January there is also the San Sebastián Street Festival (Fiesta de Calle San Sebastián), which is one long and very busy party over four days. In addition to live music there are some 300 artisans displaying and selling their work and lots of food stalls.

Carnival masks on sale in a store in San Juan. Miniature versions may lack the detail of the lifesize masks, but make for good souvenirs.

This craftsman specializes in carved wooden bird figurines. Puerto Rican markets abound with handmade crafts with a natural theme.

Art historians view the carving of santos as Puerto Rico's greatest contribution to the plastic arts. Santeros use clay, gold, stone, or cedarwood to carve figurines representing saints, usually from 8–20ins (20–50cm) tall. Perhaps the most popular group of santos are the Three Kings. Some of the best santos on the island can be seen at the Capilla del Cristo in Old San Juan.

Vejigante fiesta mask.

BEHIND THE *VEJIGANTE* MASKS

Grotesque, colorfully painted masks are one of the highlights of the island's many festivals. Artisans have been producing the horned, spike-toothed, speckled *papier mâché* creations since the 16th century – an amalgam of Spanish and African customs with some Taíno heritage thrown in. Traditionally, the masks were black, red, and yellow – symbolic of hellfire and damnation. Brightly costumed *vejigantes* don the masks and roam the streets at carnival time, in an attempt to scare sinners back into the church. Ponce and Loíza are the island's mask-making centers; their carnivals provide a chance to see masks in action. The Hatillo Mask Festival, held at the end of December, has been running since 1823 and commemorates Herod's killing of the innocent children.

A real mix and match – folk-art displays inside the Museo de la Historia in Ponce.

The late master craftsman Carmelo Martell plays an intricately decorated cuatro, Puerto Rico's national instrument.

Mural depicting a demon's mask in Piñones.

Salsa band in Old San Juan.

RHYTHM OF THE TROPICS

Salsa is king, but the sounds range from the percussion
of traditional instruments to the classical music
encouraged by Pablo Casals, who made his home here.

Just before he died, the world-renowned Argentinian composer Alberto Ginastera visited Puerto Rico in order to attend the world premiere of one of his works commissioned by the Pablo Casals Festival. During an interview at the Caribe Hilton, Mr Ginastera's thoughts turned to the song of the *coquí*, the tiny frog that is found only in Puerto Rico and is famous for its persistent and ubiquitous nocturnal calls. "It is the only natural song that I know of," said Mr Ginastera, "which is formed of a perfect seventh." The *coquí* sings a two-note song – "co… kee!" – and these two notes are a perfect seventh apart. It should come, therefore, as no surprise that the island's natural sounds have their unique man-made counterpart. The music of Puerto Rico is salsa.

The Puerto Rican sound

Puerto Ricans have always excelled in music, and the somewhat haphazard course of the island's history has given it a multitude of traditions from which to build a distinctively Puerto Rican sound. The earliest settlers were as enthusiastic about their music as any Spaniards; but, deprived of their native stringed instruments, found themselves in the position of having to create their own. As a result, there are at least half-a-dozen stringed instruments native to the island.

In the absence of many tonal instruments, the settlers were forced to make do with simple percussive ones, which are ready to hand in the various gourds, woods, shoots, and beans native to this land. The arrival of West African slaves, who brought with them a well-developed and long history of percussion-based music, accelerated this trend.

Folk music figures prominently in island life.

Bomba y plena

Even now, Puerto Ricans are very adept at making music with whatever happens to be within grabbing distance. No one *owns* a musical composition in Puerto Rico, as one does in other countries. Play a Puerto Rican a piano tune he likes in a bar room or café, and you won't believe your ears when you hear the rhythmic sounds he gets out of a spoon, a wood block, a bead necklace or even his knuckles on the table.

To be fair, there is a somewhat formalized genre of this very type of music. It's collectively called *bomba y plena*, but the two are completely different types of music that are coupled with dance. Together, they are the most popular forms of folk music in Puerto Rico.

The *bomba* is purely African in origin and came over with the black slaves who were forced to work on the country's sugar plantations. It's essentially a marriage of drumming and dancing: one egging the other on in a rhythmic competition of sorts. The northeastern town of Loíza is a particularly good place to experience a typical *bomba*.

Plena, on the other hand, is a blend of elements from the island's many cultures – even Taíno – and generally involves a handful of musicians creating different rhythms on an amazing variety of hand-held percussion instruments.

Drumming out a bomba beat.

Some resemble hand-held tympanis, some Irish *bodhrans*, some tambourines. Many of them are home-made, and have become a type of folk art, as well as functional instruments. The custom of *plena* originated in Ponce, but you can hear its distinctive sounds at any patron saint's festival and occasionally at Plaza de Armas or Plaza de la Dársena in Old San Juan.

Traditional music is still performed widely, especially during holidays and festivals. At family get-togethers, there are usually guitarists, *güiro* (gourd) players and pianists playing the long-established music of the people – particularly such standards as *Flores Negros* and *Somos Novios*. Television and radio stations showcase popular singers and groups, such as Luis Fonsi,

Kany García, and Ednita Nazario. Stars Chayanne, Ricky Martin, and Daddy Yankee command large audiences at concerts held at the Coliseo de Puerto Rico and Centro de Bellas Artes or at town plazas.

> The Spanish word salsa literally translates as "sauce": in a musical sense, salsa is the hot and spicy sauce that makes parties happen.

Contemporary music ranges from the traditional-but-modern sounds of *plena libre* to merengue singers like Olga Tañón, Elvis Crespo, and Melina León. The 21st century brought a new beat, reggaetón, a uniquely Puerto Rican fusion of hip hop, with sounds ranging from reggae to rock to salsa, all with a sophisticated beat. Artists like Wisin & Yandel, Tego Calderón, Ivy Queen, Don Omar, and Calle 13 not only hold sway in the island's top radio stations and clubs, but have crossed over into the global market as well.

Classical sounds too

This is not to neglect the achievements of this small island in the more traditional forms. It is a haven for the opera, and has its own company; Justino Díaz, the island's finest male vocalist, has impressed critics from New York to Milan, and Puerto Rico's "Renaissance Man," composer Jack Delano (who died in 1998), made his mark on the classical scene.

The Puerto Rico Ballet Company stages classics as well as original local productions at the Centro de Bellas Artes (Performing Arts) in Santurce, while the Puerto Rico Symphony Orchestra – despite being relatively young – is among the best in the Caribbean, and has premiered works by some of Latin America's finest composers, many of them at San Juan's Casals Festival, the Caribbean's most celebrated cultural event, held for two weeks in January each year. The orchestra and the Children's Chorus have drawn much attention internationally.

Pablo Casals

It is Pablo Casals who, more than any other Puerto Rican resident, is responsible for the upsurge of interest and proficiency in classical performance in Puerto Rico in recent years. Born in Catalonia in 1876 of a Puerto Rican mother, Casals was recognized around the time of World War I as one of the greatest cellists of his era. After leaving Spain in 1936 as a protest against the Civil War, he settled in the French Pyrenees, where the first Casals Festival was held in 1950. He visited his mother's homeland in 1956, and spent the final years of his life in Puerto Rico.

In 1957, at the invitation of Governor Luis Muñoz Marín, he founded the Puerto Rican Casals Festival, which must rank as the greatest cultural event in the Antilles, and a formidable one even by world standards. In later years, Casals went on to form the Puerto Rico Symphony Orchestra and the Puerto Rico Conservatory of Music. On his death at the age of 97 in 1973, he considered himself a Puerto Rican; his compatriots consider him one of their national heroes.

Salsa

Salsa is what happens when Afro-Caribbean music meets big-band jazz. Its roots may be found in the early explorations of the late Puerto Rican Tito Puente and Cuban musicians in New York City clubs following World War II. After serving three years in the United States Navy, Puente studied percussion at the prestigious Juilliard School on New York's Upper West Side. He was soon playing and composing for top bandleaders such as Machito and Pupi Campo, and he quickly proceeded to establish his own orchestra.

In an interview in *Latin US* magazine, before his death in 2000 at 77, Puente was asked to define salsa. "As you know, salsa in Spanish means 'sauce', and we use it mostly as a condiment for our foods," he said. "Salsa in general is all our fast Latin music put together: the merengue, the rumba, the mambo, the cha-cha, the guaguancó, boogaloo, all of it is salsa... in Latin music, we have many types of rhythms, like ballads (boleros), rancheros, tangos, and, of course, salsa."

The salsa band is usually composed of a lead vocalist and chorus, a piano, a bass, a horn section and a heavy assortment of percussion instruments (bongos, conga, maracas, *güiros*, timbales, claves, and the ever-present cowbell – a *jíbaro* touch). The overall effect is mesmerizing; the rhythm contagious. It is

San Juan Group guitar lessons in Old San Juan.

JUSTINO DIAZ

Internationally renowned bass singer Justino Díaz first studied at the University of Puerto Rico. He made his operatic debut in 1957 as Ben in Menotti's *The Telephone*, and later studied with Frederick Jager and at the New England Conservatory of Music in Boston.

After winning the Metropolitan Opera Auditions of the Air, he made his debut at the Metropolitan Opera House of New York in 1963 as Monterone in *Rigoletto*, beginning a long-term association with that house. He has sung 30 roles and given nearly 300 performances there.

In 1966, he starred in the role of Antony in Samuel Barber's *Antony and Cleopatra* on the occasion of the opening of the new opera house. In the same year, he made his Salzburg debut as Escamillo in *Carmen*.

In 1971, he created another new role at the inauguration of another opera house, this time as Francesco in Ginastera's *Beatrix Cenci* at the Kennedy Center Opera House in Washington D.C.. His London Covent Garden debut was also as Escamillo, in 1976, and his La Scala debut was as Asdrubale in Rossini's *La Pietra del Paragone* in 1982. He also appeared in the Zeffirelli film of Verdi's *Otello* in 1986.

On March 29, 2003, Justino Díaz retired after 40 years in the arts. For a few years he was artistic director of the Casals Festival.

highly danceable music and you will hear it everywhere.

Salsa (the center of which is now thought to have shifted *back* to Puerto Rico from New York) has firmly placed the island on the map

Miguel A. Valenzuela Morales, better known as Miguelito, is one of the most popular reggaetón artists today yet he was born only in 1999. He was the youngest person ever to win a Latin Grammy Award in 2008.

that resounded back to Spain. This highly stylized tradition of music and its accompanying dance movements are preserved by several local ensembles in Puerto Rico. The *danza* is characterized by a string orchestra, woodwind, and a formal ambience. *La Borinqueña*, the Puerto Rican national anthem, is a *danza*.

A more popular and widely practiced Puerto Rican musical tradition is the *aguinaldo*, a song performed around the Christmas and Three Kings holidays, usually in the form of an *asalto*. The *asalto* is a charming tradition that dates back to the 19th century, and

Street band in Old San Juan.

of popular music, with more and more young *salseros* getting in on the act every day – and not just in Puerto Rico.

"It's totally unexpected to see Belgians, Swedes, Finns and Danes swing to the Latin Beat... the bands there are playing more salsa than we are," said Puente.

A musical evolution

Music has played a crucial role in Puerto Rican society and culture for as long as there have been Puerto Ricans. During Spanish rule, the *danza* was the chief form of entertainment for the *criollo* aristocracy; it reached its high point in the late 19th century when Juan Morel Campos and other masters gave it a popularity

perhaps earlier. It goes along with the unrestrained partying of the holiday season. It is customary at an *asalto* to feast on *lechón asado* (roast suckling pig), *arroz con pollo* (chicken with rice), *gandules* (pigeon peas), and *palos de ron* (shots of rum). Following the feast, a group of noisy celebrants stumbles from house to house, waking the residents and singing *aguinaldos*. The members of each household are expected to join the *asalto* as it moves throughout the surrounding neighborhood.

The *décima*

The *décima* is arguably the most appealing form of traditional Puerto Rican music. It is the vehicle through which the *jíbaro* expresses his joys and frustrations; it is the poetry of the Puerto Rican soul. Instrumentation for the *décima* consists of three-, four-, and six-stringed instruments (called appropriately the *tres*, *cuatro* and *seis*).

The trademark of the *décima* is verbal improvisation. Often, two singers will alternate stanzas, trying to out boast each other with rhyming tales of luscious fruit, pretty women, or physical prowess. The verbal jousting is significantly fueled by the audience. The similarity between the traditional *décima* and the more modern verbal dueling of today's rap DJs is striking.

Willie Colón and his band have produced some of the most inspired salsa music to date. The album *Siembra*, a collaboration with Rubén Blades in 1978, is one of the hottest classics. The songs on *Siembra* show the rhythmic complexity that lies at the core of salsa, as well as the thematic motifs which tie all of salsa together. Like the *plena* singers of old, today's salsa vocalists often tell a story filled with satire or a social commentary.

Whatever the individual's taste, salsa continues to be one of the hottest forms of popular music in the world today.

Puerto Rican folk music is almost inevitably accompanied by lively dance.

Star performers

In Puerto Rico, salsa is king, but who is the King of Salsa? No one can agree, but lists generally include Willie Colón, Rubén Blades, the late Héctor Lavoe, El Gran Combo de Puerto Rico, and the Fania All-Stars. Puerto Rico's biggest salsa star is Gilberto Santa Rosa, affectionately known as "Gilbertito." In addition to salsa, merengue groups from the nearby Dominican Republic have become very popular, and some locals, led by Olga Tañón, Elvis Crespo, and Melina León, have been able to cash in on the fast-paced merengue sound. Local salsa musicians in Cuba and Puerto Rico compete in playing the most infectious melodies, but it is said that the latter are more avant-garde in their approach.

THE PUERTO RICAN CUATRO

Found in South America and the West Indies, the *cuatro* is the national instrument of Puerto Rico. Resembling a Cuban *tres*, the *cuatro moderno* is roughly violin-shaped, with five double courses and ten steel strings tuned from low to high B E A D G, with the B and E in octaves. It is played with a flat pick and it sounds like a cross between a 12-string guitar and a mandolin. An instrument of the *jíbaros* (rural farmers) it also gives its name to the music played on *cuatros* accompanied by the hollow gourd percussion instrument *güiro*. The *cuatro* is also used to accompany *aguinaldos*, the Christmas songs performed by traveling musicians.

A LAND OF FANTASTIC FESTIVALS

Puerto Ricans express their zest for life through a succession of exuberant celebrations. Many of these festivals have their origins in the island's strong Catholicism.

No matter where or when you go, Puerto Ricans always seem to be celebrating something – be it a saint's feast day or a cultural tradition. First and foremost are the *fiestas patronales*, or patron saint festivals, during which each town honors the area's patron saint. Incredibly, there are 78 of these, beginning on January 9 and continuing straight through December 12, and the festivities at each last 10 days. So, in theory, you can party your way around the island nonstop.

And this isn't even taking into consideration the *other* festivals, which all celebrate something, no matter how insignificant it may seem.

In April, for instance, Juana Díaz hosts the Maví Festival, which honors *maví*, a fermented drink made from the bark of the ironwood tree.

With farming being a dominant occupation, harvest festivals abound. Yauco and Maricao both have Coffee Harvest Festivals in February, while the picturesque western town of San Germán marks the end of the island's sugar harvest in April with an appropriate celebration.

If you have to choose, three of the best festivals are the Carnival in Ponce (February), where the *vejigante* masks were first created, the Loíza's *fiesta* of Santiago Apóstol (July), and the Hatillo Masks Festival (December).

All feature music, dancing, ornate masks and costumes, games, religious processions, shows, parades, drink, and food, food, food. It's very difficult not to join in the dancing, and easy to ditch the diet.

Poster advertising Carnival's masked ball in Ponce.

Parades feature costumed marchers, bands, floats – and generally anyone who wants to tag along.

Yauco and Maricao have both had a flourishing coffee industry since the 19th century, so it's not surprising that the island would honor this once lucrative export with a festival.

A group of vejigantes at Ponce carnival.

THE CATHOLIC CONNECTION

With all the colorful costumes and riotous behavior, it is easy to forget that many of Puerto Rico's festivals – particularly the *fiestas patronales* – have religious roots. Religious candle processions with statues, or *santos*, often kick things off, and many Masses are held throughout each festival. Christmas is celebrated here with more fervor than anywhere else in the world. Festivities go on until the Festival de Los Tres Reyes (Epiphany) on January 6. Carnival is also big news – the week before the start of Lent is filled with festivals. Easter, or Semana Santa, is the most important Catholic festival.

Puerto Rico is strongly Catholic, with many convents, monasteries, and even one or two shrines where the Virgin Mary has appeared to the faithful. But this Catholicism has, over the years, blended – like everything else in Puerto Rico – with animist elements of African and Taíno origin. Some of the elements are simple superstition: at midnight during the San Juan Bautista festival on June 24, thousands fill the beaches and walk backward into the sea (or nearest body of water – even a pool will do!) three times to renew good luck for the coming year. Beach parties, together with the usual dancing and music, round off the occasion.

The Hatillo Mask Festival, which commemorates the killing of the innocents, takes place each December. Masked performers representing King Herod's soldiers roam the streets of Hatillo looking for children.

An essential element of any festival is music and dance. Folk dances include the bomba, of pure African origin, and the plena, which blends elements from the island's many cultures.

Garishly dressed masked vejigantes roam the streets during the island's fiestas patronales to chase away evil spirits.

THE LANGUAGE OF PUERTO RICO

Although English and Spanish are both "official" languages, it is Español that rules the heart – and tongue – of Puerto Ricans. They have, however, absorbed words, phrases and mannerisms of the Taíno, Africans, and Americans to create their own version of Spanish.

The language spoken by the Taíno was very similar to that of Arawak people in South America. Much of their vocabulary still exists, particularly in place names. Their name for the island, Borikén, is still used (*La Borinqueña* is the Puerto Rican national anthem). Many Puerto Rican municipalities go by their pre-Columbian names, for example Caguas, Arecibo, Mayagüez, Yauco and Guaynabo. The Taíno feared the god Juracán, while we fear hurricanes. And the *hamacas* in which the early Indians slept are just as popular today under the name of hammocks. The word Taíno meant "good people", with "Tai" meaning "good" and "no" a plural suffix for "people". Although many of their words are still in use today, very little of their language was recorded by the Spanish.

Obliteration of the Taíno

If the Taíno welcomed the Spaniards as a strategy to ward off invading Caribs, they miscalculated. A wave of Spaniards swept across the island. Eventually there came battle and disease, which obliterated the native Taíno population. Then came integration of the races, producing the first Puerto Ricans and the first people who could claim to speak a truly Puerto Rican Spanish.

Puerto Rico's first Africans were brought as slaves, mostly from West-Central Africa. They brought with them another language; they also had many musical instruments, including the drums, which were often used for communication, and countless customs. The *baquine*, a festival of mourning for the death of a child, is a ritual of African origin, and is the scene of dancing, *lechón asado* (roast suckling pig), and a great deal of rum. By the

All is well in Arroyo.

mid-19th century, Africans made up a fifth of the population, and such customs penetrated society.

Integration has worked smoothly in Puerto Rico, and it is said that *él que no tiene dinga tiene mandinga*, a phrase which attributes some amount of African ancestry to virtually all Puerto Ricans. The Mandinga were one of the more populous of the West African tribes, brought to Puerto Rico to harvest sugar cane, coffee, and tobacco.

The farmers of those crops, black, white, and *mestizo*, gradually became the Puerto Rican *jíbaros*. Their 19th-century customs and language patterns were documented in the verses of El Jíbaro.

Quirks and oddities

For all the eccentricities of the Puerto Rican tongue, it is important to remember that the language of the island is Spanish, albeit a Spanish heavily influenced by other nationalities, and that Puerto Rican Spanish shares many oddities with the Spanish of its Caribbean and Latin American neighbors. There is a certain pronunciational sloppiness, particularly with consonants. For example, Spanish words which end in *ado* are pronounced as if the *d* were silent: *pescao* will get you fish (pescado) anywhere on the island. A good stew is an *asopao*, but if your *fiao* (credit) isn't good enough, you won't be served one in any restaurant.

> There is also a non-verbal language. Wrinkling the nose means "What is that?". Both hands raised, palms front, is "Wait a minute," and a tweak of the cheek "I like that." Pretending to wash your hands means "It's done."

"*S*" sounds are muted, and sometimes disappear altogether, at the end of syllables. Matches are *loh fohforoh* rather than *los fósforos* and *graciah* means thanks. *Yeismo* is another confusing variation; this involves pronouncing the Spanish *ll* and *y* sounds as English *js*, so as to render a word like *Luquillo*, the island's most popular beach, as "Look here, Joe."

Spanglish

The granting of United States citizenship to Puerto Ricans in 1917 signaled the advent of English as the first Germanic language to become part of the Puerto Rican dialect. The startling result of this last infusion is Spanglish, a colloquial Spanish that may be as familiar to a North American as it is to a Spaniard. Spanglish consists not only of a shared vocabulary but also of the terse sentence construction characteristic of English. The first penetration of English into Puerto Rican Spanish seems to have come from English labels on consumer products.

Poster for a Don Quixote musical in Ponce's La Perla Theater.

MANUEL ALONSO

The most famous record of the *jíbaro* was written by Manuel A. Alonso, a doctor, poet, journalist, and author belonging to the Latin American literary movement known as *costumbrismo*. In 1845, his book of poems, *El Gíbaro*, published in Barcelona, featured invaluable accounts of a *jíbaro* wedding, dances and cockfights, Christmas celebrations, and the arrival of the magic lantern in the hills. The verses examined the daily hardships and impoverished lives of farmers in Puerto Rico as well as their customs. Equally important is the portrait of mid-19th-century *jíbaro* speech patterns. In Alonso's verses we can hear the *jíbaro* dialect in its purest form. He mentions foods such as *lechón asado*, *toytiyas* (tor-tillas) and *maví* (mauby, a drink made from tree bark).

Born in San Juan in 1822, Alonso later moved to Spain to study medicine at the University of Barcelona. After practising medicine there, he returned to Puerto Rico and established a medical office in Caguas, in 1848. Working alongside other respected writers, he published the *Album Puertorriqueño*, only the second anthology of poems to be published in his home country. His work was heavily influenced by love for his country and his memory is honored by the public buildings and schools named after him. Alonso joined the Liberal Reform movement and directed its publication, *El Agente* (The Agent). He died in San Juan in 1889.

Indeed, men still sit at bars nursing *un scotch* while their children look on, chewing *chicles*. The introduction of American commerce was no less confounding in other ways. When the first American cash registers were introduced in San Juan's grocery and department stores, a whole generation stood paralyzed at checkout counters when the "No Sale" tab, marking the end of the transaction, flipped up. *No sale* in Spanish translates as "Do not leave."

Spanglish truly entered its heyday only with the mass migration of Puerto Ricans to the United States in the 1940s. This exodus created a generation of so-called *Nuyoricans*, who returned to their native island with the baffling customs and speech patterns developed on the streets of New York. Or they would send letters home with news, and, if they had no money, they would send the letter *ciodí* (cash on delivery).

Letters to the Cordillera would have to be transported by *un trok*. Perhaps there would be bad news, that a son had been *bosteado* by the *policías* for dealing in *las drogas*. More often the letters would just contain idle

Alfresco dining in Calle del Cristo, Old San Juan.

LET'S SPEAK SPANGLISH

Many terms used in Puerto Rico are now derived from modern English. Here are a few examples:

Parquear is used instead of the Spanish *estacionar*, coming from the English word "park"

Bye bye is used instead of the Spanish *adiós*

The verb *bulear* is derived from the English verb to bully

The verb *charlar* means to chat or make small talk

Troca is used for "pickup truck" instead of the standard Spanish *camioneta*

Computadora, derived from the English word "computer," is now used even in standard Spanish, despite the original Spanish term for computer, which was *ordenador*

"Hasta you later" is a corruption of the Spanish *hasta luego*, which means "until later"

The adjective *serioso* denotes the English "serious" instead of the Spanish *serio*

Norsa comes from the English word "nurse", rather than the standard Spanish *enfermera*

The word *actualmente*, meaning "currently," is very frequently misused to replace both the English terms "actually" and "in fact." The official Spanish term for "actually" is *de hecho*

Marketa is an often-used word derived from the English word "market" (as used in "supermarket") instead of the standard Spanish word *mercado*

chatter, or discussions of the decisions of the world *líderes*, or of how a brother had won a pool game by sinking the important eight ball in the corner *poquete*.

Puerto Ricans love pool, but if Puerto Rico and the Spanglish language have an official sport it has to be *el béisbol*, or baseball. Everyone knows that Roberto Clemente (from Carolina) and Orlando Cepeda (from Santurce) were Puerto Rico's greatest hitters of *jonrones* and *dobles* (home-runs and doubles). Most Puerto Ricans would say their ballplayers were *wilson*, meaning "very good." *El* or *la*

Taíno talk

The island's language has been considerably enriched by that of the ancestral Taínos, including the following words and phrases:
canoa canoe
burén ceramic grill
coa gardening instrument (hoe)
barbacoa barbecue
tibes rough stone
areyto ceremonial dance
guasábara war or fight
bija a red pigment
higüera a tree whose fruit (the gourds) are used

Street talk in Yabucoa.

Wilson can also refer to the ball itself. Some things have remained little changed, though. Dollars are sometimes called *dolares*, but more often *pesos*. Quarters are *pesetas*, nickels *vellones*, and pennies *centavos*.

Language means more to the people of Puerto Rico than just about anything else. Most Puerto Ricans fear the loss of their language through the influence of other cultures, especially if the island were to become a state of America.

One of the first questions a Puerto Rican will ask a visitor is "*¿Habla español?*" If the visitor responds positively ("*Sí, hablo español*"), then he or she will be welcomed into the fold graciously.

for utensils and musical instruments
jicotea water turtle
anón fruit tree
guanábana soursop fruit
quenepa fruit (guinep or Spanish lime on some islands, limoncillo in the Dominican Republic)
guayacán a tree with very hard wood
batata sweet potato
maní peanut
yucca cassava

Having such a rich and vibrant oral tradition, Puerto Ricans love good conversation, and, with at least four linguistic families from which to draw, they enjoy a speech that is at once cryptic and colorful.

Star basketball player, Carlos Rivera.

A SPORTING LIFE

Baseball, basketball, and volleyball fire the Puerto Ricans' competitive spirit, but there is plenty for the visitor to do on and off the island's tropical waters.

When the first ball was thrown in the Taíno *batey*, sport was born in Puerto Rico. All that remains of this early interest in sport are the ruins of the Taíno ball courts south of Arecibo at the Caguana Ceremonial Ballpark and the Tibes Indian Ceremonial Park in Ponce, where early people played a game much like soccer. The Spanish brought sports such as cockfighting, dominoes and horse racing, but were not keen on team games.

Baseball mania

In 1897, a group of Puerto Ricans and Cubans who had lived in the US, introduced baseball to the island. Two clubs were started and in 1898 the first match was held. After the Spanish American War, US soldiers brought more sports to the island, as they used boxing and basketball as part of their training, and played baseball against the local teams. After a slow start, the game later became overwhelmingly popular. The Puerto Rico Baseball League is the main professional league, playing from November to January, and its champion goes through to play in the Caribbean Series in February against teams from the Dominican Republic, Venezuela and Mexico. Teams come and go according to ability and finance, but currently the league consists of the Criollos de Caguas, Gigantes de Carolina, Indios de Mayagüez and the Leones de Ponce.

The best players are recruited to play for US teams. The game has produced such luminaries as Roberto Clemente, Orlando Cepeda, and Rubén Gómez, with more recent stars including Iván "Pudge" Rodríguez, Carlos Delgado, Carlos Beltrán, Bernie Williams, and Jorge Posada. In 2011 Roberto Alomar became the third Puerto Rican to be enshrined in the Baseball Hall of Fame, after Clemente and Cepeda.

New York Yankees star Carlos Beltrán hails from Puerto Rico.

Basketball

Although baseball has been the sport most identified with Puerto Rico, basketball ranks a close second, drawing much interest because of success in international competitions such as the Olympics and the Pan-American Games. Puerto Rican teams have even given the powerful US entries a run for their money. The Baloncesta Superior Nacional (Superior Basketball League) fields 10 teams. There is also a successful women's league. The season runs through spring and summer, adjusted annually to accommodate international participation in the Olympics, Pan-American Games, and other events. In 2011 Juan José Barea became the first Puerto Rican to play in the NBA Finals for a winning championship team when he played for the Dallas Mavericks.

Boxing for gold

Puerto Rico's boxers have won gold medals in international competition and boxing is right up with basketball and baseball in the island's affections, having produced more amateur and professional champions than any other sport. More than 50 professional pugilists have held champion status in every weight category except heavyweight (unless you include John Ruiz, an American of Puerto Rican descent). There are eight Puerto Ricans in the Boxing Hall of Fame. Three-time world champions include Wilfredo Gómez, Wilfredo Benítez, and Felix "Tito" Trinidad. Hector "Macho" Camacho has won world championships in three different weights. In women's boxing, Ada Vélez and Amanda Serrano are the current holders of the IBF super bantamweight and super featherweight titles respectively.

Courts and courses

Puerto Rico has also produced champion tennis players, golfers – and even a horse that won the Kentucky Derby, Bold Forbes. Horse racing

The Trump International Golf Club in Río Grande is superb.

THE HIGHS OF SKYDIVING

For those thrill-seekers who thrive on the adrenaline rush of extreme sports, Puerto Rico has it all. From skydiving to caving or rock climbing, there is something for you. The northern town of Arecibo and the eastern town of Humacao are known for skydiving. You can jump from more than 10,500ft (3,200 meters) and free fall at more than 100mph (160kmh) while enjoying a scenic view, from the mountains to the sea. While you can skydive any time of year, in February the Xtreme Divers professional school (tel: 787-852 5757, www.xtremedivers. com) hosts the annual Puerto Rico Freefall Festival, which attracts thousands of divers and spectators.

draws great interest, even though there is only one race track, Camarero in Canóvanas. Tennis courts abound on the island, and the public may use hotel and resort facilities for a fee. A few internationally known tennis players have emerged from the local courts, such as Charlie Pasarell and Gigi Fernández. The Baldrich Tennis Club in Hato Rey provides 10 regulation courts for use at a nominal cost.

Golf is a natural for the island, with 26 courses of varying standards including 19 championship courses. Public courses are available at reasonable rates in Punta Borinquen and Aguirre, with a public driving range in Bayamón and a golf academy and range in San Juan. All hotel courses are available at higher rates. Puerto Rico's most famous golfer is Juan "Chichi" Rodríguez, who has his own golf resort, El Legado, in Guayama).

Water sports

Water sports of all types feature, naturally, and marinas are at Isla Grande, Boca de Cangrejos, Fajardo, Ponce, and Mayagüez. Surfing has become a way of life in areas like Rincón, where international events have been held. Windsurfing is a natural choice for the waters of the Atlantic and the Caribbean. Ocean kayaking has gained popularity in recent times, with kayaks for rent on the placid Condado Lagoon. Scuba diving and

Although cockfighting is now illegal in all 50 US states and Washington D.C., it remains legal in Puerto Rico, where contests are held between November and August.

Trail rides

In four-legged sports, a favorite weekend activity is *cabalgatas*. Derived from the Spanish word for horse – *caballo* – these are trail rides that range from elegant *paseos* on fine *paso fino* horses accompanied by catering vans along the way, right

Surfing is very popular throughout the island.

For a country that is considered machista, Puerto Rico's fascination with women's volleyball is notable, with full crowds for semi-pro leagues, and even high school matches receive a great deal of media attention.

snorkelling are offered by many companies with probably the best diving off Vieques and Culebra. Visibility can be affected by run-off from rivers on the main island, but they have the advantage of attracting a wide range of fish. Anglers can indulge in all types of fishing, although deep-sea fishing is particularly good, with billfish plentiful. Marlin as heavy as 500lbs (227kg) have been reeled in.

through to raucous four-legged pub crawls that include anyone who's managed to raise a horse in his backyard. There are sedate horseback trail rides for tourists, which are a good way to see the island, or you can trust in your own legs and go hiking, which is very popular in El Yunque forest.

For those who prefer speed, there are mountain bike trails around the island and several companies offering guides and equipment hire. Some trails are quite technical, twisty single tracks with roots and rocks; there are some steep downhills, and several pleasant routes that end at the beach – so all levels are catered for. Other adventure sports such as caving, canyoning, tubing, body rafting, rock climbing, rappelling, and even skydiving are available for the active traveler.

Mountains in the mist in the Cordillera Central.

Colorful facades in Old San Juan.

Puerto Rico offers an array of family-friendly beaches.

INTRODUCTION

A detailed guide to the entire island, with principal
sites clearly cross-referenced by number to the maps.

*Playa Las Palmas, Punta la
Galiena.*

Puerto Rico is small enough that you can base
yourself somewhere and still manage to visit the
rest of the island if you hire a car. You will need
more time, however, to include the charming islands
of Vieques and Culebra.

San Juan, the capital and business center, is also
the most populous area. Old San Juan harks back
to the 16th century and the colonial city is not to
be missed, with its fortresses, grand mansions, museums, and art galleries. The vari-
ous districts of metropolitan San
Juan house the high-tech offices of banks and trading companies, the university, convention center,
hotels, casinos and beaches, making this a modern
city in a Caribbean environment.

The northeast of the island is the most geographi-
cally diverse. Its range of terrain, from mountains
and rainforest to secluded islands, is staggering.
Here, too, you'll find most of the island's best
beaches and some of the finest yachting. Ferries will
take you to the slower-paced Vieques and Culebra,
where pristine sand and transparent waters are perfect for diving and snorkeling.

View from the Ruta Panorámica.

Heading west from San Juan, exploration of the
northern part of the island reveals one of the largest cave networks in the
Western Hemisphere, as well as the oddly scaled karst mountain region.
Limestone formations rise above the island's most historic cities – Arecibo, Lares, and San Sebastián.

The western reaches of Puerto Rico feature beautiful beaches,
surfers' paradises and towns worth discovering, such as metropolitan Mayagüez and architecturally rich San Germán. In the south of
the island, you'll realize fully the relaxed pace of life in Puerto Rico.
There's Ponce, a gem of a city on the coast, where you'll never be at a
loss to find a quiet place to sit in the sun.

The heart of the island is the Cordillera Central. Here, the Ruta Panorámica will take the adventurous driver from one end of the mountain
range to the other, affording spectacular views. This area contains a range
of natural and cultural attractions to delight any visitor.

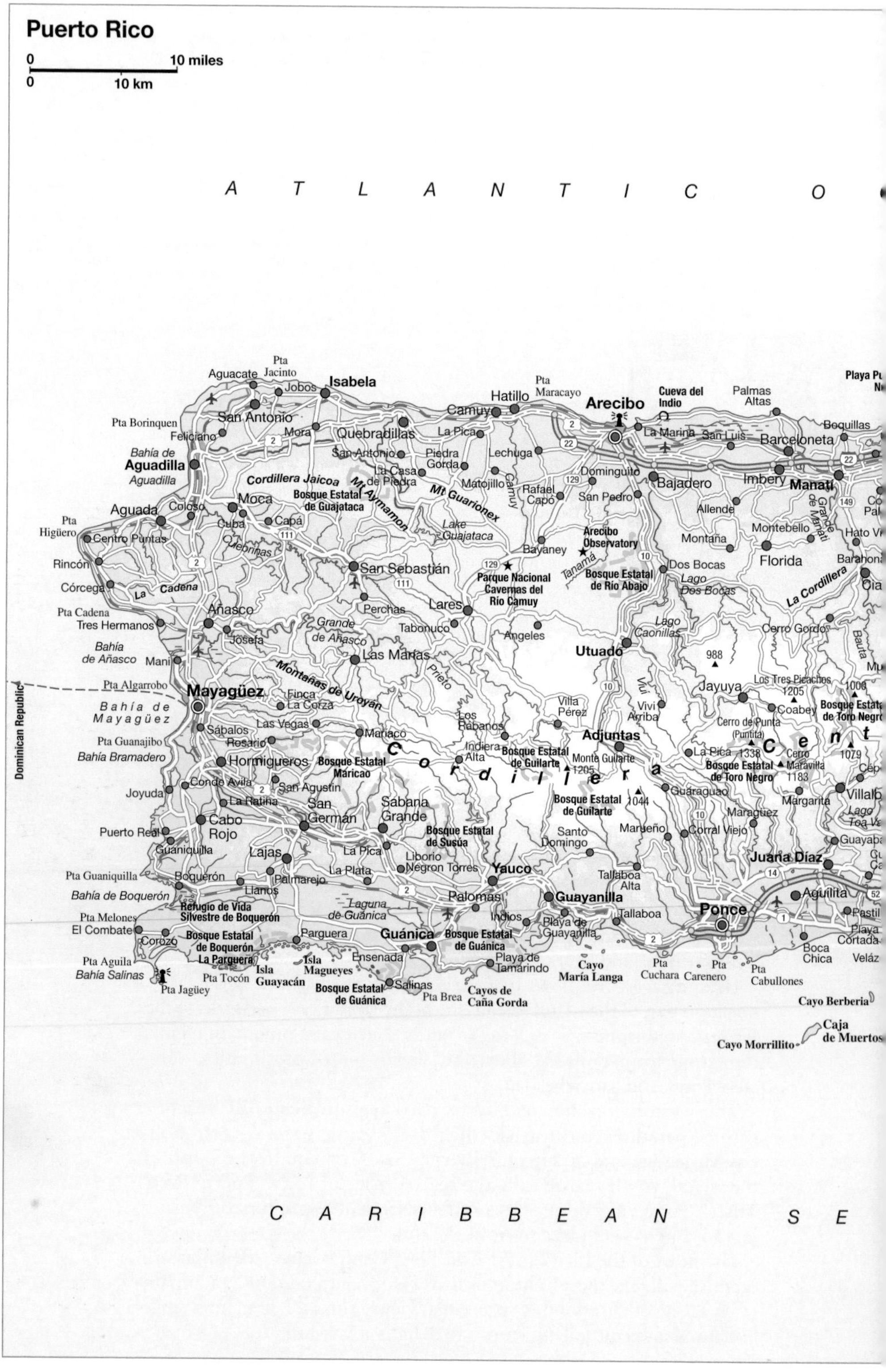

Puerto Rico

```
0                 10 miles
0        10 km
```

ATLANTICO

Isabela
Arecibo
Aguadilla
Mayagüez
Manatí
Ponce

Pta Jacinto
Aguacate
Jobos
Hatillo
Camuy
Pta Maracayo
Cueva del Indio
Palmas Altas
Playa Pu
Ne
Pta Borinquen
San Antonio
Feliciano
Mora
Quebradillas
La Pica
Arecibo
Indio
Boquillas
Bahía de Aguadilla
Aguadilla
San Antonio
Piedra Gorda
La Casa de Piedra
Lechuga
La Marina
San Luis
Barceloneta
Cordillera Jaicoa
Bosque Estatal de Guajataca
Matojillo
Rafael Capó
San Pedro
Dominguito
Bajadero
Imbery
Co
Pal
Aguada
Coloso
Moca
Capá
Cuba
Lake Guajataca
Arecibo Observatory
Allende
Montaña
Montebello
Hato V
Pta Higüero
Centro Puntas
Lebrijas
Bayaney
Dos Bocas
Lago Dos Bocas
Florida
Barahona
Rincón
Córcega
La Cadena
San Sebastián
Parque Nacional Cavernas del Río Camuy
Bosque Estatal de Río Abajo
La Cordillera
Cia
Pta Cadena
Tres Hermanos
Añasco
Perchas
Lares
Tabonuco
Angeles
Lago Caonillas
Cerro Gordo
Bahía de Añasco
Mani
Josefa
Grande de Añasco
Las Marías
Utuado
988
Los Tres Picachos
1205
1006
Coabey
Pta Algarrobo
Montañas de Uroyan
Prieto
Villa Pérez
Vivi Arriba
Jayuya
Bosque Estat de Toro Negr
Finca La Corza
Las Vegas
Mariaco
Los Rábanos
Cerro de Punta (Puntita)
1079
Cep
Pta Guanajibo
Bahía Bramadero
Sábalos
Rosario
Indiera Alta
Bosque Estatal de Guilarte
Monte Guilarte
1205
Adjuntas
La Pica 1338
Cerro Maravilla 1183
Joyuda
Conde Avila
San Agustín
Bosque Estatal Máricao
Guaraguao
Villalb
Margarita
Lago Toa Va
Cabo Rojo
San Germán
Sabana Grande
Bosque Estatal de Guilarte
1044
Marueño
Corral Viejo
Guayaba
Puerto Real
Guaniquilla
Lajas
Bosque Estatal de Susúa
Santo Domingo
Maragüez
Juana Díaz
Gu
Pta Guaniquilla
Boquerón
La Pica
Liborio
Negrón Torres
Yauco
Tallaboa Alta
14
Aguilita
52
Pastil
Bahía de Boquerón
Pta Melones
El Combate
Refugio de Vida Silvestre de Boquerón
Llanos
Palmarejo
La Plata
Laguna de Guánica
Palomas
Guayanilla
Tallaboa
Ponce
1
Playa Chica
Corozo
Parguera
Guánica
Bosque Estatal de Guánica
Indios
Playa de Guayanilla
Boca Chica
Veláz
Pta Aguila
Bahía Salinas
La Parguera
Isla Guayacán
Isla Magueyes
Ensenada
Playa de Tamarindo
Cayo María Langa
Pta Cuchara
Pta Carenero
Pta Cabullones
Pta Jagüey
Pta Tocón
Bosque Estatal de Guánica
Salinas
Pta Brea
Cayos de Caña Gorda
Cayo Berbería
Cayo Morrillito
Caja de Muertos

Dominican Republic

Bahía de Mayagüez

CARIBBEAN SE

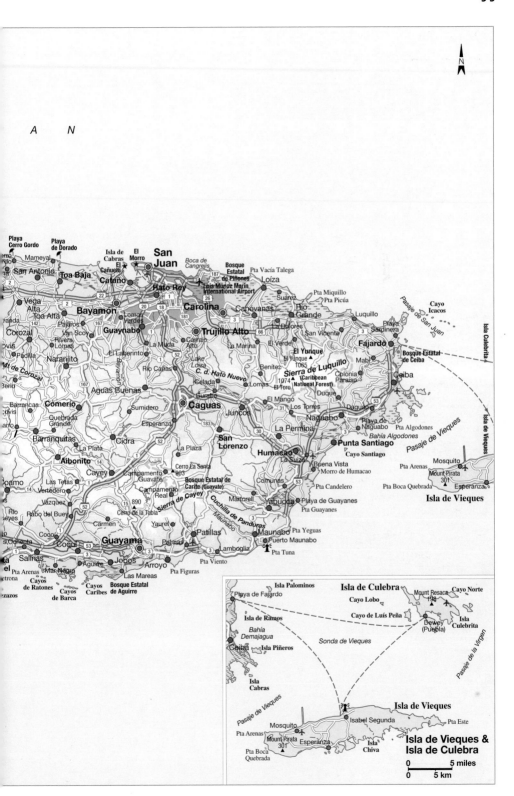

A   N

Playa
Cerro Gordo
Playa
de Dorado
Isla de
Cabras
El
Morro
San
Juan
Boca de
Cangrejis
Mameyal
El
Cañuelo
187
Bosque
Estatal
de Piñones
Pta Vacía Talega
San Antonio
Toa Baja
Cataño
Luis Muñoz Marín
International Airport
Loíza
Hato Rey
Suárez
Pta Miquillo
Pta Picúa
Cayo
Icacos
Vega
Alta
2
Bayamón
20
18
Carolina
Cañovanas
Río
Grande
Luquillo
Toa Alta
181
La Dulores
Playa
Sardinera
Corozal
Pájaros
Van Scoy
Guaynabo
Rivera
Lomas
La Muda
Carraío
Alto
San Vicente
El Verde
Fajardo
Padilla
Naranjito
El Laberinto
Río Cañas
52
Lake
Loíza
La Marina
Benítez
El Yunque
El Yunque
1065
Sierra de Luquillo
Mabí
Bosque Estatal
de Ceiba
Aguas Buenas
C. d. Hato Nuevo
Celada
Gurabo
El Toro
1074
El Mango
(Caribbean
National Forest)
Colonia
Paraíso
Ceiba
Comerío
Sumidero
Caguas
Juncos
31
Los Torres
Duque
53
Quebrada
Grande
Esperanza
183
Naguabo
Playa de
Naguabo
Pta Algodones
Barranquitas
Cidra
La Plata
La Plaza
San
Lorenzo
30
La Permina
Punta Santiago
Cayo Santiago
Aibonito
14
Humacao
La Suiza
Buena Vista
Morro de Humacao
Pta Arenas
Mosquito
Mount Pirata
301
Cayey
Campamento
Guavate
Cerro La Santa
903
Bosque Estatal de
Carite (Guayate)
Comunas
53
Pta Candelero
Pta Boca Quebrada
Esperanza
Campamento
Real
Martorell
Yabucoa
Playa de Guayanes
Isla de Vieques
Vázquez
15
890
Cerro de la Tabla
Cuchilla de Panduras
Pta Guayanes
Rabo del Buey
52
Carmen
Yaurel
Patillas
Pta Yeguas
Maunabo
Puerto Maunabo
Cogol
Coqui
53
Guayama
Palmas
Lamboglia
Pta Tuna
Salinas
Jobos
Arroyo
Pta Viento
Aguirre
Las Mareas
Pta Figuras
Pta Arenas
Mar Negro
Cayos
de Ratones
Cayos
de Barca
Cayos
Caribes
Bosque Estatal
de Aguirre

Isla Palominos
Isla de Culebra
Mount Resaca
198
Cayo Norte
Playa de Fajardo
Cayo Lobo
Cayo de Luís Peña
Isla de Ramos
Dewey
(Puebla)
Isla
Culebrita
Bahía
Demajagua
Sonda de Vieques
Ceiba
Isla Piñeros

Isla
Cabras

Isla de Vieques

Pasaje de Vieques
Mosquito
Isabel Segunda
Pta Este
Pta Arenas
Mount Pirata
301
Esperanza
Isla
Chiva
Pta Boca
Quebrada

**Isla de Vieques &
Isla de Culebra**

0   5 miles

0   5 km

Old San Juan

```
0          200 yds
0          200 m
```

ATLANTIC OCEAN

C. San Miguel

Bastión de Santo Tomás

Bastión de San Sebastián

(Boulevard de Valle)

Sebastián

Calle Tanca

Abraham Lincoln

Calle Sol

C. J. L. Acosta

C. del Toro

C. Tamarindo

Calle Luna

Calle O'Donell

San Juan National Historic Site Headquarters

El Castillo de San Cristóbal

36

Plaza San Juan Bautista

Avenida Muñoz Rivera

El Capitolio

tensores a la Fe

Capilla Franciscana

Plaza Salvador Brau

Calle San Francisco

Callejón de la Capilla

Casa del Callejón 4

Calle Fortaleza

C. Gambaro

Columbus

Plaza Colón 1

Avenida

Muñoz Rivera

Carnegie Library

Ateneo Puertorriqueño

Casa de España

General Archives and National Library of Puerto Rico

Old Casino of Puerto Rico 3

Avenida Ponce de León

Paseo de Covadonga

Calle

Calle Tanca

Teatro Tapia 2 (Tapia Theater)

Paseo de Covadonga

Depto. de Hacienda

Calle Tetuán

Calle General Pershing

Calle Harding

C. del Muelle

Calle Recinto Sur

Banco Popular de Puerto Rico

Sur

Antigua Edificio Federal Correo (Old US Post Office)

Calle Comercio

C. Braumbaugh

C. Nolascorubio

Calle Marina

a de tos

Plazoleta de San Juan

Plaza Darcenas

La Casita

Pier 2

Customs House ficio de Aduana)

Pier 1

Pier 3

Pier 4

Muella Turista 3 (Cruise Ship Pier)

Cataño

Nuevo San Juan

OLD SAN JUAN

There's a wealth of architectural treasures on the spit of land that is Old San Juan, from sturdy fortresses to pretty pastel painted houses, with museums, shops, restaurants and bars for all to enjoy.

Old San Juan, walled within the island capital, is the second-oldest European settlement in the Americas. Built by Spanish colonists in 1521, it exhibits magnificent colonial fortresses such as El Morro, San Cristóbal and La Fortaleza, superb examples of 16th- and 17th-century colonial architecture with blue cobblestoned streets.

No matter how much history is crammed within the *adoquín*-lined streets of Old San Juan, it is something altogether more spiritual that attracts Puerto Ricans and visitors alike. There is something that traps travelers and forces them to move at the city's pace. If you've rushed through Old San Juan, you certainly have not been there. Get a good pair of walking shoes and ramble; a car is a liability here.

Old San Juan has an endless supply of undiscovered attractions to enjoy. It is to these that second-time visitors call a taxi for as soon as they step off the plane at Luis Muñoz Marín International Airport. The 7-mile (11km)-square city was declared a World Heritage Site by Unesco in 1983. A cultural center, fine dining and shopping district, and nightlife center, the islet is also home to 395,000 people.

Plaza Colón

As Puerto Rico's Spanish history begins with Columbus, an exploration of Old San Juan could naturally begin in the **Plaza Colón ❶**, or Columbus Square. Built in the 17th century as Plaza Santiago, it was first named after the patron saint of Spanish soldiers, Saint James. In front of the quadrangle lay the Puerta de Santiago and the walls surrounding the city, most of which were demolished in the 19th century. For the 400th anniversary of his arrival on Puerto Rico, a statue of Christopher Columbus was commissioned in 1893, and it was unveiled at the remodeled *plaza* in 1894.

Main Attractions

Plaza Colón
Teatro Tapia
La Fortaleza
Calle del Cristo
San Juan Cathedral
Museo del Niño
El Morro
El Castillo de San Cristóbal

Cruise ship on the waterfront.

It is here that the high-speed, heavily trafficked Ponce de León and Muñoz Rivera avenues give way to the narrow grid that is Old San Juan. If you're without a car this will be your last stop on the municipal bus, or *público*. If you are driving, you should now start looking for a place to park.

Located at the southeastern corner, Plaza Colón is an ideal spot for fanning out on a walking tour of the city. The square itself offers a good introductory stroll.

On its south side is the **Teatro Tapia** ❷ (Tapia Theater; tel: 787-721-0180 or 787-721-0169). This neoclassical gem may be the oldest freestanding theater stage building that is still in use in the US territories. It takes the form of a horseshoe-shaped opera house and there are three tiers of wooden seats, providing enough space for 700 people. The theater has served as a cultural center since 1832, when construction finished on the public theater originally named the Teatro Municipal de San Juan.

Despite the fact that it had seen the likes of singers and performers such as Adelina Patti and Anna Pavlova, it fell into a period of neglect during the 1940s that nearly resulted in its demolition. Fortunately, Felisa Rincón, then mayor of San Juan, saw the need to preserve this Puerto Rican treasure. The restorations were finished in 1949 and it was renamed after renowned local playwright Alejandro Tapia y Rivera (1826–82). Soon the theater was in full use once again. In 1975 and 2008 the building went through more extensive restorations, keeping in line with its original architectural glory and adding state-of-the-art technology.

Today the venue continues its traditional use by serving as host to ballets, concerts, operas, theatrical performances, and cultural events. It is also used for meetings and presentations.

Across the street from the theater on the plaza's eastern side is the **Old Casino of Puerto Rico** ❸. Built in 1917 in the style of a French mansion of the Louis XVI era, it sits on the spot of the old Puerta de Santiago, also referred to as Puerta de Tierra, and part of the walls surrounding

Busy sidewalk in the Old City.

the Old City. Built by an elite social club of the time, the most glamorous events were celebrated at the casino and it now functions as the State Department Reception Center. Other notable buildings east of Plaza Colón along Avenida Ponce de León include the Carnegie Library, the Ateneo Puertorriqueño, the Casa de España and El Capitolio.

Calle Fortaleza

Calle Fortaleza is the usual route into the old city from Plaza Colón and is, at least for three blocks, cluttered with souvenir shops, jewelry shops, and shoe stores. Fortunately, Calle Fortaleza is just as crowded with architectural wonders. The first right along the street is **Callejón de la Capilla**, a romantic, lantern-lit alleyway that arcs uphill to Calle San Francisco.

At the corner of Fortaleza and Callejón de la Capilla, the **Casa del Callejón ❹**, an 18th-century residence, houses two charming museums – one dedicated to pharmacology and the other to the Puerto Rican

family. Located on the first floor of the building, the **Museo de la Farmacia** (tel: 787-977-2700; Tue–Sat 8.30am–4.20pm; free) houses a valuable collection of crystal and porcelain flasks as well as furniture and other objects that were typical of drugstores in the mid-19th century. The second floor is home to the **Casa de la Familia Puertorriqueña** (tel: 787-977-2700; Tue–Sat 8.30am–4.20pm; free). This museum illustrates, with its decor and furnishings, the times and daily routines of domestic life for middle-class Puerto Rican families of the 19th century.

Continuing on Calle Fortaleza, you can turn right on to Calle Tanca for a bit of relaxation in the sloping Plaza Salvador Brau, or make a left toward the piers of San Juan Port. Nearby at the waterfront, **Plazoleta de San Juan** teems with eager visitors who purchase souvenirs and folk art from the local artisans.

San Juan port, which takes more cruise traffic than any other port in the Caribbean, not only benefits from the tastefulness of its more

TIP

A good way to get around the Old City is by using the free trolleys that travel all over Old San Juan from 7am to 6pm weekdays, 9am to 7pm weekends. Stops (paradas) are clearly marked. All four routes start from opposite cruise ship pier 4.

A rainbow of facades.

The Spanish flavor of Old San Juan's architecture is evident from any angle.

The lovely Plaza de Armas.

utilitarian maritime buildings (the pink, mock-colonial **US Customs House ❺** is a good example of this), but has a beautiful cityscape too.

The waterfront has become even more attractive with its **Frente Portuario** complex. This Mediterranean-style mega-project offers 200 condo apartments across three buildings, the large Sheraton Hotel and Casino, two office towers, a 603-space parking garage, and a large amount of retail space.

Frente Portuario, designed to blend in with the rest of Old San Juan, features picturesque cobblestone-like paved boulevards lined with wrought-iron lamps and red-tiled roofs. Visitors can browse through art galleries, eateries, and boutiques.

There are half a dozen cruise-ship piers along the waterfront. Some of the world's largest cruise ships regularly call here. From Pier 2 you can also take the ferry to Cataño, home of the Bacardi rum distillery. At 50 cents a passenger, this ferry is truly one of Puerto Rico's great bargains.

Plaza de Hostos

Plaza de Hostos is an oasis of shade in a square full of *adoquines*. Named for the 19th-century scholar, it provides a haven for sunburned tourists and locals alike; the square must be the dominoes capital of the Caribbean. Looming over the plaza is the original office of the **Banco Popular de Puerto Rico ❻**, which has to be one of the great modern architectural triumphs of the Caribbean region. This brawny, 10-story edifice, built in the mid-1930s, is a fine example of Art Deco. Heavy cameo eagles brood over the impressive main entrance, which is lettered in sans serif gilt intaglio. Elongated windows with prominent pastel mullions run the full height of a faintly apsidal facade. The bank presents various exhibits of historical interest during the year.

The area is particularly fortunate in its culinary offerings. Calle Fortaleza has a number of first-rate restaurants and also hosts an annual food festival when tables are pulled out onto the street and there is wall-to-wall eating,

shopping and entertainment day and night. South Fortaleza Street is known as SoFo.

Whether approaching uphill on Calle Cruz from Plaza de Hostos, or via Calle Fortaleza from Plaza Colón, almost all travelers pass through the workaday heart of Old San Juan. At its center, on **Calle San Francisco**, a friendly mix of tourist shops and government buildings, is the **Casa Alcaldía** ❼ (City Hall; tel: 787-724-7171, ext. 2391; Mon–Fri 8am–4pm; free) and the adjacent **Plaza de Armas** ❽. Construction on Casa Alcaldía began in 1604 and was completed in 1789. The building, of neoclassical design, was remodeled in the 1840s to replicate the facade of the City Hall in Madrid, with two towers overlooking the plaza. Casa Alcaldía is currently home to the office of the mayor, is open to the public, and has periodic art and cultural exhibitions. There is also a visitor information center.

The plaza, originally known as Plaza Mayor, is no less historic. Built in 1521, it was the first square in the newly established city. It also served, in the days before soldiers were permanently billeted in San Juan, as the training field for Spanish soldiers sent out from Europe to defend the island – hence its current name. Stone paving of the plaza began in 1840 and was completely remodeled in the late 1980s.

Anchoring the plaza is the Fuente de las Cuatro Estaciones, the Fountain of the Four Seasons. Each statue represents a different season.

La Fortaleza

Calle Fortaleza grows more dignified as it approaches **La Fortaleza** ❾ itself (tel: 787-721-7000 ext. 2211; Mon–Fri 9.30am–3.30pm). This blue and white wonder of a fortress is the oldest continuously inhabited executive mansion in the Western Hemisphere. Its construction began in 1532 and was completed in 1540, and it serves to this day as the residence of the Governor of Puerto Rico. It is an architectural wonder, but strategically it was always inadequate. This was apparent even to the Spanish architects, who decided

FACT

Adoquines are blocks of slag, from the lowland smelting mills of Spain's 16th-century empire. The cobblestones were brought over by the Spanish as ballast for their ships.

Strolling down Calle del Cristo.

that the gnarled peninsula on which La Fortaleza was being built did not command enough of San Juan Bay to protect completely against invasion from the sea. Accordingly, construction of the massive fort at the tip of the San Juan Peninsula – **El Morro** – began in the 1540s.

The 1588 sinking of the Spanish Armada made the West Indian possessions of the Spanish Crown more vulnerable than ever, with the result that even more Puerto Rican colonists clamored for greater fortification. By 1595, Queen Elizabeth I had dispatched Sir Francis Drake, whose ambitions included not only a great bounty of gold, but all the Spanish lands of the New World as well. Drake arrived in San Juan in late November of that year. He stopped across the bay at Isla de Cabras, and launched several dozen ships from there. Ten would never go back to England, and a total of 400 English sailors would rest forever beneath San Juan harbor. Drake's own cabin was torn apart by a mortar shell during the invasion.

Perhaps the Spanish grew complacent after the first thwarted invasion of their colonial capital, for in June 1598 the Earl of Cumberland was able to land a force of about 1,000 men in the area of Puerta de Tierra, and then march into San Juan. The 400 Spanish soldiers defending the city were suffering from tropical diseases but put up valiant resistance, enduring a 15-day siege inside El Morro before capitulating. The British flag flew over the walls of La Fortaleza. The British were hounded by Spanish colonists almost immediately, but it was less Spanish resistance than British *lack* of resistance to the same diseases that led them to give in. In a matter of several weeks after the invasion, Cumberland sailed for home, having lost over 400 men, to leave San Juan to recover in peace for another 27 years.

The year 1625 saw the final occupation of La Fortaleza during colonial times. A Dutch fleet under the command of Boudewijn Hendrikszoon swiftly moved into San Juan Bay and set up a beachhead between El Morro and La Fortaleza. The Dutch burned much of the city to the ground, including a large portion of La Fortaleza. Reconstruction began in 1640; the building was expanded in 1800 and 1846.

Calle del Cristo

Calle del Cristo (Christ's Street) is the most alluring of Old San Juan's thoroughfares, an intoxicating avenue of sights and sounds, of romance and history. Running from a point high above San Juan Bay, Calle del Cristo arches to an even higher perch above San Juan's Atlantic shore, where El Morro looks sternly out to sea. It can claim Old San Juan's most popular park, underrated museum, and famous chapel.

This adventure in *adoquines* begins at the **Parque de las Palomas** ❿ (Pigeon Park), a part of the city walls which thousands of pigeons have

The light-filled interior of San Juan Cathedral.

made their home. Fabulous views of San Juan Bay and the distant suburbs of Bayamón and Guaynabo make Parque de las Palomas a popular spot for lovers and an even more popular spot for any aspiring ones.

Cristo Chapel

Love almost certainly played a decisive part in the construction of the quaint **Cristo Chapel** or Capilla del Cristo ⓫ (Tue 10am–3.30pm; free), which contains some beautiful Campeche paintings. Romantic legend has it that, during an 18th-century horse race, one of two competing riders failed to make a left turn onto Calle Tetuán and fell over cliffs, seemingly to his death. When he survived, astounded locals constructed a chapel to commemorate Christ's intercession.

Others claim that the race was really a duel over a comely young woman between two chivalrous *enamorados*. One fell to his death, and the chapel was built both to commemorate the tragedy and to block off Calle del Cristo to prevent such a mishap from ever occurring again.

The peninsula stretching below the Cristo Chapel is known as **La Puntilla**. Today it accommodates the **Arsenal de la Marina** (tel: 787-724-1877; times vary depending on exhibitions; free), a former Spanish naval base that now houses the Plastic Arts Divisions of the Institute of Puerto Rican Culture. This complex houses offices and ample gallery space where diverse art exhibits are held year-round. The gardens and patio are also used for cultural activities.

A short walk up Calle del Cristo on the right is one of Puerto Rico's most enchanting and least-known museums. The **Casa del Libro** ⓬ (tel: 787-723-0354; Mon–Fri 11am–5pm, closed public holidays; free) is a breezy, parqueted sanctuary which is dedicated to the history of books and printing. Within its walls are nearly 5,000 rare sketches, illustrations, and ancient manuscripts, as well as work by local artists. Two of the museum's most prized possessions are royal mandates, signed in 1493 by Ferdinand and Isabella of Spain, concerning the provisioning

TIP

Guided tours of the public areas of La Fortaleza (several times a day in English and Spanish) depart from the main gate on Calle Fortaleza most weekdays. Call ahead (tel: 787-721-7000 ext. 2211) as schedules are subject to change. Photo ID required.

Entrance to La Fortaleza.

ARCHITECTURE IN THE OLD CITY

From an architectural standpoint, La Fortaleza really captures the essence of all of Old San Juan: it is an amazing blend of building styles through the ages, from its 16th-century core to its 19th-century facade. La Fortaleza and El Morro – both Unesco World Heritage Sites – are perhaps the most outstanding, but throughout the streets of the Old City are fine examples of medieval, Gothic, Baroque, neoclassical, and even Moorish architecture. Most buildings are in excellent condition, partly owing to the painstaking efforts of those who restored them (working from many original plans and using, whenever possible, original materials, like *ausubo*, or ironwood, beams) and partly because Old San Juan's sandstone walls and fortresses prevented any modern expansion.

There are some 400 historically important structures in this part of the Puerto Rican capital city, some of which are considered to be the finest examples of Spanish colonial architecture anywhere in the New World. Those of particular note include San Juan Cathedral, with a Baroque facade but a medieval core; San José Church, the only truly Gothic structure under the United States flag; and the Dominican Convent, a 16th-century white building that now houses the National Gallery.

of Columbus's fleet for his second voyage, which resulted in the discovery of Puerto Rico. Another precious work is one of only six known copies of the first printing of the Third Part of the *Summa* of St Thomas Aquinas, dating from 1477.

Next door, the **Centro Nacional de Artes Populares y Artesanías** or Popular Arts and Crafts Center ⓭ (tel: 787-721-6866; Mon–Sat 9am–5pm; free), run by the Institute of Puerto Rican Culture, houses a collection of paintings from the 18th century to the present. Island crafts are for sale at the shop inside. Other attractions at this end of Calle del Cristo include restaurants, cafés, art galleries and shops.

San Juan Cathedral

Ascending Calle del Cristo, even the most skeptical travelers will begin to see what they came to San Juan for. On the right, usually bathed in sunlight in the afternoon, is **San Juan Cathedral** ⓮ (daily 8am–4pm, Sun until 2pm; donation), a fabulous beige-and-white structure built in

The much-photographed cupolas of San Juan Cathedral.

1540 and carefully restored in the 19th and 20th centuries. The beauty of its exterior is immediately perceptible. Three tiers of white pilasters and arches mount to a simple cross at the cathedral's pinnacle. The three brick-red and white cupolas are among San Juan's most photogenic sights.

The cathedral is in regular use; Mass is held, along with many other religious activities. It is also a very popular venue for weddings, and has held funeral services for prominent local figures.

Among its highlights are **Ponce de León's marble tomb**, with an understated virgin warrior glancing down at the body and the red script of the epitaph, and the glittering blue statue of **La Virgen de Providencia**, Puerto Rico's patroness, located nearby. A relic of St Pius, a Roman martyr, is in a glass case containing a macabre plaster figure of the saint, behind the altar. There's another such effigy, of a prostrate Jesus, in the **Chapel of Souls in Purgatory**, which is in the cathedral's right nave.

Directly across Calle del Cristo is **Hotel El Convento ⑮**, established in 1651 as the first Carmelite convent in the Americas. It housed the nuns for 252 years until closing a few days before Christmas in 1903. Vacant for a decade, the abandoned building served as a retail store, a dance hall, and, for the next 40 years, a flophouse without running water, sanitary facilities, or electricity. Opened in 1962 as El Convento Hotel, it offered a tranquil, European-style alternative to the glitzy hotels lining the Condado strip. It was restored in 1996 and turned into a four-star, 100-room luxury hotel with a casino – much to the anger of the nuns, who argued that slot machines were a sacrilege to the memory of their sisters buried underneath. Though few of the fixtures are originals, the decor fits harmoniously with the concept of a nunnery-turned-hotel and serves as a fine example of restoration of Spanish colonial architecture and design.

Museo del Niño

Next door and across the street from the San Juan Cathedral in a 300-year old colonial home is the **Museo del Niño ⑯** (tel: 787-722-3791; Tue–Thu 10am–3.30pm, Fri 10am–5pm, Sat–Sun noon–5.30pm, ticket office closes 1.5 hours before closing time), which has interactive exhibits and covers topics such as dinosaurs, space, music, and the human body, complete with a giant replica of a human heart. Three floors of exhibits also include an opportunity to talk to youth in other countries on a short-wave radio, a miniature town square, and an extensive explanation of the benefits of recycling. The Children's Museum is a non-profit organization involved in preserving the island's cultural heritage and presenting subjects in a rich and interesting way for children.

One block away from El Convento, the **Center for Advanced Studies on Puerto Rico and the Caribbean** – built in 1842 as a religious school for young men – is a private research institute housing a fine library. Besides its academic value, the center can be a haven for weary tourists and locals.

Campeche paintings and a gold-and-silver altar can be seen through the Cristo Chapel's glass doors.

The Paseo de la Princesa offers great views.

EAT

El Picoteo (tel: 787-723
9020; www.elconvento.
com), located in Hotel El
Convento on Cristo
Street, delights its
patrons with delicious hot
and cold tapas and the
paella is considered to be
the best in Puerto Rico.

*Modern sculpture in an
ancient city: dramatic
lines of La Rogativa.*

Nun's Square and Old City Walls

Across Cristo from San Juan Cathedral, between the fork of two of San Juan's oldest and most pleasant cobblestoned streets, lies the lush **Plazuela de las Monjas** (Nuns' Square), a perfect spot for an urban picnic. The square looks out not only on the cathedral and El Convento but on the **Casa Cabildo**, San Juan's original City Hall, which now houses an interior design company.

A walk down **Caleta de San Juan** will take you to the massive wooden **San Juan Gate** ⓱, built in the 18th century and the only one of three original portals remaining. Sailors weary from their voyages used to moor their ships in San Juan Bay, ferry themselves ashore, enter through the gate, and walk to prayer services via Caleta de San Juan, which describes a conveniently straight line between the gates and the main altar of the cathedral.

Through the gate is **Paseo de la Princesa**, a romantic bay-front promenade that skirts the **Old City Walls** ⓲, or *murallas*. Built of sandstone from 1635 to 1641, it measures up to 20ft (6 meters) in thickness and at one time completely surrounded the colonial city, guarding it against enemy attacks. Along the *paseo* – an immaculate, landscaped pedestrian boulevard facing the sea – are statues, a large fountain, and kiosk vendors selling everything from cotton candy to *guarapo de caña* (sugar cane juice). Various family activities, such as concerts and children's theater, are scheduled here on many weekends. The old **La Princesa** ⓳ jail (Mon–Fri 8am–4.30pm; free) built in 1837, midway along the promenade, now houses the Tourism Company offices and an art gallery.

Continuing up Recinto del Oeste, past more examples of fine colonial architecture, you reach a modern sculpture, **La Rogativa** ⓴, showing the Bishop of San Juan followed by three torch-bearing women, which commemorates the failure of an English siege of the city in 1797. The legend runs that General Sir Ralph Abercrombie led a fleet of British ships to take San Juan in a

rapid, all-out assault by land and sea. When this plan failed, Abercrombie ordered a naval blockade, which lasted two weeks, while the residents of San Juan began to suffer from dysentery, losing hope of the arrival of Spanish reinforcements from the inland settlements. The governor called for a *rogativa*, or divine entreaty, to the saints Ursula and Catherine. All the women of San Juan marched through the town carrying torches, to the loud ringing of tocsins. Abercrombie, believing reinforcements had arrived, quit San Juan, never to return.

Home of Doña Fela

A short walk back down Recinto del Oeste brings you to the **Casa Museo Felisa Rincón de Gautier** ㉑ (tel: 787-723-1897 or 787-724-7239; www.museofelisarincon.com; Mon–Fri 9am–4pm; free). This little museum is the former home of Felisa Rincón de Gautier, or "Doña Fela," one of San Juan's most popular mayors, who led the city from 1946 to 1968 and was noted for her flamboyant style. The home-turned-museum contains many items belonging to the late Doña Fela, including her impressive collection of hand fans – as well as a film clip from the 1950s, which shows the mayor bringing a plane-load of snow to the island from New York so that the children of San Juan could have a snowball fight.

The walk back to the cathedral on **Caleta de las Monjas** is full of surprises, chief among them the "step streets" leading up to the left toward *calles* Sol and San Sebastián. At the top of the first, **Escalinata de las Monjas**, is the old Palace of the Bishop of San Juan. The second, **Calle Hospital**, is a favorite of artists and photographers.

Calle San Sebastián

With all the historical legacy San Juan offers, it's easy to forget to view the city as its natives view it: a place to have fun. **Calle San Sebastián** is perhaps the pre-eminent place in the Old City in which to do just that. Perpendicular to the top of Calle del Cristo, it's a place of museums and old homes whose many bars and spacious plaza make it a mecca for *sanjuanero* youth. In the third week of January, for four days from Thursday to Sunday around January 20, the day of Saint Sebastián, a huge street party is held here, known locally as **SanSeb**. There are parades in which you will see the vejigantes (masked, clown-like characters), the gigantes (stilt walkers), and the cabezudos (huge, papier mâché heads). Then there is music, both traditional folkloric and modern, going on well into the night, although everything closes down at midnight on Thursday and Sunday and at 1am on Friday and Saturday, so residents can get some sleep. There are food stalls and crafts stalls in adjacent streets and plazas, and the ban on drinking in the street is lifted. Thousands of people attend, so don't even think of driving anywhere near the area.

Plaza San José ㉒ is the focal point of the street, paved with rosy

Ponce de León stands proudly on Plaza San José.

FACT

After Ponce de León's death in Cuba in 1521, his body was brought to Puerto Rico and laid to rest in San José Church, where his descendants worshipped. Later, in 1908, his remains were moved to San Juan Cathedral.

The informative Museo de las Américas.

Spanish conglomerate around a statue of Ponce de León made from English cannons melted down after the first invasion. The plaza draws strolling locals on warm weekend evenings, and fun-loving tourists throughout the year. Live concerts of traditional music often take place here.

San Juan's **Dominican Convent** ㉓ dominates the plaza. Built in 1523, this imposing, elegant building has seen as much history as any on the island, having housed both English and Dutch occupying forces over the centuries.

The convent now houses the Galería Nacional (National Gallery), run by the **Institute of Puerto Rican Culture** (tel: 787-725-2670; Tue–Sat 9.30am–noon, 1–5pm, guided tours sometimes available), the body which, more than any other, has been responsible for the renaissance in Puerto Rican scholarship and art over the past several years. Under its auspices the parts of the convent not used for office space have been converted to cultural use. This is the place to come to see many of the great Puerto Rican works of art

by major artists such as Campeche, Oller, and Frade. A beautiful indoor patio is the scene of many concerts and plays. The old convent library has been restored to its original 16th-century decor.

Next to the Dominican Convent is the stunning and unusual **San José Church** ㉔. Built in stages from 1532 to the 18th century by the Dominicans as part of the San Aquinas Monastery, it was renamed when the Jesuits took over the monastery in 1865. Ponce de León was interred in the crypt here from 1559 to 1836, when he was moved to the Cathedral, but his coat of arms is still visible near the main altar and his grandson of the same name still lies in the crypt. The artist José Campeche is also buried here. One of the earliest churches built by the Spanish in the New World, San José is a fine example of 16th century Gothic architecture. A wooden crucifix of the mid-16th century, donated by Ponce de León, is one of the highlights, as is the 15th-century altar brought from Cádiz.

Ballajá Infantry Barracks

Across from the Plaza San José is the **Cuartel de Ballajá** ❷❺ or Ballajá Infantry Barracks Building, constructed by the Spanish Army between 1854 and 1864. One of the most impressive structures erected by Spain in the New World, it stands as the last example of monumental military architecture by the Spanish monarchy in the Americas.

Located on a lot of approximately 3 acres (1.2 hectares), it occupies six city blocks that were expropriated and demolished in 1853. Used until 1898 as infantry barracks and permanent housing for approximately 1,000 troops, it consisted of rooms for officers, soldiers and their families, storage, kitchens, dining rooms, jail cells, and stables for horses. The ascending vaulted Gothic ceilings above the main staircase are unique in Puerto Rico, and its vast interior patio is a striking example of 19th-century architectural prowess.

After the change of sovereignty, the Americans also used the facilities as barracks until 1939. Then it became the Rodríguez Hospital. In 1986 renovation work began. The three-story structure was the centerpiece of the restoration of Old San Juan in time for the 500th anniversary in 1992 of Columbus's arrival in the New World. Today it is a cultural center including schools of music and dance. On top of the building is a picturesque eco-garden with a water feature and 720 solar panels.

Ballajá's first floor is occupied by the **Museo Pablo Casals** ❷❻ (tel: 787-723-9185; Tue–Sat 9.30am–4.30pm) which displays memorabilia of the legendary cellist who moved to Puerto Rico in 1956 and lived here until his death in 1973. It includes manuscripts, instruments, texts of his speeches to the United Nations, photographs, and cassettes of his music which can be heard on request. A Casals Arts Festival takes place every year in the Santurce district of the city. (See page 250.)

On Ballajá's second floor is the **Museo de las Américas** ❷❼ (tel: 787-724-5052; Tue–Sat 9am–noon, 1–4pm, Sun noon–5pm), which provides an

TIP

If your feet need a break, consider a ride on a *calesa* (horse-drawn carriage) reminiscent of old colonial days. The carriages are based just off Pier 1 at the San Juan Harbor front. Night rides are particularly enchanting.

Taking a break in the shade.

overview of cultural development in the New World. Among its colorful exhibits of crafts in the Americas are a replica of a country chapel and examples of Haitian voodoo and *santos*. The permanent exhibits include artifacts and samples of the arts and crafts pertaining to daily life, such as clothes, tools, musical instruments, religious objects, and so on. There are also permanent exhibition rooms dedicated to African heritage, the Indian in the Americas, and Conquest and Colonization. The temporary exhibits change throughout the year.

Plaza del Quinto Centenario

Directly in front is the three-level **Plaza del Quinto Centenario** , which looks out over the Atlantic. Dominating this plaza, at the center of an eight-pointed pavement design, is the Tótem Telúrico, a 40ft (12-meter) terracotta-colored granite and ceramic totem pole sculpture by local artist Jaime Suárez that symbolizes the blending of Taíno, African, and Spanish cultures. Commissioned in 1992,

nearby is a fountain with 100 jets of water; it is supposed to symbolize five centuries of Puerto Rican history since the arrival of Columbus.

Across the plaza from the Cuartel de Ballajá, along unmarked Calle de Beneficencia, is the stately **Antiguo Asilo de Beneficencia** Old Home for the Poor. The building, constructed in the 1840s to house the destitute, today serves as headquarters for the Institute of Puerto Rican Culture.

El Morro

The Spanish colonists considered San Juan chiefly as a military stronghold, and held military architecture as their first priority. It is not surprising, then, that contemporary *sanjuaneros* are proudest of the breathtaking forts, unique in the Western world, that their antecedents left them.

El Castillo San Felipe del Morro, simply known as **El Morro** (tel: 787-729-6777; www.nps.gov/saju; daily 9am–6pm except New Year's Day, Christmas Day and Thanksgiving), features a maze of secret access tunnels, dungeons, lookouts, ramps,

Puerto Rico's most famous silhouette: El Morro fort in Old San Juan.

LA PERLA:

In 1978, singer Ismael (Maelo) Rivera had a hit song, called "La Perla," written by his childhood friend, Catalino Curet Alonso (1926–2003), one of the greatest salsa composers of the 20th century. Rivera (1931–87) was dubbed "El Sonero Mayor" by the great Cuban singer Benny Moré, and despite a spell in prison for drugs possession, he was a hugely popular singer. His greatest hit was another song by Curet, "Las caras lindas (de mi gente negra)." He was also active in promoting the contribution made to local culture by black Puerto Ricans. After his death the government declared his birthday, October 5, Ismael Rivera Day. In Santurce, where he is buried, there is a statue in the Plaza de los Salseros dedicated to Rivera.

barracks, and vaults. Declared a World Heritage Site by the United Nations, El Morro falls under the auspices of the US National Park Service. Free tours in English and Spanish are given daily.

This, the larger of the city's two forts, commands San Juan Bay with six levels of gun emplacements and walls that tower 140ft (43 meters) over the Atlantic. Its guns were capable of aiming at any ship within El Morro's field of vision, no matter the distance, and the walls themselves, connected with the system that encircles Old San Juan, are 20ft (6 meters) thick.

The fort's first battery was completed in the 1540s, but it was not until 1589, when Juan Bautista Antonelli arrived with a team of other Spanish military engineers to begin raising a true bulwark along the edge of the peninsula, that the fort was completed. When Sir Francis Drake attacked in 1595 he was roundly repulsed, but Cumberland's land attack from the Condado succeeded in piercing El Morro's still vulnerable rear approach.

The English held the fort for three months, until dysentery took the lives of nearly half their men. It would be the last time El Morro would fall, even holding out against the Dutch siege of 1625 and the American gunnery fire which rained upon it during the Spanish-American War of 1898.

Today, visitors appreciate El Morro (which means "headland" in Spanish) more for its breathtaking views and architecture than for the protection it gives them. The approach to the fort is over a vast, 27-acre (11-hectare) parkland, once the former drill square for the soldiers and currently a haven for kite flyers and strolling lovers. A gravel path through the green leads over a moat and into the massive structure, crossing El Morro's main courtyard surrounded by beautiful yellow walls and white archways. Here you will discover a souvenir shop and a museum, both of which are useful in orienting the traveler to the fort's layout and long history.

The massive archway facing over San Juan Bay on the west side of the courtyard is the entrance to what

San Juan Cemetery boasts the most scenic of locations.

The atmospheric Plaza del Mercado has a great nightlife, with cafés and bars open until late.

looks like the longest skateboard run in the world: a huge, stone, step-flanked ramp leading to the lower ramparts. This is the most popular of the fort's various sections, affording views of the surf crashing below, and profiling the fort from the ocean side, as its invaders saw it.

Back on the upper level of El Morro, a left turn through the courtyard patio leads to another ramp, this one twisting rightward toward the **Port of San Juan Lighthouse**, which was destroyed by an American mortar shell during the Spanish-American War but later restored.

San Juan Cemetery

San Juan Cemetery ㉛, considered by many to be the most picturesque resting place for old bones in the world, sits on a broad, grassy hummock of land tucked between El Morro's walls and the pounding surf. The cemetery's highlight is a tiny, 19th-century circular chapel, set among the bleached-white gravestones. Abutting El Morro's grounds, the **Casa Blanca** ㉜ (tel: 787-725-1454; house Tue–Sun

8am–noon, 1–4.30pm; garden daily 8am–4.30pm) is the oldest house in Puerto Rico, having been built for Ponce de León in 1521. Used in the years preceding the construction of La Fortaleza as a shelter against the attacks of savage Carib tribes, it was owned by the conquistador's family until the late 18th century and is now a museum of 16th- and 17th-century family life, with an interesting ethnographic section.

The nearby **Casa Rosa** ㉝ (also referred to as Casa Rosada) is a lovely pink building overlooking the bay and serves as a day-care center for government employees' children.

La Perla

A glance down the beachfront from El Morro will show one of the most bizarre and colorful coastal city-scapes imaginable. One- and two-story shacks, seemingly piled one on top of another, crowd the coastline all the way from El Morro to San Cristóbal, running along the battlements which formerly connected the two castles. This is **La Perla** ㉞, the

---

EATING OUT IN OLD SAN JUAN

With so many places to go and things to do right in their own neighborhood, it's a wonder Old San Juan residents ever leave their walled haven. When it comes to food, most travel experts will tell you to take a cue from the locals.

For a hearty breakfast or lunch with excellent coffee, stop at **Caficultura** (401 San Francisco Street; tel: 787-723-7731; daily from 8am). **Cafeteria Mallorca** (300 San Francisco Street; tel: 787-724-4607; Mon–Fri from 9am, Sun from 11am) is an ideal place to try sweet treats with *café con leche*. The cafeteria also serves sandwiches, toasts, delicious *mallorcas* (pastries) – and heavier Puerto Rican fare.

There are plenty of lunch spots, but once again there is one restaurant on most people's list of favorites. **El Jibarito** (280 Sol Street; tel: 787-725-8375) is a mecca for the masses that seek popular Puerto Rican staples like rice and beans, roast pork, fried plaintains, and more. This cozy establishment also offers an outdoor café space.

Known for its "mojito" chicken breast and succulent

seafood as well as great *mofongos*, **Mojito's** (323 Recinto Sur Street; tel: 787-439-8078; daily lunch and dinner although hours vary) is a quaint locale that packs a lunch crowd. Their classic Cuban cocktail with fresh mint is excellent.

Old San Juan is a thriving nightlife spot and people pour into the city from all over the island, but there are plenty of restaurants to go around. **La Madre** (351 San Francisco Street; tel: 787-647-5392; dinner daily from 5pm, Sat–Sun also lunch from noon) is one of the best options in the city for Mexican food lovers. Sampling one of many types of margarita served there is not be missed.

Fortaleza Street has seen a boom in fashionable restaurants, and one place that always attracts the dinner crowd is **The Parrot Club** (363 Fortaleza Street; tel: 787-725-7370; www.oofrestaurants.com), a colorful restaurant with a modern take on Puerto Rican and Latin cuisine where you can sometimes listen to live Latin jazz (call for days and times).

So, no need to leave the city walls, then...

so-called "world's prettiest slum." It grew up in the 19th century outside the city walls, where the city's slaughterhouse was located away from the main center of habitation, and is now home to over 300 people.

Set against the backdrop of an aquamarine Atlantic, it looks at first glance delightful, but it is not a tourist attraction and is notorious for drugs trafficking and crime, a reputation which the community is trying to shed with weekly salsa and reggaeton concerts. Along Calle Norzagaray, the **Museo de San Juan** ❸❺ (tel: 787-480-3555; Tue–Sun 9am–noon, 1–4pm; free) beckons visitors for a look. Its construction as the Plaza del Mercado, or farmers' market, from 1853 to 1857, served to align the streets and allowed for uniformity of facade for its surrounding structures. In 1979 it was converted into a museum. The galleries feature plastic art exhibits, a collection of *santos* and the interior patio hosts cultural activities year-round. There is also a video documentary shown on the hour throughout the day detailing the history of the city.

El Castillo de San Cristóbal

Though overshadowed by its more famous neighbor to the west, **El Castillo de San Cristóbal** ❸❻ (tel: 787-729-6777; www.nps.gov/saju; daily 9am–6pm except New Year's Day, Christmas Day and Thanksgiving) makes as fascinating a trip as El Morro. What El Morro achieved with brute force, San Cristóbal achieved with much more subtlety.

Sitting 150ft (45 meters) above the ocean waves, the fort reflects the best of 17th-century military architectural thought, and has a fascinating network of tunnels that was used both for transporting artillery and for ambushing luckless invaders.

Begun in 1634, San Cristóbal was completed in 1678 (although modifications continued well into the 18th century) as a means of staving off land attacks on San Juan, like the

one the English made under the Earl of Cumberland to capture El Morro in 1598. But the fort as it is known today is the product of the acumen of two Irishmen, "Wild Geese" who had fled from the Orange monarchy and were in the employ of the Spanish Army.

Alejandro O'Reilly and fellow Irishman Colonel Thomas O'Daly designed a system of battlements and sub-forts that ensured no one could take El Castillo de San Cristóbal without taking all of its ramparts first. No one ever did. The first shot of the Spanish-American War was fired from San Cristóbal's walls.

Frequent guided tours explain how San Cristóbal's unique system of defense worked, and also point out some of the fort's big attractions, like the **Garita del Diablo** (**Devil's Sentry Box**), a *garita* at the end of a long tunnel that runs to the waterline.

Views from the battlements are outstandingly spectacular, particularly in the direction *sanjuaneros* described as "towards Puerto Rico": Condado, Hato Rey, and El Yunque.

A tunnel inside El Castillo de San Cristóbal.

View over Condado at night.

METROPOLITAN SAN JUAN

Condado, Ocean Park, and Isla Verde have fine beaches,
Santurce is a genuine marketplace, and Bayamón has a
maverick quality. This urban sprawl contains huge
shopping malls, the university, art galleries, hotels,
and casinos, and is the commercial heart of the island.

I t's easy to try to relegate **Puerta de Tierra ❶** to the status of a sort of buffer zone between San Juan's body and its soul, separating as it does the brawn of Santurce from the historical grandeur and romance of Old San Juan. Puerta de Tierra means "gateway of land," and to many it can seem just that, as vehicles speed through it without pause on the access roads to the old city.

El Capitolio

Commanding a fabulous view of beach and water, straddled by Puerta de Tierra's two main thoroughfares, **El Capitolio ❷**, Puerto Rico's Capitol building, serves as the centerpiece to the whole peninsula. Constructed between 1925 and 1929, El Capitolio is a grand, white classical structure resembling the Capitol building in Washington, on a rather smaller scale and with wonderful ocean views. The large rotunda features four corner sections done in Venetian mosaic with gold, silver, and bronze, depicting some of the most important events in Puerto Rico's history. In the very center of the dome is a lovely stained-glass rendering of Puerto Rico's seal. Near the main entrance is the original Constitution of Puerto Rico, signed in 1952 and brought back to the island in 1992 after spending nearly five years in a Washington restoration laboratory.

The ornate Casa de España.

Landmark buildings

Nearby are a number of buildings which, though less imposing, are no less beautiful. The ornate **Casa de España ❸**, just down the hill toward Old San Juan from El Capitolio, is a blue-tiled, four-towered edifice built in 1935 and paid for by the Spanish expatriate community. Once a popular gathering spot for local men, it now has a restaurant and is the site of cultural events. Of interest inside are the tiled paintings of Don Quixote and the Salón de

Main Attractions
El Capitolio
Ocean Park
Museo de Arte de Puerto Rico
Piñones
Río Piedras/Jardín Botánico
Bacardi Rum Plant, Cataño
Bayamón

1 2 4

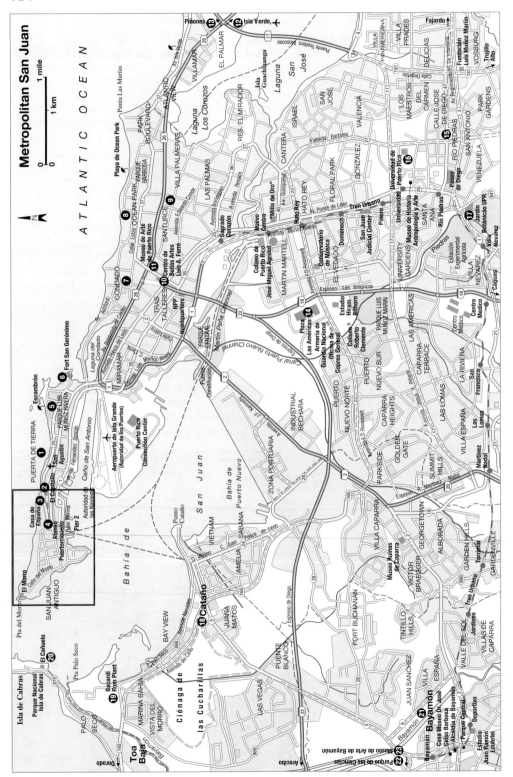

Metropolitan San Juan

ATLANTIC OCEAN

Fajardo

Piñones · Isla Verde

VILLA
PRADES
PAN AMERICANA

Puente Teodoro Moscoso

VILLA
VOSBURG
DELICIAS
Trujillo
Alto.

Fundación
Luis Muñoz Marín

PARK
GARDENS

VENEZUELA

San
José

Laguna
San
José

Calle Delgado

LOS
MAESTROS

CALLE JOSE
DE DIEGO

SAN ANTONIO

Laguna
Los Corozos

Laguna
La Torre

RES. EL MIRADOR

Isla Guachinanga

SAN
JOSÉ

VALENCIA

RÍO PIEDRAS

Paseo
de Diego

Jardín
Botánico UPR

VILLA
NEVÁREZ

Caguas

PARK
BOULEVARD

VILLA PALMERAS

LAS
PALMAS

ISRAEL

CANTERA

Avenida Barbosa

HATO REY

GONZÁLEZ

FLORAL PARK

Universidad de
Puerto Rico

UNIVERSITY
GARDENS

Museo de Historia
Antropología y Arte

VILLA
NEVÁREZ

Playa de Ocean Park

PARQUE
BARBOSA

Museo de Arte
de Puerto Rico

"Milla de Oro"

Conservatorio
de Música

San Juan
Judicial Center

Estación
Experimental
Agrícola

Villa
Nevárez

OCEAN PARK

Centro de
Bellas Artes
Luis A. Ferré

Nuevo
Centro

Coliseo de
Puerto Rico
José Miguel Agrelot

MARTÍN MARTELL

Domenech

EL VEDADO

Piñero

Piedras

SANTA
ANA

CONDADO

SANTURCE

Sagrado
Corazón

Av. Ponce de León

Tren Urbano

Río Piedras

Centro
Médico

Escambrón

Fort San Gerónimo

TRAS
TALLERES
NPP
Headquarters

PARQUE
CENTRAL

Canal Puerto Nuevo Channel

Estadio
Hiram
Bithorn

PARQUE LUIS
MUÑOZ MARÍN

Centro
Médico

PUERTA DE TIERRA

MIRAMAR

Plaza
Las Américas

Coliseo
Roberto
Clemente

Armería de
Guardia Nacional

Oficina de
Copreo General

CAPARRA
TERRACE

LA RIVIERA

Puerto Rico
Convention Center

Aeropuerto de Isla Grande
(Autoridad de los Puertos)

ZONA PORTUARIA

PUERTO
NUEVO

PUERTO
NORTE

NUEVO SUR

San
Francisco

VILLA ESPAÑA

Las
Lomas

Martínez
Nadal

Casa de España

El Capitolio

Autoridad de
las Navieras

INDUSTRIAL
BECHARA

CAPARRA
HEIGHTS

GOLDEN
GATE

PARKSIDE

SUMMIT
HILLS

Ateneo
Pier 2

San
Juan

Bahía de
San Juan

Bahía de
Puerto Nuevo

Punto
Cataño

SABANA

VIETNAM

AMELIA

VILLA CAPARRA

GEORGETOWN

ALBORADA

GARDEN HILLS

GARDENVILLE

Puertorriqueño

El Morro
SAN JUAN
ANTIGUO

Pta del Morro

Calle del Morro

Cataño

JUANA
MATOS

Museo Ruinas
de Caparra

VICTOR
BRAEGGER

TINTILLO
HILLS

Tren Urbano
Jardines

VILLAS DE
CAPARRA

BAY VIEW

Bacardi
Rum Plant

El Cañuelo

Isla de Cabras

Parque Nacional
Isla de Cabras

Pta Palo Seco

PALO
SECO

Toa
Baja

MARINA BAHÍA
VISTA DEL
MORRO

Ciénaga de
las Cucharillas

JUANA
MATOS

PUENTE
BLANCO

LAS VEGAS

FORT BUCHANAN

VALLE DE SOL

JUAN SÁNCHEZ

VILLA
ESPAÑA

Bayamón

Casa Museo Dr. José
Celso Barbosa

Alcaldía de Bayamón

Parque Central

Museo de Arte de Bayamón

Parque de las Ciencias

Estadio
Juan Ramón
Loubriel

Parque
Deportivo

Dorado

ATLANTIC OCEAN

1 mile

1 km

Los Espejos (Hall of Mirrors) with its painted wooden ceiling.

Down Avenida Ponce de León is the lovely **General Archives and National Library of Puerto Rico** (tel: 787-724-0700). Now run by the Institute of Puerto Rican Culture, the building, constructed in 1877 as the last major Spanish architectural effort on the island, was originally designed as a hospital.

Another landmark along the boulevard is the **Ateneo Puertorriqueño ❹** (tel: 787-721-3877), which promotes cultural activity through conferences, lectures, films, and the like. Next door is the **Carnegie Library** (tel: 787-722-4739; Mon and Fri–Sat 9am–5pm, Tue–Thu 9am–9pm), established by the Carnegie Foundation and now run by the Department of Education.

Further east, **Parque Luis Muñoz Rivera ❺** is a 27-acre (11-hectare) recreational and national park. In 1919, land was set aside to create a park for local people. It once composed part of the third line of defense for the city. The powder house built in 1769 (El Polvorín) which supplied

Fort San Jerónimo (Condado) is still located in the park. It is a pleasant place to relax where kids can let off steam, but best avoided at night for safety reasons.

Escambrón Beach is a pleasant, Blue Flag beach with a fine view along the coast to the Capitolio and El Morro. If you walk east along the shore you can see all along the coastline from Condado to Isla Verde. The reef offshore ensures that the waves are small and swimming is safe for children, although lifeguards are on duty 8.30am–5pm, just in case. There are picnic benches under the trees, also a restaurant and beach vendors. Access to the beach is off Avenida Muñoz Rivera and there is secure parking (charge) at Balneario El Escabrón.

The **Caribe Hilton** sits on several acres of beautifully landscaped grass and sand, overlooking a little beach-lined cove that stretches to Condado. The hotel has a historical asset in **Fort San Gerónimo ❻**, a small but crucial element of the old Spanish fortifications which stymied a British invasion

TIP

The Condado beaches are said to be the best in the city. Snorkeling is good, and a wide range of water sports equipment can be hired. But be warned that it is not advisable to walk along the beaches at night.

El Capitolio stands as a powerful symbol of self-government.

The Caribe Hilton and Fort San Gerónimo.

of the region in 1797. Unfortunately, the fort has recently fallen into decay but efforts are underway to prevent it deteriorating further. Adjacent to the fort, a huge Paseo Caribe retail and entertainment center, comprising luxury apartments, restaurants, shops, and a waterfront promenade, is being constructed.

Condado

Condado ❼ in Spanish means "county," and many Puerto Ricans still refer to the glittering strip of land between the Condado lagoon and the Atlantic Ocean as "*the* Condado." If the appellation is meant to convey anything rustic about this part of town, it grossly misses the mark. A trip across the Puente San Gerónimo from Puerta de Tierra takes one out of history and into the tourist zone, where gambling, dining, drinking, and dancing are the main activities of the evening. **Ashford Avenue**, Condado's main thoroughfare, looks as though it is trying to run for election as the sixth borough of New York City, or perhaps as an annex of Miami Beach. In a large measure, it succeeds. Its lengthy oceanfront is lined with chic boutiques, banks, restaurants, and – most conspicuously – hotels.

Quality hotels

Condado is known for its luxury, glitzy hotels and casinos, but there are plenty of alternatives in the mid-range and a few lower budget places to stay. The casinos aren't exclusive: non-hotel patrons are welcome at the tables. Restaurants, both hotel-affiliated and otherwise, tend to be of good quality. However, there is a price to pay for quality in Condado, and it is a high one. Some of the restaurants in town are almost legendary – for both their food and their prices – but they are definitely worth it for the experience. The Condado area is constantly changing: old hotels are being knocked down and replaced by newer, bigger, more modern ones, or a public park.

To go to the beach in Condado implies more than taking the sun and riding the waves. People-watching is

the chief popular pastime, and there is certainly a fine variety of types to watch, enjoying the warm, unpolluted water and the gentle waves. The Condado beaches are mostly pockets of sand tucked behind the major hotels, and, although all beaches are public by law in Puerto Rico, they are less accessible. The big hotels aren't going to go out of their way to show anyone the easy route to the beach, but the determined visitor, of course, will usually find the way.

Ocean Park

Heading east on Ashford Avenue, you approach **Ocean Park** ❽, the most popular beach in the area, where sunbathers, dogs, kiteboarders, and children co-exist in happy harmony. From here, the high-rises give way to residential houses, and the beaches become less crowded. This is one of the more scenic of San Juan's beachfront panoramas, with views stretching from the palm-lined point at Boca de Cangrejos to the bright white high-rise wall of Ashford Avenue's hotels.

South of Condado

A knot of highways and main roads, **Santurce** ❾ connects the more touristy and more picturesque areas of the metropolis. It can't claim a seacoast; in fact, one could almost define the area as the set of neighborhoods one encounters moving south from more fashionable Condado and Ocean Park. It hasn't the history of Old San Juan, having been founded only about a century ago as a fashionable suburb. But Santurce does have its own appeal, making it well worth a visit.

Santurce is considered by most to be the heart of San Juan, and not just in the sense that it's the source of the city's main traffic arteries, but it survives as a true marketplace. The quaintest manifestation of this ethic is in the **Plaza del Mercado** on Calle Canals, where vendors sell fruit and vegetables and on Friday evenings the neighboring streets come alive with music and dancing.

While many *sanjuaneros* come to work in Santurce, a surprising proportion come to eat, too, at the many

TIP `

If you fancy seeing an arthouse film while in Puerto Rico, your best bet is in Santurce. Try the Metro or the Fine Arts Cinema – all on Avenida Ponce de León.

Governor Luis Muñoz Marín.

FUNDACIÓN LUIS MUÑOZ MARÍN

The Luis Muñoz Marín Foundation (Route 877 Km 0.4, Trujillo Alto; tours Mon–Fri 10am–2pm, Sat–Sun 10.30am–1pm; tel: 787-755-7979, ext. 22 to arrange; donation) is a non-profit organization preserving the values and ethics of the first directly elected Governor of Puerto Rico. Located in his family home where he lived from 1946–80, the house contains about a million documents and memorabilia relating to the public and private life of the man considered to be the architect of modern Puerto Rico.

Born in 1898, Muñoz Marín grew up surrounded by politics, poetry and journalism and was a founding member of the Popular Democratic Party of Puerto Rico. He became Governor in 1949 and held office in three subsequent elections. He retired from politics in 1970 and died in 1980.

Muñoz Marín was a tireless advocate of the working class, promoting legislation for agricultural reform, industrialization and economic recovery. These policies were the basis of Operation Bootstrap, which transformed the island from high dependency on sugar cane to a diversified, industrialized economy with tax breaks for investors in labor-intensive light industry such as textiles. He also launched Operation Serenity, promoting education and the arts, and encouraged birth control and migration to the US to ease population pressures.

elegant restaurants, and the appealing little *fondas*, as low on price as they are on pretentiousness. The arts thrive in Santurce as well, and the construction in 1981 of the attractive **Centro de Bellas Artes Luis A. Ferré** ❿ (box office tel: 787-620-4444), at the corner of *avenidas* Ponce de Léon and de Diego, has brought the neighborhood a share in San Juan's cultural wealth with a 1,800-seat Festival Hall, 760-seat Drama Hall, 210-seat Experimental Theater and 1,300-seat Symphony Hall.

Further along Avenida de Diego is the $60-million-plus, state-of-the-art **Museo de Arte de Puerto Rico** ⓫ (tel: 787-977-6277, ext. 2215 for 60-minute guided tours; www.mapr. org; Tue–Sat 10am–5pm, Wed until 8pm, Sun 11am–6pm; free Wed 2–8pm), which traces the history of Puerto Rican art from José Campeche to the present. The facade of the former hospital has been retained and its graceful columns are echoed in the modern construction behind. The museum has a lovely sculpture garden, a fine collection of prints, and revolving exhibitions featuring international and local artists.

Isla Verde

Almost everyone arrives in Puerto Rico at Luis Muñoz Marín International Airport on **Isla Verde** ⓬. Technically part of the municipality of Carolina, this San Juan suburb takes on a look of affluence that few areas as close to such booming noise, annoying traffic snarls, and transient lifestyle possess – big, chalk-white blocks of high-income apartment houses choke one of the most beautiful beachfronts on the island, giving Isla Verde one of the most Miami-Beachesque aspects this side of… well, Miami Beach.

Isla Verde is very rich, but a bit dull. The usual airport businesses – car rental agencies, vinyl cocktail lounges, and the like – have overrun the place, and suburbs separate the area from the historical charms of the older parts of San Juan, while water separates it from the allure of Piñones. An array of fine hotels lie just west of the airport while along Avenida Isla Verde, the many low-priced guesthouses, restaurants, fast-food emporia, the cock-fighting arena, and garish stores give the area a honky-tonk look.

The golden sandy beach at Isla Verde stretches for over a mile to the north of the airport. To the east are the lovely coral reefs at **Boca de Cangrejos**, and farther on the surf is formidable, especially in winter, rolling into the area known as **Piñones** ⓭, a popular hangout for young locals, especially on weekends, when a twisting road along 5 miles (8km) of beaches becomes the site of an ongoing party, and roadside kiosks sell raw oysters, seasoned pork and coco frío. On this wild piece of coastline, hotels have not yet begun to encroach on, and replace, the natural mangrove forest where visitors can go for a 7-mile (11km) bicycle ride (see page 140).

The Museo de Arte de Puerto Rico in Santurce mixes old and new harmoniously.

The Golden Mile

Most of the money in the Antilles is filtered through a group of banks and financial institutions clustered on a section of Avenida Luis Muñoz Rivera in Hato Rey known as Milla de Oro (The Golden Mile).

A mile west of the business district on Route 23 (Avenida Franklin Delano Roosevelt) is **Plaza Las Américas** ⑭ (tel: 787-767-5202; www.plaza lasamericas.net; Mon–Sat 9am–9pm, Sun 11am–7pm), the largest shopping mall in the Caribbean. Locals flock here to stroll amid its fountains and flowered walks and to buy everything from *guayaberas* (traditional Puerto Rican shirts) to guava juice. The mega shopping center includes flagship stores Macy's, Sears, and JC Penney among over 300 shops.

Río Piedras

To the south is the university town of **Río Piedras** ⑮ where concrete and plate-glass give way to cobbled paths and flower gardens. With 25,000 students and distinguished faculty from all parts of the world, the

Universidad de Puerto Rico (UPR) ⑯ is certainly unique in the American university community. The octagonal clock tower, which soars out of the palms at one side of the campus, has become something of a symbol for Río Piedras. Among those who've taught here have been Juan Ramón Jiménez, Pablo Casals, and Arturo Morales Carrión. At the intellectual heart of the university on Avenida Ponce de Léon is the **Museo de Historia**, **Antropología y Arte** (tel: 787-763-3939; Mon–Fri 9am–4pm, Wed until 8.30pm, Sun 1.30am–4.30pm; free, guided tours by appointment). Important exhibits include Francisco Oller's masterpiece *El Velorio* (The Wake) and the only Egyptian collection in the Caribbean.

The Botanical Garden

The highlight of any visit to Río Piedras must be the **Jardín Botánico** ⑰ (Botanical Garden; tel: 787-758-9957; daily 6am–6pm; free) at UPR's Agricultural Experimental Station, a mile south of the university and reached by following the signs after turning

EAT

The Fine Arts Café in Hato Rey is perfect for catching the latest independent or foreign film. First-class leather seats and a wine and beer bar that serves up hummus and sushi really make the movie-going experience a treat.

The sandy beach at Isla Verde.

off at the intersection of Avenida Muñoz Rivera and Route 847. Hundreds of varieties of tropical and semi-tropical plants, including many from Australia and Africa, make up this extensive park. The gardens comprise 200 acres (80 hectares) and it's hard to imagine a botanical garden landscaped as imaginatively or as subtly as this one. Ponds, lilies, ferns, and ubiquitous *yautía* compete for attention with an exceptional orchid garden. At the southern end of the Botanical Garden is a Sculpture Garden (daily 8am–5pm; free) containing colossal works by international and Puerto Rican artists in metal, granite, steel, and other media.

Río Piedras is not, however, all ivory towers and ivied lanes. Its **Paseo de Diego** is the largest pedestrian market in San Juan, with all the haggling frenzy of an Arab *souk*.

Cataño

Crossing from Old San Juan on the Cataño ferry allows excellent views of windswept San Juan Bay. **Cataño** ⓲ itself is by no means a picturesque town, but it does have a pleasant enough beachfront area and unrivaled views of the Old City.

It also has rum. In the most remote corners of the world, people know the name Bacardi. That they automatically associate it with Puerto Rico is all the more surprising, considering that Bacardi isn't the island's only rum, or even its best. Yet few tourists visit Puerto Rico without making a pilgrimage to the sprawling **Bacardi Rum Plant** ⓳ (tel: 787-788-1500; www.casabacardi.org; guided tours alternating in Spanish or English, Mon–Sat 9am–6pm, last tour 4.15pm, Sun 10am–5pm, last tour 3.45pm; free), five minutes west on Route 165. The distillery has a capacity of 100,000 gallons (454,000 liters) a day and is the largest rum distillery in the world, but you do not get to see inside it. From the entrance, you are taken from the waiting area/outdoor pavilion by trolley to the Bacardi Visitor Center, where you are told about sugar cane, rum manufacture, and the history of the Bacardi family. Then you are taken back to the pavilion in the spacious grounds with a view across the bay, where complimentary drinks are waiting. There is, of course, a gift shop, where rum prices are much the same as in supermarkets on the island although with a greater selection.

North of the distillery and bathed in the warm aroma of Bacardi's molasses, **Palo Seco** used to have an almost unbroken string of seafood restaurants, parallel to the ocean, many named after local pirate Roberto Cofresí. Now, however, numbers are down to a handful, but it is still a good place to come for seafood and local dishes.

Isla de Cabras

Just north of Palo Seco, at the end of a pine-flecked spit of land, is **Isla de Cabras**, once a leper colony but now a recreational area and hangout for local fishermen. The island originally housed the long-range artillery of Fort San Juan de la Cruz, better known as

The Bacardi distillery and visitor center.

El Cañuelo ⑳, built in 1610 in wood, but later rebuilt in stone in the 1670s after the Dutch burned it down. Strategically placed across the water from El Morro, the two forts were able to catch invading fleets in their crossfire. You can walk around the walls of the square fortress, but not enter. Cabras also boasts a beautiful – but unswimmable – beach. Hedonists should head further west on Route 165 to **Punta Salinas**, which is flanked by two pretty beaches.

Vaqueros of Bayamón

To the south of Cataño is the Island's second largest city, **Bayamón** ㉑, whose inhabitants are referred to as *vaqueros* or "cowboys." This is due to a sort of maverick quality that has put the city in friendly opposition to others on the island and has been adopted as the name of the local basketball team, Vaqueros de Bayamón.

Founded in 1509 by a group of settlers led by Ponce de León, it was named either after the cacique Bahamon, or after the river Bayamongo, now known as the Bayamón River.

Bayamón labors under the stereotype of a sort of glorified shopping mall and, indeed, has more shopping malls per capita than any other Puerto Rican town. It is a place where the antiquated *fincas* and plantations of an older Puerto Rico are set in sharp juxtaposition to some of the most innovative civic architecture.

Bayamón has been fastidious about retaining its regional customs and cuisine. Along almost every road leading into the city are *bayamoneses*, food vendors selling roast chicken, bread, and the most legendary of all local treats – the *chicharrón*, deep-fried pork rinds or crackling in cholesterol-hiking, molar-cracking hunks. There is even a chicharrón festival in July. (Male visitors should know that *chicharrón* has a connotation which makes it inadvisable to ask a local woman if she'd like a taste.)

The first sight of Bayamón is the eight-story **Alcaldía de Bayamón**, which spans five lanes of highway. Built in 1978 of concrete, glass and steel, it is the only building so suspended in the entire Caribbean.

More than 700 cruise ships arrive every year at the Port of San Juan, the busiest ocean terminal in the West Indies.

The famous bat symbol.

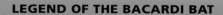

LEGEND OF THE BACARDI BAT

The next time you pick up a bottle of Bacardi rum, take note of the bat pictured on the label. When Don Facundo Bacardí experimented with the rum-making process in his tiny shed in Cuba back in the 19th century, colonies of fruit bats hung over his head and watched the strange proceedings with interest.

The wine merchant and importer ended up inventing a whole new process, distilled his very first bottle of rum and never looked back. For the Bacardí family, the bat became a symbol of good luck, prosperity, and tradition – and was made the Bacardi corporate symbol in 1862. Business was so good that Don Facundo quickly expanded it; by 1936 the family had decided to open a distillery in Puerto Rico.

In 1959, Fidel Castro came to power in Cuba. Shortly after, the Communists confiscated the family's extensive holdings – worth an estimated $76 million at the time – and the Bacardís were forced to shift production to Puerto Rico, Bermuda, the Bahamas, and elsewhere.

Today, Bacardi is truly a global empire, with plants in more than a dozen countries. Through a web of companies that include Bacardi Corporation, Bacardi & Company, Bacardi Limited, and half a dozen others, the empire now accounts for 75 percent of US – and 50 percent of all the world's – rum consumption.

Bayamón museums

Nearby, the **Parque Central** is dedicated to recreation, with historical and cultural displays. In the placid **Paseo Barbosa**, numerous shops are ranged about the restored 19th-century house now housing the Casa Museo Dr. José Celso Barbosa (16 Barbosa Street; tel: 787-977-2700; Tue–Sat 8.30am–4pm; free). Barbosa (1857–1921) was the first mulatto to attend the prestigious Jesuit seminary on the island and was the first person to practice medicine on the island with a US medical degree. While working as a doctor, he introduced an embryonic health insurance scheme paid for by employers, and during the Spanish American War of 1898 treated the wounded in dangerous conditions as a member of the Red Cross. In 1899 he formed the Puerto Rico Republican Party and became known as the father of the statehood movement in Puerto Rico, later founding the first bilingual newspaper, then serving first as a member of the executive cabinet and then as a senator. His many awards, books, and other possessions are displayed in his house, where one room is a re-creation of his consulting room. Another Bayamón native, Francisco Oller, was Puerto Rico's greatest artist; some of his work is at the **Museo de Arte Francisco Oller** (tel: 787-785-6010; Mon–Fri 8.30am–4pm; free) in the Old Alcaldía on Calle Degetau. Showcasing the art and cultural legacy of the metropolis, the gallery contains sporting relics, santos, Taíno pieces, and other memorabilia as well as art.

Two other museums on Calle Degetau are the **Museo de Archivo Histórico** (tel: 787-780-5552 ext. 2000) chronicling the history and development of the municipality, and the **Museo de Muñecas** (tel: 787-785-6010) containing Prof Catalina Hernández' collection of 952 dolls.

Not far from here, on Route 167, is the **Parque de las Ciencias** ㉒ (tel: 787-740-6868). Much more than just a science museum, this is a major theme park complex with numerous interactive and educational features. It is currently undergoing renovation, but the Museo de Arte de Bayamón (tel: 787-740-6868; Tue–Sat 9am–4pm; free) remains open to the public. The museum has nine exhibition rooms and its permanent collection features works by mainly Puerto Rican artists, from the 18th century to today, including the rococo artist José Campeche.

If you take Highway 2 east from Bayamón back to San Juan, at Km 6.4 you come to the **Museo Ruinas de Caparra** (tel: 787-781-4795; Mon–Fri 9am–noon, 1–4.30pm; free), containing the ruins of the first settlement on the island (see page 32). Excavations during the construction of the highway in 1935 uncovered the remains and the subsequent archaeological dig revealed the outline of the original buildings. The small museum here displays items found at the site and from around the island.

Modern architecture in Bayamón.

RUM – HOLDING ITS OWN IN THE SPIRITS WORLD

As Puerto Rico is the world's leading producer of rum, it's no surprise that it is the national drink – but few realize its versatility and broad range of flavors.

It is Christopher Columbus who can be thanked for the fine Caribbean rums today, because he happened to bring some sugar cane with him on his second voyage to the New World in 1493. It wasn't long before large cane plantations sprang up to meet the growing world demand for sugar. But the Spanish settlers discovered that sugar was not the only profitable substance produced from cane when they found that its by-product, molasses, fermented naturally.

Not satisfied with the flavor and proof of this "molasses wine," the Spaniards distilled it, filtering out impurities and increasing the concentration of alcohol. Rum was born.

There are four essential steps in the making of rum: fermentation, distillation, aging, and blending. Aging is most commonly done in used bourbon barrels made of white American oak. Puerto Rican law states that rum must age untouched for at least one year; there are, in fact, rigid standards for every step of the rum-making process.

Puerto Rican rum is distinguished from other Caribbean rums by its light body and smooth flavor. Its premium-aged rum competes admirably in the upper end of the spirits world and has a broad range of flavors comparable with single malt Scotch.

Spanish settlers planted sugar cane on the island in 1515, later discovering how to turn a sugar by-product, molasses, into rum.

Rum is a drink of many colors: it can be a light, dry white (a replacement for gin or vodka in cocktails), smooth amber (often mixed with cola), or mellow gold ("on the rocks").

A stunning display of the famous bottles.

Stainless-steel stills produce the cleanest rum and are most widely used. Premium-age rums are distilled in copper to bring out more aroma and flavor.

Barrilito specializes in premium-aged rums.

THE ROLLS-ROYCE OF RUMS

If you think rum is only good for fancy cocktails, think again. Gold, premium-aged rums can, at the very least, be a suitable substitute for whiskey: consumed straight or on the rocks. At their best, gold – or *añejos* – rums rank right up there with the finest cognac. There is more than one añejo out there, of course – Bacardi has its "Gold Reserve"; Serrallés has "El Dorado." But many rum connoisseurs point to Ron del Barrilito, who only makes premium-aged rums, as a real leader in the field with its unblended three-year-old Two-Star and blended six- to ten-year-old Three-Star – both coming in at 86 percent proof. Located in Bayamón, only 10 minutes away from the ultra-modern Bacardi facility in Cataño, Barrilito rum is blended and aged on a 200-year-old Fernández family farm called Hacienda Santa Ana. Instead of using white American oak bourbon barrels for aging like most rums, they traditionally used only sherry casks, and this practice continues to this day. So put away those paper umbrellas and get out your snifter: these are rums to be savored.

The island is full of inviting places to relax and sample the national drink in some of its many guises. Flavored rums are tasty and can be paired in much the same way as vodka. Brands include Bacardi Apple, Bacardi Coco, Don Q Limón, and Don Q Passion.

Caribbean classic. Reputedly invented in Puerto Rico, the piña colada remains a favorite rum libation. It's made with cream of coconut, white rum, and pineapple juice.

La Mina Falls, El Yunque.

Lush El Yunque.

THE NORTHEAST

Loíza is a center of authentic African culture, El Yunque is
a protected rainforest, Luquillo is arguably the island's
finest beach, and Icacos is the most popular cay.

nyone with only a few days to
spare in Puerto Rico would
be well advised to hire a car
or guide to explore east from San
Juan. It is not that the northeastern
corner of the island contains all the
island's attractions; that would be
impossible. It is only that the variety
of landscapes and societies – none of
them farther than 45 minutes from
San Juan – is astonishing. The ease
with which one can move from one
landscape to another, which bears
no resemblance to the previous one,
and the variety of sights and activities in the area, will make exploration
hugely rewarding.

Route 187: road of contrasts

Nowhere are the island's contrasts
more apparent than on Route 187
just east of San Juan. Here, the highway that links the metropolis with
the Caribbean's most modern international airport passes over a bridge
and heads for **Boca de Cangrejos** ❶
(Crabs' mouth), as exotic a spot as one
will find within 20 minutes of any
major city in the world. The further
you get from the Metropolis, the more
rural and isolated the beaches become.
The flocks of sheep and herds of cows
in the area belong to the residents of
nearby settlements around the *municipio* of Loíza. The shacks on the beach

are not residences by any stretch of
the imagination, rather seaside food
emporia. Boca de Cangrejos is where
sanjuaneros retreat for a *coco frío* – ice-
cold coconut water, which is served in
its own shell.

Long beaches under luxuriant
pine groves are what draw visitors
to Boca de Cangrejos. Surfers are
devoted partisans and can be seen
riding the waves at the part called
Aviones (Airplanes) for the flights
from Isla Verde that roar over all day.
A protected marina in the laguna

Main Attractions

Boca de Congrejos
Piñones
Loíza
El Yunque
Luquillo
Fajardo
El Faro
Icacos

Beach fun at Boca de Cangrejos.

TIP

It's advisable to stay away from any deserted beach. There is no police presence along this coast (resources are allocated to the more touristy areas of Isla Verde and Condado) so exercise caution, watch your belongings and do not hang around after dark.

also draws the boating crowd out from the city.

Piñones

At **Piñones** ❷, the Bosque Estatal de Piñones (Forest Reserve) has beaches with beautiful sand dunes, lookout towers and boardwalks. A 7-mile (11km) bike trail goes from end to end and through mangroves – extremely popular, especially because most of the seaside route is dotted with kiosks serving cold drinks. Bikes can be rented in Boca de Cangrejos and guided bike tours are available. Turtles nest on the beach at Piñones so avoid disturbing their nesting sites.

Piñones grows more eerie, rustic, and beautiful as one moves further eastwards. At its farthest point from San Juan is **Vacia Talega Beach**, a breathtaking finger of rock capped by palms and carved into strange formations by eons of surf.

On to Loíza

Puerto Rico's largest mangrove swamp, the massive and mysterious woodland of **Torrecilla Baja** ❸, lies east of Piñones, stretching inland and along the coast to the **Río Grande de Loíza**, the island's widest, roughest, and only navigable river. The coastal Route 187 traverses the forest and crosses the river to reach Loíza Aldea. Just 6 miles (10km) east of metropolitan San Juan, predominantly Afro-Puerto Rican **Loíza** ❹ (population 30,000) has maintained its separateness from the capital thanks to these natural barriers.

Loíza is arguably among the purest centers of true African culture in the Western world, tracing its ancestors to the Yoruba tribe of West Africa. Even today, two thirds of the population is black, a higher percentage than in other Puerto Rican towns. It was settled in the 16th century by black slaves sent by the Spanish Crown to mine a rich gold deposit in the area. When the gold ran out they became cane-cutters and, when slavery was abolished in 1873, many black residents turned to farming.

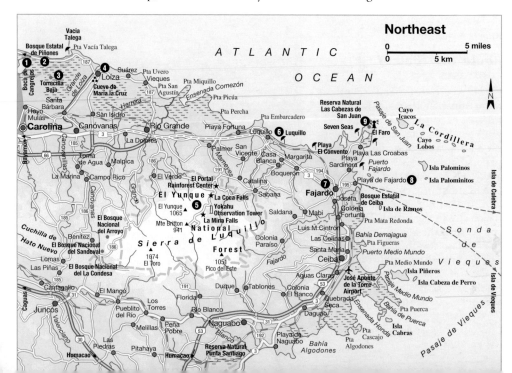

They learned Spanish and became Catholics, but in the subsequent fusion of African culture with Spanish and Indian, the African certainly won out – although the town's Church of San Patricio (St Patrick), also known as Espírito Santo (Holy Spirit) is the oldest in continuous use on the island, dating from 1670. St Patrick's Day in March is a popular local festival.

Fiesta de Santiago Apóstal

Such influence is most visible during the Fiesta de Santiago Apóstol, when the people of Loíza gather to praise Saint James, patron of the town. The week-long celebration commences each July 25, when citizens dress in ceremonial costumes strikingly and significantly similar to those of the Yoruba.

Participants include masqueraders, ghouls, and *viejos* (old men), and the making of costumes for the ceremonial rites is ordered by a social hierarchy.

The most distinctive festival attire, however, belongs to the *vejigantes*, most of them young men, who dress in garish costumes and parade through the streets. Their religious purpose is generally taken to be that of frightening the lapsed back into the Christian faith, though they can be just as much a source of celebration and mirth.

Most true *vejigante* masks are fashioned from coconuts or from other gourds and carved into grimaces like those of the most sinister jack-o'-lanterns. Sometimes aluminum foil is used to make a mask's teeth appear even more eerie.

Loíza is a poor area, where two-thirds of the population live below the poverty line, but it is rich in music and the arts. The African drumming of the Bomba can be heard at any festival, of which there are several, including carnival in October, and local people spontaneously get up to dance, gyrating their hips in a fast, tribal African movement quite unlike the Latin salsa more commonly seen. The best local African-influenced food makes an appearance at the fiestas patronales,

El Yunque's flora and fauna are spectacular. Fifty varieties of fern, more than 20 kinds of orchid, and some 240 types of tree are just some of the fantastic flora to be found here, as well as over 30 species of amphibian and reptile.

Town square mosaic in Loíza, known for its rich African heritage.

The tiny coquí tree frog.

but specialties can usually be found any time in local fondas.

Studios where the artisans make the colorful masks and bomba drums are open to the public and works of art can be bought here. Some to look out for are the Hermanos Ayala, who make things out of coconut, the Boria family who use coconut and make cloth dolls and the Parrilla Pérez family, who make masks. Samuel Lind is an artist who sells his paintings and sculptures with Afro-Caribbean themes at his studio on Route 187 (tel: 787-876-1494).

While much is made of the Afro-Caribbean culture and heritage here, it is worth remembering that the area was inhabited long before colonial times. One of the earliest signs of human habitation was found at Loíza in the Cueva de María la Cruz (Calle San Patricio, off Route 187; tel: 787-886-5757). In 1948, Ricardo Alegría and archaeologists from the Centro de Investigaciones Arqueológicas discovered evidence that archaic man used the cave for shelter when they

found rudimentary tools made of stone and shell. Their findings are displayed in the Museo de Antropología e Historia at the university in Río Piedras. The cave has been used for centuries as a burial site, a dwelling, a hurricane shelter and as a source of fertilizer. It got its name after a US missionary, María de la Cruz Walker, lived there as a hermit in the 1940s. More recently, the cave was used as a film location in 2011 for the TV movie adaptation of *Treasure Island*, starring Eddie Izzard as pirate Long John Silver, Elijah Wood as castaway Ben Gunn, and Donald Sutherland as Captain Flint.

El Yunque rainforest

As you continue east, a turn-off at the town of Palmer, known in Spanish as Mameyes, along Route 191, points toward El Yunque, the rainforest that attracts many visitors to the island. Route 191 used to lead straight through the forest to Naguabo, but a gate now blocks access at Km 13.5 because of a landslide in the 1980s.

The only tropical rainforest in the USDA National Forest system, and the only part of Puerto Rico administered by the US Department of Agriculture, the **El Yunque National Forest ❺** – named after the good Taíno spirit Yukiyú – is home to all the mystery and wonder that comes in the color green. These 28,000 acres (11,000 hectares) of bucking mountain at the highest part of the Sierra de Luquillo offer great biodiversity with distinct and varied ecological zones within a comparatively small area (tel: 787-888-1880; www.fs.usda. gov/elyunque; 7.30am–6pm). At **El Portal Rainforest Center** (tel: 787-888-1880; 9am–4.30pm; www.elyunque. com/elportal.htm; donation), visitors can learn about the unique beauty and history of El Yunque and the forest environment through interpretive displays, discussions, and a 15-minute documentary film.

Rainforest flora and fauna

To begin with, there is the rain. The massive, low-lying, purplish-black clouds one sees moving across the Atlantic onto Puerto Rico's northeast coast dump most of their cargo when they hit the northern flank of the Sierra de Luquillo, with the result that this is far and away the rainiest section of the island.

El Yunque gets upward of 240ins (600cm) of rain annually. However, rain does not bother the hundreds of different animal species that make El Yunque their home, among them 26 endemic to the island. Puerto Rico's most familiar animals are here, like the mellifluous tree frog known as the *coquí*. And more exotic ones are here as well, such as the colorful but endangered Puerto Rican parrot, and the rare Puerto Rican boa, the island's largest snake, which can grow up to 7ft (2 meters) long. The oldest natural reserve in the Americas, named a forest reserve in 1876 by King Alfonso XII of Spain, it is home to 150 fern species and 240 tree species, of which 88 are found only in Puerto Rico and 23 of those are found only in El Yunque.

La Coca and La Mina falls

Rising gradually, Route 191 hits one of El Yunque's premier attractions at a bend in the road not far into the forest. **La Coca Falls**, at Km 8.2, is a blurry cascade of ice-gray river rushing down a wall of beautiful moss-covered stones. El Yunque's second great waterfall, **La Mina**, is just off the road a mile (1.6km) ahead. Unfortunately, it's invisible from Route 191 and can be reached most easily from the Palo Colorado Recreation Site at Km 12. On your way there, you will pass the **Palma de Sierra Visitors' Center**, which also houses a food concession.

El Yunque recreational trails

Over the years, landslides on Route 191 have left El Yunque much less accessible by car. Hiking is the best way of getting around and there are 24 miles (38 km) of recreational trails.

The view from El Yunque's Yokahu Tower is spectacular.

Many trails criss-cross El Yunque.

THE MANY FACES OF THE FOREST

El Yunque – with an intensity characteristic of Puerto Rico's sub-climates – offers a startling diversity of vegetation and "forest types." Most widespread is the Tabonuco forest, which ranges around the warmer, drier parts of El Yunque at altitudes of under 2,000ft (600 meters). Higher up is the Palo Colorado forest, which is mossy and more humid. Then there is Sierra Palm forest which, although taking up less than a fifth of El Yunque's territory, is the "rainforest" that gives the area its reputation. Perhaps this is because its beauty is so unexpected and almost unnatural; perhaps it's because Route 191, which most tourists take through El Yunque, never gets above 2,500ft (760 meters), where the palm forest stops.

Sierra palms, which account for most of the sub-climate's vegetation, can grow in very slippery and unstable soil. Thus they can be found in the most dramatic locations: half-submerged in river beds or jutting from cliffsides. Areas above the palm forest are even more bizarre and fascinating. This cloud forest with moss-covered dwarf trees represents less than 1,000 acres (400 hectares) and gets the full brunt of the island's sometimes intense weather. The view from El Yunque's Yokahu Tower is spectacular: Luquillo and Fajardo in the foreground, the islands of Vieques and Culebra far off on the horizon, and the lush rainforested peaks of El Yunque all around.

The **Tradewinds National Recreation Trail** connects with El Toro Trail to form the island's longest nature trail, at about 4 miles (6.5km). Commencing a few hundred yards beyond the gate on Route 191, it bypasses El Yunque's big attractions, but it has the advantage of going through all the major ecosystems and vegetation areas of the forest, reaching the highest peak in the Luquillo mountains. The **Big Tree Trail**, leaving from the first parking lot along Route 191, gives a good bird's-eye view of La Mina Falls before meeting the road again at the Palo Colorado Recreation Area.

Perhaps most spectacular of all is the **El Yunque Trail**, which you may access from **Caimitillo Trail** (Route 191 Km 12) for three of the most spectacular vistas in the forest. To get to **Los Picachos Lookout Tower**, continue along El Yunque Trail. When you get to the junction with the Mount Britton Trail, a left will take you to Mount Britton Tower. A right turn will keep you on El Yunque Trail where you will encounter another

right that will bring you to Los Picachos Trail. A left turn just before reaching Los Picachos leads you to the lookout tower at **Pico El Yunque** and the fabulous vistas at the remote **El Yunque Rock**.

The forest can also be accessed from the southern part of Route 191 coming from Naguabo, where there is parking, picnic shelters, and restrooms.

Not all the action takes place in the forest, however, and there are several activities that can be enjoyed in the foothills of El Yunque. If you turn off Route 3 on to Route 992 (between the turning for El Yunque and the kioskos at Luquillo, you can visit Hacienda Carabalí (tel: 787-889-4954; www.carabalirainforestpark.com), where you can go horse riding or mountain biking on trails through the forest and across the 600-acre ranch, drive an ATV vehicle or race a go-kart. Further along the same road is Yunke Zipline Adventure (tel: 787-242-3368; www.yzapr.com) if you want to get up close and personal with the forest on a higher level.

*The stunning Playa
Luquillo.*

Luquillo

Shimmering **Luquillo** ❻ is just 35 minutes east of San Juan on either Route 66 or Route 3, and considered by many to be the island's best beach. The clean, golden sand stretches for about a mile, backed by a grove of coconut palms, earning the locals the nickname of *Los come cocos* (the coconut eaters). In the distance you can see the dramatic peaks of El Yunque rainforest cloaked in purple thunder clouds. Occasionally, some of the rain intended for the forest falls on Luquillo, and there are times when the beach is under heavy cloud cover.

On the eastern end of the beach is Mar Sin Barreras (sea without barriers), a park specially constructed for people with physical impairments. Personnel are on hand to help disabled visitors enjoy one of Puerto Rico's best strands.

The only liability of a trip to palm-fringed Luquillo is that it can get very crowded. It is usually included in day tours after a visit to El Yunque and is popular with people escaping San Juan at weekends. As much as the beach, what draws the San Juan crowd are the kioskos along the road – a seemingly endless string of *friquitines*, or kiosks sellings delectably rich local seafood specialties. These family-run businesses, ranging from shacks to more elaborate buildings with proper seating, sell everything from fruit to fritters, and many keep going into the evening with live music at weekends.

Fajardo

To some, the town of **Fajardo** ❼, the next sizeable destination beyond Luquillo, is merely an overcluttered dockfront town, ranking third behind Brindisi in Italy and Hyannis in Massachusetts in the "Grim Ferry Ports of the World" rating. To others it is an eminently glamorous resort, a charming community, gateway to a handful of fabulous islands and home to some of the finest sailing in the Caribbean.

The first major town along Puerto Rico's northeast coast, in the late 18th century Fajardo was a popular supply port for many pirate and contraband vessels and now is a mecca for

TIP

It is wise to allow at least a day to appreciate El Yunque fully. If you're planning on hiking, the staff at the Yunque-Catalina Service Center (tel: 787-888-1880 or 787-888-1810) can provide hiking information and, with notice, can help plan overnight treks into the forest.

The marina at Fajardo.

yachting enthusiasts. The town itself is somewhat unprepossessing compared with the area's natural attractions – the calm, clear waters and cays and coral reefs of Vieques Sound. **Playa de Fajardo ❽**, a waterfront community at the east end of the town, is the docking-place for the ferries headed to Culebra, Vieques, and a small island marina nearby. Flights to the islands go from Ceiba airport a few miles south, which used to be a US Naval Station, Roosevelt Roads, and has a huge runway.

Just north of Fajardo, two condominium high-rises, architectural anomalies here, loom over the small fishing village of **Playa Sardinera**. Hundreds of fancy motorboats and yachts of all descriptions crowd the two waterfront marinas nearby. Local fishermen line the beach in the middle of the village with boats and tents; they supply the half-dozen expensive seafood restaurants in the town.

Laguna Grande at **Las Croabas** (sometimes called Bio Bay or Fajardo lagoon) in the northeast is a great place to come on a kayaking tour at night to experience the bioluminescence in the water. Microscopic plankton light up when touched like thousands of tiny stars. There are many companies offering tours and no experience is necessary although you have to be comfortable paddling along a dark channel through the mangroves to get to the lagoon.

Reserva Natural Las Cabezas

Nearby, right off Route 987, **Seven Seas Beach and Campground** (tel: 787-863-8180; Apr–Aug daily 9am–5.30pm, Sept–Mar Wed–Sun 9am–5pm) on Bahía las Cabezas, is a lovely crescent of sand shaded by almond trees and palms. The Balneario here ensures that in summer the beach is cleaned and the washrooms have water, but at other times of the year services are sometimes lacking. Northeast of here, the **Reserva Natural Las Cabezas de San Juan ❾** (tel: 787-722-5882; www.paranaturaleza. org; Sat 7am; birdwatching tours only by reservation) is a 316-acre (128-hectare) environmental paradise

Icacos cay and surrounding coral beds.

run by the Para La Naturaleza, part of the Conservation Trust of Puerto Rico, with some of the Caribbean's most stunning landscapes. Admission to the reserve is by guided tour only. In addition to some rewarding birdwatching, you can observe nearly all of Puerto Rico's natural habitats – coral reefs, thalassia beds, sandy and rocky beaches, lagoons, a dry forest, and a mangrove forest.

Another important attraction at Cabezas de San Juan is the lighthouse, known simply as **El Faro**. Built in 1880, this pristine white neoclassical structure with black trim is one of only two operational lighthouses on the island. The view from Las Cabezas de San Juan is head-spinning. As you look back toward the heart of Puerto Rico, El Yunque towers over the island. In the other direction a chain of cays ranges like enticing stepping stones to the islands of Culebra and Saint Thomas.

Cays and islands

The dozens of cays and islands off Fajardo provide Puerto Rico's best boating. A protective reef stretching from Cabezas de San Juan to Culebra and beyond keeps the waters calm, while swift Atlantic trade winds create perfect sailing conditions. You can charter a yacht from one of Fajardo's marinas, such as Puerto del Rey Marina, and spend the day sailing, sunbathing, and snorkeling. There are dive shops for forays underwater and several excellent golf courses, while large resorts also offer spas and casinos.

Icacos, the largest and most popular cay, offers a narrow stretch of bone-white beach, making it a great spot for picnicking or even camping. A coral underworld descends to the sandy bottom 20ft (6 meters) below, providing all the action: elkhorn, staghorn, brain, star, and other corals host legions of underwater plant and animal life.

Other popular cays, somewhat less readily accessible, include **Culebrita**, **Cayo Lobos** (wolves), **Diablo** (devil), **Palominos** (doves) and **Palominitos** (take a wild guess). These and many smaller cays are ripe for underwater exploration among the coral, caverns, and tunnels.

TIP

Isla Palominos may be small, but it will astonish you with all the activities it has in store for you. There's snorkeling, horseback riding, volleyball, windsurfing, rafting, kayaking, and sailing.

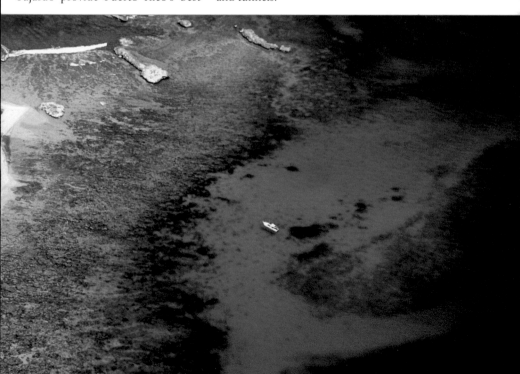

Ecotourism

Beyond the cities, the sun, the sand, and the water, Puerto Rico is an eden for nature lovers.

Puerto Rico is among the most industrialized and heavily populated of the Caribbean islands, yet there are still areas where you can escape modern life and imagine the island as it must have been before the arrival of the Spanish. Less than 1 percent of the land is virgin forest, yet there are several reserves preserving the fauna and flora of primary and secondary forests. For the visitor, many of these protected areas are easily accessible.

The rainforest of El Yunque National Forest encompasses approximately 28,000 acres (11,000 hectares), where you can find a variety of plant and animal species living in several different ecosystems depending on the altitude. It is home to more than 240 kinds of trees, 20 varieties of orchids, 150 species of ferns, and a plethora of flowers. You can also find around 17 endemic species of birds, including the endangered Puerto

La Mina waterfall in El Yunque.

Rican parrot and the Puerto Rican lizard-eating cuckoo or *Pájaro Bobo*. The tiny *coquí* frog, which derives its name from its distinctive chirp and is a 0.25–1ins (6–25mm) in size, also lives in El Yunque, although it is found all over the island.

Whether you want to go birdwatching or would simply like to enjoy the variety of plants, El Yunque has 24 miles (38km) of hiking trails across the park (see page 143). Visitors can also explore areas where crowds and tour buses cannot go. Several companies offer private guided ecotours of El Yunque, day or night. Some companies hold special permits to be in the forest after 6pm.

Subtropical dry forest

Visitors can also find other types of forests throughout the island, such as the Guánica Biosphere Reserve and State Forest, west of Ponce. A subtropical dry forest, with upland deciduous forest, semi-evergreen forest and scrub forest, it is home to around 700 plant species, of which 48 are endangered and 16 exist nowhere else in the world. It was designated a forest reserve in 1919 and the UN declared it a Biosphere Reserve in 1981, considering it the best example of a dry forest in the Caribbean.

Approximately half of Puerto Rico's birds and nine of the 16 endemic bird species are also found here, including the Puerto Rican woodpecker, the Puerto Rican nightjar and the Puerto Rican emerald hummingbird. There are 12 marked trails here, covering 37 miles (58km) but remember to take plenty of drinking water, sun protection, and mosquito repellent with you as the forest is very hot and the trails do not always have shade. Along the Ballena Trail you will find an ancient guayacán tree, whose trunk spans 6ft (2 meters) across and is believed to be 700 years old.

Mangroves

The Aguirre Forest Reserve at Guayama on the south coast protects mangroves, tidal flats, lakes, and bird nesting sites. Bordering it is the Jobos Bay National Estuarine Research Reserve. The estuary is dominated by seagrass beds, coral reefs, and mangroves as well as mudflats and evergreen littoral forest. Boardwalks through both reserves allow you to see the ecosystem up close, or you can paddle a kayak through the canals and along the coast. If you're lucky, you may also see manatee and sea turtles. The mangroves on the south coast tend to die behind the outer fringe because not enough water is received to wash away the salt. This leaves areas of mud and skeletal trees that flood at times of spring tide making a popular feeding ground for water birds; in winter many ducks stop on their migration routes at Jobos. The mangroves on the north coast, at Piñones Forest, stretch inland for a considerable distance. Here you can hire bikes (or kayaks) and cycle or hike along a boardwalk which runs along the coast and inland into the mangrove forest.

Caves to be explored

Puerto Rico also boasts an intricate system of caves called the Río Camuy Cave Park in Camuy. It is one of the largest cave systems and the third-largest underground river in the world, which runs through a network of caves, canyons, and sinkholes. There are guided tours to see stalactites, stalagmites, and multitudes of bats.

For those who seek a little more adventure, private companies offer expeditions to other caves that are not accessible to the public. Near the Camuy Cave Park, you can find Cueva del Infierno, which has around 2,000 caves, where you can find 13 species of bats, *coquí* frogs, crickets, and an unusual arachnid called the *guavá*, among many other species.

Bioluminescence Puerto Rico has several bioluminescent bays, also referred to as phosphorescent bays, where you can see the water glow at night thanks to microscopic organisms called dinoflagellates. It is one of the few places on the planet where you can enjoy this phenomenon almost every evening. However, the effect can only be seen properly in pitch darkness, so try not to go on the night of a full moon.

On Vieques, just off the coast of Fajardo, you can find the Puerto Mosquito Bioluminescent Bay Natural Reserve, considered to be one of the most spectacular in the world for its brightness. You can either take a kayak-guided tour of the bay or opt for an electric pontoon boat. La Parguera Bioluminescent Bay, in the southwestern town of Lajas, is popular. Once you arrive at the area of La Parguera, you will find countless boating services that offer excursions to see the bay. Las Croabas lagoon in the northeast is also bioluminescent. Tour guides take you through the lagoon on kayaks rather than on polluting motorboats. Both La Parguera and Las Croabas have suffered from pollution and it is now forbidden to swim at Las Croabas. This has already had a beneficial effect on the dinoflagellate population and numbers have increased.

Exploring the Río Camuy Cave Park.

Casa Cautiño in Guayama, formerly a plantation owner's residence, retains the original rooms and furnishings.

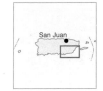

THE SOUTHEAST

The mountains give way to miles of flat land in the southeast stretching to the Caribbean Sea. Formerly sugar country, there is now industry and, of course, tourism along the palm-fringed coast.

The southeastern section of Puerto Rico – thought by many to be one of the prettiest parts of the island – has the interesting characteristic of having some of the most heavily developed, as well as some of the least developed, parts of the country. It is largely residential and quiet, blessed by the pleasant Caribbean trade winds that blow steadily in this region all year, stabilizing the weather. During the "rainy" season, from about May to September, the southeast may get some 9ins (23cm) of rain a month, while during the December to April "dry" season, monthly rainfall averages 3–5ins (7–12cm).

A major town in the region is **Humacao ❶**, which, although an industrial center, does have its charms. Previously subsisting off agriculture, Humacao is now the gateway to the major resort area on the island. Only a 45-minute drive from San Juan via Route 30, Humacao is within 2 miles (3km) of some of the most dazzling beachfront that Vieques Sound has to offer. Add to that its convenience as a starting point for excursions in the southeast, and it earns its standing as a serious holiday resort.

One of the few attractions in the town itself is the T-shaped **Casa Roig Museum** (tel: 787-852-8380; Wed–Sun 10am–4pm; free), the former home of a wealthy sugar cane landowner,

Antonio Roig. Built in 1920, it was designed by Antonín Nechodemo, in the style of Frank Lloyd Wright and is one of the few remaining buildings by Nechodemo.

A local specialty are the *frituras* called *granitas* made in the *barrio* of Patagonia in Humacao. Made out of a paste of rice flour with a chunk of cheese in the middle, they are molded into a canoe shape (or an oversized grain of rice) and then deep-fried. You can find vendors selling them in the Plaza del Mercado and around town,

Main Attractions
Playa Humacao
Cayo Santiago
Punta Tuna
Bosque Estatal de Carite, Arroyo

Stopping for a chat in Arroyo.

FACT

The Festival del Azúcar (Sugar Festival) takes place in Yabucoa each May – one of half a dozen festivals held in the town throughout the year.

and people come from all over the island to buy them.

Tour of the beaches

The best way to begin a beach tour of this part of the island is to head north to **Playa Humacao** ②, probably the best-equipped public beach on the island. It boasts not only miles of bright sand and a handful of offshore cays, but also a veritable arcade of lockers, refreshment stands, and other amenities. The beach benefits from its size, drawing heavily enough from local and tourist groups alike to ensure that there's always something going on, if only a pick-up volleyball game: join in. On Route 3, just south of Punta Santiago, you will see the entrance to the Reserva Natural de Humacao, now officially called Reserva Natural Punta Santiago (tel: 787-852-6058; Mon–Fri 7.30am–3.30pm, Sat–Sun 9am–5pm; free). There are pleasant trails for walking and cycling through the forest, where many of the trees are labelled. Parking is free and there are toilets

and picnic tables, but no restaurant. Kayaking can be arranged here and while paddling on the interconnecting lagoons you can see lots of birds and a large number of iguanas lounging in the trees or swimming in the water. The area was once a sugar plantation and at that time the lagoons were drained to grow sugar cane.

Monkey Island

A little less than a mile off the coast of Playa Humacao lies a 39-acre (16-hectare) island that few people have had the opportunity to visit. This place, **Cayo Santiago** ③, or Isla de los Monos (Monkey Island) is home to approximately 950 rhesus macaques. With a grant from Columbia University, 409 animals were brought from India to Puerto Rico in 1938 for research into primate behavior. Never before had such a social troupe of monkeys been transported into the Western world and placed in semi-natural conditions. Despite the comfortable climate and undisturbed environment

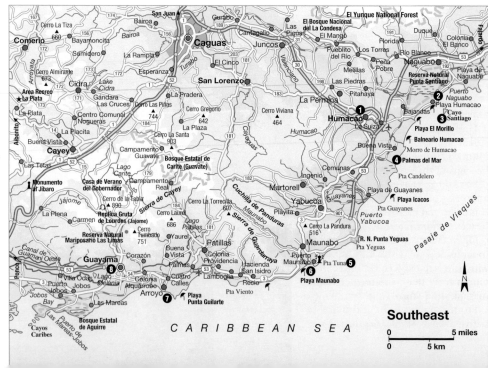

Southeast

0   5 miles
0   5 km

of Cayo Santiago, many experts remained skeptical on the question of whether the primates could survive and breed.

For two years, tuberculosis scourged the colony. Then, during World War II, grant money ran out and the monkeys faced the threat of starvation. Townspeople from Playa de Humacao helped the colony by regularly taking bananas, coconuts, and other foods out to the island for the duration of the war.

Today, the island is administered by the University of Puerto Rico, and scientists from the Caribbean Primate Research Center there spend many, many hours studying the behavioral patterns of these fascinating creatures.

Due to the ongoing research and possible health hazards (and the fact that rhesus monkeys can be very aggressive at times), visitors are not allowed on the island. However, the island is about 30 minutes away if you can take a kayak tour, paddling slowly around about 30ft (10 meters) offshore so you can see the monkeys on the beach. The tour includes a snorkeling stop at a sunken barge where there are lots of fish on the reef. Alternatively there is a motorboat, *La Paseadora*, with shade and bench seating run by Captain Frank (Paco) López out of Punta Santiago or Palmas del Mar (tel: 787-316-0441; www.lapaseodora.yolasite.com), also with a snorkeling stop.

Halfway down the eastern coast and a 10-minute drive south from Humacao is **Palmas del Mar** ❹ on (www.palmasdelmar.com), Puerto Rico's largest vacation resort. The self-appointed "New American Riviera," this 2,700-acre (1,100-hectare) holiday heaven comprises just about everything: 20 tennis courts, two gorgeous beachfront golf courses, riding stables, fine beaches, deep-sea fishing, 19 restaurants, numerous bars, a casino, a marina, and so on.

From Humacao to **Yabucoa** (a native Indian term meaning "Place of the Yuca Trees"), rolling hills, semi-tropical forests, sugar cane fields, and cow pastures highlight an exceedingly pleasant drive. Yabucoa used to be a sugar town but now marks the beginning of an industrial circuit that continues south-westward. Taking advantage of low-wage labor and liberal tax laws, oil refineries, pharmaceutical companies, textile manufacturers, and industrial chemical plants border the smaller towns all the way down the coast.

Leaving Yabucoa, Route 30 to Route 901 takes you on a scenic drive southward (part of the Ruta Panorámica) through arid coastal headlands which form part of the Cuchilla de Panduras mountain range.

Balneario Lucía

A few miles away from town along the **Balneario Lucía** shore, abandoned seafood restaurants indicate that, at one point, this spot was believed to have potential as a popular bathing retreat. Now, it is wild; few bother with it. Rows of planted coconut palm trees grow in awkwardly misshapen

Beach at Humacao.

directions along the beach. The trunks of these trees are wrapped with sheet metal, apparently to prevent rats from climbing them.

The rats have joy-riding in mind, according to a native writer: "When there are no such bands, rats with a penchant for primitive piloting climb the trunks, nibble a hole in the coconuts, lap out the milk, crawl through the hole into the nut, gnaw off the stem and sit inside the shell as it makes its break-neck descent to the ground."

Route 901 curves upward into a series of hills overlooking rugged shoreline and an expanse of the Caribbean Sea, with the island of Vieques visible in the distance.

The road descends to **Punta Tuna** , where one of Puerto Rico's two active lighthouses stands. Built in the 1890s by Spain, the lighthouse is now run by the US Coast Guard. Adjacent to Punta Tuna, a little-known beach ranks among the nicest on the southeastern coast.

Former movie theater in Guayama.

Farther down the road, on the other side of Punta Tuna, another good beach arches for nearly a mile around tiny **Puerto Maunabo** . Pack a picnic and have a lunch break on one of the lovely beaches; camping is also allowed here.

The Ruta Panorámica continues past the town of Maunabo and winds up a narrow road past cliffside houses and damp verdure over the Cuchilla de Panduras and back to Yabucoa.

Unspoiled interior

Turn inland at **Patillas** and head up into the Sierra de Cayey on Route 184 to **Guavate**, known for its *lechoneras*. Open air cafés on either side of the road offer delicious suckling pig roasted on a spit, usually served with rice and beans, making a hugely popular excursion for *sanjuaneros*, particularly in the summer months, when you can expect queues. Many families leave the city at 3am to get away for the weekend and at least one of the *lechoneras* is serving roast pork by 4am.

Route 184 runs right through the **Bosque Estatal de Carite** (Visitors' Center at Route 184, Km 27.5; tel: 787-747-4545; Mon–Fri 7am–3.30pm;

AMERICAN LANDING AT GUÁNICA

During the Spanish-American War, American forces under the command of General Nelson A. Miles landed at Guánica near Ponce on July 26, 1898. The landing surprised the United States War Department no less than the Spanish, as Miles had been instructed to land near San Juan (the War Department learned of the landing through an Associated Press release).

However, en route to Puerto Rico, Miles concluded that a San Juan landing was vulnerable to attack by small boats, and so changed plans. Ponce, said at the time to be the largest city in Puerto Rico, was connected with San Juan by a 70-mile (110km) military road, well defended by the Spanish at Coamo and Aibonito.

In order to flank this position, American Major General John R. Brooke landed at Arroyo, just east of Guayama, intending to move on Cayey, which is northwest of Guayama, along the road from Ponce to San Juan. General Brooke occupied Guayama on August 5, 1898, after slight opposition, in the Battle of Guayama. On August 9, the Battle of Guamaní took place north of Guayama.

A more significant battle, the Battle of Abonito Pass, was halted on the morning of August 13 upon notification of the armistice between the United States and Spain.

free): a 6,680-acre (2,703-hectare) humid, sub-tropical forest with a network of trails for hiking through the palms, ferns, and pine trees. Opportunities for birdwatching are good here, particularly at first light. There are campsites so you can be on hand for the dawn chorus (camping permit required). There are also gazebos and picnic spots for day trips. A popular spot is the **Charco Azul** (Blue Pool) where you can cool off in the mountain-fed stream (Charco Azul Recreation Area; Route 184, Km 16.6, 9am–5pm; Guavate Recreation Area, Route 184, Km 27.3, 9am–5pm; free). A rare and possibly extinct inhabitant of the Sierra de Cayey is the endemic *coquí dorado* (*Eleuthe rodactylus jasperi*), a tiny frog found in areas of dense bromeliad growth at an altitude of between 2,120 and 2,570ft (650–785 meters).

Arroyo

Five miles (8km) west along the coast from Patillas off Route 3, Samuel Morse installed the first telegraph line in Puerto Rico in **Arroyo 7** in 1859, and the **Old Customs House Museum** (tel: 787-839-8096; Wed–Sun 9am–4pm; closed for lunch; free) on Calle Morse 65, holds memorabilia of the event. The seaside town was left behind when Guayama was developed as an industrial center and has a laid-back feel. At the end of Calle Morse is a charming boardwalk, the Malecón, which has palm trees and the sea on one side and seafood restaurants on the other. The Tren del Sur, a narrow gauge railroad which used to run through sugar cane fields, is temporarily closed for renovation.

Balneario Punta Guilarte (tel: 787-839-3505) is the most popular tourist destination in this area, with an enormous government-run vacation center. There isn't much sand on the beach but there's a good grassy area where children play; safe, shallow water, and lots of facilities such as beach volleyball courts and accommodations from camping to villas.

Guayama

Guayama 8, about 4.5 miles (7km) further west along Route 3, has one of Puerto Rico's best-preserved and loveliest plazas, and the church of **St Anthony of Padua** beside it is the only neo-Romantic church on the island. A clock painted on the right tower points to 11.30, the exact time the church was "baptized." The Art Deco cinema still shows first-run films, while **Casa Cautiño**'s facade is a riot of neoclassical creole embellishments. Built in 1887 as the house of a rich sugar-producing family, it's now a museum (Tue–Sat 9am–4.30pm, Sun 10am–4pm; free).

About 5 miles (8km) north of Guayama is a non-profit butterfly reserve, **Reserva Natural Mariposario Las Limas** (Route 747, Km 0.7; tel: 787-391-3777; Mon–Fri 9am–1pm; groups only, reservation required; free). There are trails through the forest, heliconia gardens, a museum and, of course, butterflies, making this a rewarding excursion if you can get a group together.

The Sheraton Hotel and Casino dominates the plush Palmas del Mar resort.

Waves pounding the north-coast shore.

THE NORTH

The north coast is blessed with a string of beautiful beaches backed by resorts, golf courses, wetlands, and nature reserves. Inland is the remarkable karst country with limestone sinkholes and caves to explore.

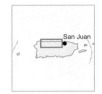

Driving west from San Juan on Route 2, as the landscape opens up a bit and the first hills begin to rise, first-time visitors may begin to feel they have left the metropolis and are about to penetrate Puerto Rico's fabled countryside. That is, until you hit sprawling, congested Bayamón; then you begin to wonder if the big cities will ever stop. They stop in **Dorado ❶**, 10 miles (16km) west of San Juan, the first town that can claim to be out from under its shadow.

Dorado is a pleasant, quiet, unassuming little town. You'll miss it if you stay on the highway, and may have to look twice for it even if you take the detour on Route 165, which leaves Route 2 and runs north across emerald marshlands before looping back to it.

The friendly little town of **Toa Baja** signals the turn-off. Dividing Toa Baja from Dorado is the sluggish, meandering **Río de la Plata**, with grassy banks and clay river bed which has turned the stream's waters a rugged brick red.

Easygoing Dorado

Dorado follows Route 165 loosely on both sides. There are no cross-streets to slow traffic enough to draw attention to the small main plaza by the roadside, and the town's businesses are admirably free of gaudy billboards and other "Welcome to..." bric-a-brac.

Cheerful northerner.

"Urban" Dorado is just clean, slow-paced and friendly, and a disproportionate number of its business establishments – bakeries, bars, juice stands – have camaraderie as their *raison d'être*.

Two sites that stand out are the **Santuario del Cristo de la Reconciliación**, whose temple holds the third-largest statue of Jesus Christ in the Caribbean, and **La Casa del Rey** (Calle Méndez Vigo 292; tel: 787-796-1030; Mon–Fri 8am–4.30pm; free). Both were built in 1823 and are

Main Attractions
Dorado
Playa de Vega Baja
Arecibo
Karst country
Parque Ceremonial Indígena de Caguana
Parque Nacional Cavernas del Río Camuy
Guajataca Forest Reserve
Playa Guajataca

The Casa del Rey in Dorado dates back to the founding of the city.

the oldest buildings in Dorado. The church statue, at 25ft (7.6 meters), was created by Puerto Rican sculptor Sonny Rodríguez.

Right next to City Hall, La Casa del Rey was originally built as a parador, providing housing for Spanish government officials and then used as the regional military headquarters with a small prison cell. The first mayor of Dorado, Jacinto López Martínez bought it in 1848 for use as his home and extended it, building on two wings to create an interior patio. In 1871 the house acquired another notable owner, the romantic writer, Manuel Alonso y Pacheco. After a period of neglect in the first half of the 20th century, it was restored in 1978 by the Institute of Puerto Rican Culture to become a local history museum. It exhibits mid 19th-century furniture and fixtures. It is listed on the US Register of Historic Places.

Another stop on the downtown trail is the **Museo de Arte e Historia de Dorado** (tel: 787-796-1030; Mon–Fri 8am–noon, 1–4pm, Sat 9am–2pm;

free). Located on Méndez Vigo at Juan Francisco, the building has three galleries holding exhibits of art, archeological artifacts, and a presentation on the history of Dorado.

The **Plaza de Recreo** houses a remarkable landmark, a statue showing three life-sized figures: Spanish, African, and Taíno. This is the **Monumento a las Raíces**, sculpted by Dorado native Salvador Rivera Cardona.

Dorado beaches

Dorado is known for its inviting beaches, easily accessible via the buses that leave from near the town plaza. A mile (1.6km) northwest of town, through a spinney of mangroves and a bone-white graveyard on Route 693, is the irresistibly lovely beach at **Playa Dorado-Sardinera**, and also nearby is **El Ojo del Buey** (The Ox's Eye), a seaside recreational area that takes its name from a large rock bearing an amazing resemblance to the head of an ox.

In the first half of the 20th century, the Rockefeller family bought plots of land in the area, converting

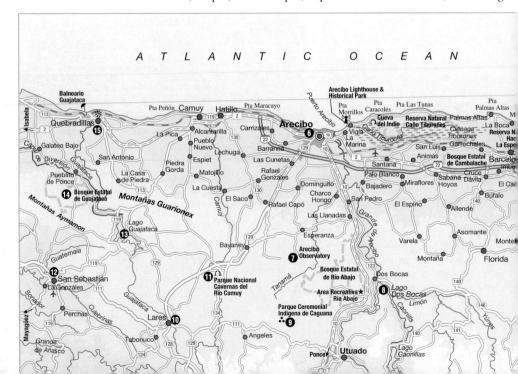

them into a huge private vacation compound. Subsequently, Laurence Rockefeller used this land to build the luxury Dorado Beach hotel, which opened in 1958. In its heyday the hotel, once owned by Clara Livingston, Puerto Rico's first woman pilot and head of the Air Civil Defense, welcomed celebrities and dignitaries from around the world. Over the years, however, economic difficulties and opportunities brought the construction, closure, redevelopment, and reopening of hotels in the area. A luxurious, low-rise, low-density hotel, the Ritz-Carlton Dorado Beach Resort & Spa, opened in 2012 on the site of the old hotel. Dorado Beach's four championship golf courses, at one time administered by Juan "Chichi" Rodríguez, are open for business to club members and guests.

The Cibuco river

West of here there is a string of palm-fringed, horseshoe-shaped bays, including Playa Los Tocones and Playa Cerro Gordo with access from the coastal road, Route 693, and the village of Breñas. Further west, a fast, 35-minute drive from San Juan on routes 2 and 686, **Playa de Vega Baja** ❷ is one of the most popular beachfronts on this stretch of coast, and is dotted with cabins belonging to the local residents. It benefits not only from spectacular juxtapositions of sand and sea, but also from lush and unusual surrounding countryside. The beach itself draws most attention for its weird and haunting rock formations, which are actually a string of coral islands running parallel to the seashore for 2,500ft (760 meters), from the palm-lined cove of **Boca del Cibuco** to craggy **Punta Puerto Nuevo**. This odd, almost unique formation has sheltered most of the beach, while causing its western end to resemble at times a sort of preternaturally large Jacuzzi.

The Cibuco, one of the rivers that cross such fertile land, is a variation of the name "Sebuco," a chief or cacique Taíno Indian of the region. The Taíno often settled on the banks of rivers, for the fresh water and fish.

FACT

The nickname for Vega Baja is melao-melao, meaning "molasses-molasses," because of the large quantities of molasses produced here. An annual marathon in October is the Maratón Melao-Melao.

The beach at Punta Las Tunas.

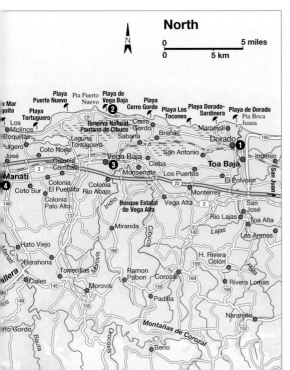

Centuries before Spanish settlers first set foot on what is now Vega Baja, the area was populated by as many as four different civilizations from different ages in history, of which the Taíno were the most recent. Relics of tribal civilizations from the vicinities of Vega Baja are considered among the most archeologically important in the area. Taíno carvings have been found on the exposed reefs in the vicinity of the Cibuco river. Among them, one depicts a face and others are shaped as fish, indicating these reefs were frequented for spearfishing and other activities. The Cibuco river fosters a rich diversity of ocean life and reefs.

Vega Baja

The town of **Vega Baja** ❸ has grown into a fairly modern and uniform Puerto Rican municipality sitting in the middle of the fertile coastal flatlands west of San Juan. Visitors will be rewarded with long vistas over cane fields and marshes, and an array of deciduous foliage: most impressive in an island full of tropical trees.

Playa Mar Chiquita is a good swimming beach.

Founded in 1776 by Antonio Viera as "Vega-baxa del Naranjal de Nuestra Señora del Rosario," the name was eventually shortened to Vega Baja. The town's patron saint is "Nuestra Señora del Rosario," and her saint's day on October 7 is celebrated with religious processions, food and dancing.

One of the oldest houses in the town has been restored and converted into a museum: **Museo Casa Alonso** (Calle Betances/Acosta 34; tel: 787-855-1364; Tue–Sat 9am–3pm). Although the foundations are 18th century, the current two-story building dates from the 19th century, a fine example of neoclassical design which has been used as a film location many times because of its typical colonial features. The house is furnished with antiques, including the kitchen and bathroom, while one room is devoted to the library of the political activist, Pedro Albizu Campos, and another is full of musical instruments, records, radios, phonographs, and other items devoted to popular Latin American music.

Further west along the coast, and accessible by Route 686, which runs near the bottom of it, is **Playa Tortuguero**, the largest and most palm-lined of the beaches. Half a mile inland, **Laguna Tortuguero**, while not officially a nature reserve, provides a haven for birdlife. Though an old-time favorite for picnicking, boating, and fishing, the lake is now habitat to caimans, and its use for water sports has consequently diminished.

The Manatí area

Continuing west, the **Manatí** ❹ area produces most of the island's pineapple products as well as coffee, textiles, shoes, and pharmaceuticals. Vendors offer fresh pineapples along the road (Route 2). The town is believed to have been named after the manatee, although some say it was baptized after the Taíno-named river, the Manatuabón. Known as the Athens of Puerto Rico because of its cultural and literary heritage, there is a fine library, the Biblioteca Nacional Francisco Alvarez, next door to the Salón de los Poetas on the Paseo de Atenas.

A short drive from town takes you to **Playa Mar Chiquita** ❺, an unusual semi-circular beach almost entirely blocked off from the sea by a row of high rocks. The surf comes pounding through a gap to produce a most dramatic effect, while the resulting sheltered lagoon provides excellent swimming.

West of Manatí are the ruins of **Hacienda La Esperanza** (tel: 787-722-5882; www.paranaturaleza.org), one of the largest, wealthiest, and most advanced sugar plantations in Puerto Rico in the 19th century. It was owned by José Ramón Fernández (1808–83), Marqués de La Esperanza, one of the most powerful sugar barons on the island. Extending over 2,278 acres (922 hectares) of an alluvial plain, it has ten different ecosystems and includes cemented dunes, limestone karst formations, a manor house, and a sugar mill. Excavations on the site have revealed four pre-Columbian ceremonial plazas, petroglyphic carvings, and a burial ground. Check the website for details of tours, including an historical trail,

TIP

At the foot of the Arecibo Lighthouse is La Poza del Obispo (Bishop's Pool), created by an opening in rocks. Waves crash through and over the rocks but the pool is calm and protected.

The streets of Manatí.

The century-old Punta Morrillos lighthouse in Arecibo is now restored as a museum focusing on the city's heritage. For more details, call the Puerto Rico Tourism Company on 1-800-866-7827.

The region is dotted with excellent golf courses and resorts.

river, karst, wetland and coastal trail, bird- and bat-watching and activities including workshops, volunteering, citizen science, and other participatory events. Check the website or call for details of tours, including the "From Slavery to Hope" tour of the hacienda (Wed–Sun 1.30pm; in English; 75 mins; reservations required), the river, karst, wetland and coastal trail, as well as bird- and bat-watching tours (in Spanish).

Coastal roads and vistas

There are prettier cities on this island, but few present a more beautiful approach than **Arecibo** ❻. Route 2 takes a tortuous turn 48 miles (77km) west of San Juan and reveals the prosperous city – a hub for the island's pharmaceutical industry as well as other manufacturing – backed by the blue Atlantic. All the roads from San Juan hug the shoreline here, giving pleasant views of the city from afar. Those roads were put here for a reason: to the east recede swamps of unmeasured depth and gloom. Be warned that the surrounding area is

chockablock with mosquitoes in the wet season. Directly to the south of Arecibo lies karst country, with typical landscapes of pine and mahogany in the Río Abajo forest.

The western end of the expressway (PR 22) affords another dramatic perspective of the island's north coast, this one just west of Arecibo in Hatillo. Travelers are treated to a spectacular, unobstructed view of the Atlantic Ocean's crashing waves, fronted by acres of palm trees. This is Puerto Rico unspoiled. Navigation via the expressway obliges you to double back east to reach the town of Arecibo. However, it is not an unpleasant trip: Route 2 is packed with shopping malls and fast-food outlets, but in just a few miles you return to the town's historic area, all the while enjoying glimpses of the ocean to the north.

The coastal road, Route 681, is the road the expressway left behind. It meanders, meaning you won't get to Arecibo quickly, but you will enjoy the view from the cliffs. The drive runs from Palmas Altas through Islote, past Desvío Valdés and to

Punta Caracoles (Seashell Point), site of **La Cueva del Indio** (Indian Cave; tours by appointment, tel: 787-295-8878). A short walk leads to the hole in the cliff, inside which are some pre-Columbian drawings.

The lighthouse and beyond

Further ahead, off Route 655 to your right at Punta Morrillos, you'll find the **Arecibo Lighthouse and Historical Park** (tel: 787-880-7540; www.arecibolighthouse.com; Mon–Fri and public holidays 9am–6pm, Sat–Sun 10am–7pm). The excursion is both fun and educational for children and adults alike. An expansive deck with a children's play area accompanies a restored museum that includes replicas of a Taíno Indian village, Christopher Columbus's ships and African slave quarters. A pirate's cave and a pirate's ship, together with a mini zoo, complete the facilities, along with the lighthouse itself, which was the last one built by the Spaniards, in 1898. From the top you can get a great view of Arecibo and the ocean, with whale watching in season if you're lucky.

Arecibo

Arecibo forms a semi-peninsula pointing northeastward at the delta of two rivers: the **Río Grande de Arecibo** and the **Canal Perdomo**. The waterfront drive is quite lovely, with views of the lighthouse and the Atlantic coast, although the *malecón* (boardwalk) is somewhat sad. This is not a city with much interest for tourists, but it is a pleasant enough place to live. Its streets are broad, there are cafés and theaters, and there is a good shopping district. **Calle Alejandro Salicrup**, at the tip of the semi-peninsular wedge, is one of the best thoroughfares on which to see the old local timbered architecture, which is as unique to Arecibo as the southwestern townhouse style is to San Germán.

The **Museo de Arte e Historia de Arecibo** (tel: 787-879-4403; Mon–Fri

9am–noon and 1–3.30pm; free) on calles Juan Rosado and Santiago Iglesias, is a former transportation center, and displays art and photography of the area including old postcards of early Arecibo. Built in 1919, it was once used as a warehouse to store rum, and was painstakingly restored and re-inaugurated in 2006.

Arecibo Observatory

Anyone who has ever taken sixth-grade science should have some familiarity with Arecibo. On one of those big, full-page spreads that fill up space in astronomy textbooks, the **Arecibo Observatory** ❼ is generally featured prominently. A complicated trip 20 miles (32km) south of the town of Arecibo into the karst country will bring you to this mammoth complex. From downtown Arecibo, follow de Diego to Route 129. Bear left on Route 651 and follow it for the 4 miles (6km) before it becomes 635. Travel about the same distance until you come to a T-intersection, at which you will turn right (onto Route 626) and

Arecibo's Playa de Los Morrillos.

TIP

If you have the time, take advantage of the 45-minute free boat trips on Lago Dos Bocas provided by the Transportation and Public Works Department (tel: 787-854-1010 for departure times).

travel a few hundred yards before making a left turn onto 625, at the end of which is the renowned observatory. (see page 175.)

Karst country

The northwest of Puerto Rico has an intriguing area known as the karst country, where the land rises in regular green-and-white hillocks and appears to be boiling.

Karst is the name for one of the world's oddest rock formations and can occur only under the most fortuitous circumstances. Some geologists claim there are only two other places on earth where rock formations resemble those of Puerto Rico: one just across the Mona Passage in the Dominican Republic, and one in Slovenia.

Karst is formed when water sinks into limestone and erodes larger and larger basins, known as "sinkholes." Many erosions create many sinkholes, until one is left with peaks of land only where the land has not sunk with the erosion of limestone: these are *mogotes*, or karstic hillocks,

The Cueva Clara sinkhole.

which resemble each other in size and shape to a striking extent, given the randomness of the process that created them. All this leads you to realize that the highest point on the highest *mogote* in the karst country is certainly below the level that the limestone ground held in earlier days when the first drop of rain opened the first sinkhole.

It's hard to say where the karst country begins. Some say at Manatí, though there are two hills not 10 minutes' drive west of San Juan that look suspiciously karstic. From Manatí, they carry on as far west as Isabela, and are at their most spectacular a short drive (5 miles/8km) south of the major cities of Puerto Rico's northwest.

These hills are impressive mountains only 100ft (30 meters) high – they are probably the grandest landscape within which humans can feel a sense of scale. They encompass a startling variety within their regularity; certain *mogotes* can look like the Arizona Desert tucked in for bed in the Black Forest.

THE KARSTIC FORESTS

Puerto Rico's Department of Natural Resources has recognized the beauty and fragility of its unique karstic landscape. It has created four national forests in which it is protected: Cambalache (east of Arecibo, with plantations of eucalyptus, teak, and mahoe trees), Guajataca (west of Arecibo, offering some 25 miles/40km of hiking trails), Río Abajo (south of Arecibo, and home to 223 plant and 175 wildlife species; 70 trails crisscross its 5,780 acres/2,300 hectares), and Vega Alta (west of Toa Baja).

Not all the karst country is limited to these forests; in fact, they are woefully small, comprising only about 4,000 acres (1,600 hectares) in total, with Río Abajo accounting for over half of these. All are ripe for hiking, yet the trails in the karst country never seem as crowded as those up El Yunque and other Puerto Rican mountains. Perhaps this is owing to the dangers involved with this sort of landscape. Sinkholes are not like potholes, but they can come as unexpectedly, especially in heavy brush.

Get a trail map from the visitors' center at whatever reserve you try. Otherwise, *The Other Puerto Rico* by Kathryn Robinson offers helpful advice, and one read of it will convince you that there's nowhere in Puerto Rico that's not worth risking a little danger to see.

A karst country drive

Arecibo is the capital of the karst country, and some fine drives can begin from there. The easiest to undertake is certainly Route 10 south to Utuado. From there you can take Route 111 to Lares and return on Route 129, which is flanked by *colmados* (grocery stores), or continue to San Sebastián. From there you can pick up Route 119 to **Lago Guajataca** for perhaps the finest views of the water and limestone that made the whole unfathomable but evocative landscape possible. Route 119 eventually meets up with the coastal Route 2 after an exhaustive tour of the karst country.

Make it a point, if at all possible, of getting out to the karst country. The unique beauty is staggering, and is worth a visit by itself. Even more, though, the sight of karst will add another dimension to this tropical paradise too often labeled as a place for a "beach vacation."

Lagos Dos Bocas

Route 10 follows the course of the Río Grande de Arecibo upstream to Lago Dos Bocas ❽ (Two-Mouthed Lake) on its way to Utuado. The lake curves into a U-shape around steep hills. At Km 68, Route 10 skirts the lakeshore. From there, a launch service carries passengers back and forth across the lake at the weekends, while restaurants situated by the lake also pick up passengers in their private boats to take them across for lunch.

On the other side of the road is the forest reserve, **Bosque Estatal de Río Abajo** (tel: 787-880-6557; daily 9am–5pm), where there is also a recreation center and the nearby José Luis Vivaldi Lugo Aviary. There is an important program here to preserve the endangered Puerto Rican parrot and if you are lucky you may see the parrot flying in the forest, one of 34 bird species found here. The subtropical wet forest is spectacularly beautiful, with trails running through it, leading you to limestone caves and streams, or you can take a cooling dip in the lake. There is also a Visitor's Center, parking, bathrooms, basic camping facilities, and gazebos.

EAT

Make sure to stop in at the Heladería de Lares (Lares Ice Cream Parlor), a famous ice-cream store located in front of the town square of Lares. Founded in 1968 by Salvador Barreto, it has an array of over 1,000 flavors ranging from the traditional, such as vanilla or chocolate, to savory, such as rice and beans, carrot, salt cod, avocado, and corn).

Arecibo, one of the oldest and most prosperous towns in Puerto Rico.

Caguana Indigenous Ceremonial Park

West of Utuado on Route 111, the **Parque Ceremonial Indígena de Caguana** ❾ (Caguana Indigenous Ceremonial Park; tel: 787-894-7325; daily 8.30am–4.20pm) should not be missed as it is one of the most important archeological sites in the islands of the Caribbean. Built by the Taínos nearly a millennium ago, some 30 bateyes (ball courts) have been identified, on which the early Indians played a lacrosse- or pelota-like game in a blend of sport and religious ceremony. Several have been restored to their original state and there are large monoliths brought from the nearby River Tanama as well as petroglyphs dotted between the ball courts. There is a small museum displaying Taíno artifacts and a botanical garden growing crops the Taíno would have harvested, such as corn, yucca, and sweet potatoes.

Overlooking the courts, a small rocky peak, **Cemí Mountain** (Montaña Cemí) has been guarding the park for centuries. The Taíno believed that their gods lived there and it is thought that they built their ball courts here for that reason. Strange sounds echo back and forth over the landscaped grounds. An owl hoots. A dry leaf rasps across one of the bateyes. The Taíno gods Yukiyu and Juracán continue to make their presence felt here.

A few seconds from the entrance to the park, a rural road off Route 111 leads to Batey del Cemí Zipline Adventure (tel: 787-484-3860; www.bateydelcemi.com). For the adventurous this is a great way to get up close and personal with the karst country, where a variety of tours offer hiking, ziplining, rappelling and caving, including the underground river cave, Portillo. Bring a spare set of clothes as you will probably get wet and muddy even if it doesn't rain.

Lares

If this tiny island has a frontier town, surely **Lares** ❿ must be it. It sits at the western edge of the Cordillera Central's main cluster of peaks, and rests at the southernmost spur of the karst country. Lares is as far from the sea as you can get in Puerto Rico, and to its west a placid corridor of plains runs just to the north of the hills of La Cadena and south of Route 111 and the sleepy Río Culebrinas.

Like many of the towns in this area, where plains meet uplands to produce eerily spectacular vistas, Lares is as scenic to approach as it is to leave. Arriving from the south on either Route 124 or Route 128, you are greeted by a tiny, close-packed community perched on a gentle rise across a valley and shadowed by rugged twin karstic *mogotes*. Emerging from the east on Route 111 from the karstic clusters of the Río Abajo Forest Reserve, you are taken by surprise at Lares's anomalous urbanity.

The town itself is an attenuated cluster of little businesses, bars and shops snaking along two main one-way streets that run in opposite

Petroglyphs inside the Taíno Ball Courts.

directions. In the central **Plaza de la Revolución** stands an imposing 19th-century Spanish colonial church, Iglesia San José, with a pale pastel facade and gracefully arched roof.

As the scene of the "Grito de Lares," Puerto Rico's glorious and ill-fated revolt against Spanish colonial rule, the town is generally considered to be the birthplace of modern Puerto Rican political consciousness.

Parque Nacional Cavernas del Río Camuy

One of the largest cave systems in the Western world can be found northeast of Lares on Route 129 heading back to Arecibo. The cave system is actually a series of karstic sinkholes connected by the 350ft (106-meter) -deep Río Camuy, which burrows underground through soft limestone for much of its course from the Cordillera to the Atlantic. The largest of these entrances has been developed as a tourist attraction, with inducements of the "fun for the whole family" variety.

The **Parque Nacional del Río Camuy** ⓫ (Río Camuy Cave Park;

tel: 787-898-3100; Wed–Sun, public holidays 8.30am–5pm, last trip at 3.30pm), contains one of the most massive cave networks in the Western Hemisphere. This 268-acre (106-hectare) complex includes three crater-like sinkholes and one cave. The Taínos considered these formations sacred; their artifacts have been found throughout the area. The park's main attraction is the 170ft (52-meter) -high and 695ft (210-meter) -long **Cueva Clara**, which is specially lit and accessible only by trolley and in guided groups. This is a very popular attraction and can get crowded with school groups and other tour parties. The trolley runs every 30 minutes and there is a short video to entertain you while you wait, as well as a gift shop. Visit in the morning if you can as afternoon rain raises the water level and tours are often suspended. The cave is cool and the concrete walkways are wet and can be slippery, so dress appropriately and wear trainers or shoes with good grip.

The cave is home to a unique species of fish that is completely blind

A plaque that commemorates the 1868 revolution in Lares.

Bathing in Lago Dos Bocas.

and a colony of half a million bats, which will be asleep during your visit, but you will smell the guano. The entrance looks like a cathedral facade, with a broad row of toothy stalactites descending from the bushy hillside. Far below you can see and hear the river rushing through the deeper caves. Dozens of river cave systems lie beneath the spectacular karst landscape.

At Km 18.9 on Route 129 there is a camping ground with showers, toilets and other facilities. Along the road you have the Restaurante El Taíno, where they pride themselves on traditional Puerto Rican cuisine, bilingual waiters, a family atmosphere, and fairly reasonable prices. The house specialty is arroz con guinea (rice with guinea hen), served with beans, and amarillos (fried bananas) for dessert.

Cueva de Camuy

Monument honoring Emeterio Betances on the Plaza de la Revolución in Lares.

If you're an avid spelunker, there's still more for you to see: close to Río Camuy is the privately owned **Cueva de Camuy** (daily 9am–5pm, Sun until 8pm) on Route 486. Although smaller and less interesting, it too has guided tours as well as family-centered activities that include a swimming pool and waterslide, amusements, a café, ponies, and go-karts.

Day-long caving, rock climbing and rappeling trips (abseiling down sinkholes) can be organized through Aventuras Tierra Adentro (tel: 787-766-0470; www.aventuraspr.com), which include floating down underground rivers solely by the light of headlamps. Some 2,000 caves have been discovered in the karst region. They provide homes for 13 species of bat, the tiny *coquí*, the *guavá* (an arachnid), crickets, and other species.

San Sebastián

Northwest of Lares in the fertile lowlands is the provincial town of **San Sebastián** ⑫, linked by history to Lares through the 1868 attempted revolution. A cornucopia of food products come from the region, for this is the heart of many of the island's oldest and most traditional food industries. The weekly Friday

---

THE GRITO DE LARES

The "Grito de Lares" (Shout of Lares) was not merely a Puerto Rican historical event; its roots lay in the serious political grievances that were to sweep Spain's Caribbean colonies in the mid-19th century and result, some decades later, in their ultimate loss. When, in 1867, native Puerto Rican guards demonstrated in protest at discrepancies between their own salaries and those of Spanish guards, many liberals were expelled from the island, including Ramón Emeterio Betances, a distinguished physician and certainly the most prominent voice in Puerto Rican politics at the time. He went to New York, Santo Domingo, and Saint Thomas, where he rallied support for abolition and self-determination.

On September 23, 1868, hundreds of Emeterio Betances' followers seized Lares and began to march on nearby San Sebastián. There they were met by Spanish forces, and easily routed. Though Emeterio Betances was merely exiled to France, and the revolution came to nought, the "Grito de Lares" led Puerto Ricans to think differently of their land and their aspirations for it, and the spirit of that September day lives on – not only in the streets of Lares but also in the hearts and on the tongues of Puerto Ricans throughout the island. There is a monument to the revolutionary leader in the Plaza de la Revolución and every year there are festivities on September 23 organized by Independistas to mark the event.

bazaar at Plaza Agropecuaria is a big attraction in town, as is the Hammock Festival in July.

San Sebastián is surrounded by green and moist rolling grassland, and stood as one of Puerto Rico's sugar-boom towns in the cane industry's heyday. Now the area is given over to scattered dairy farming and various agricultural pursuits that used to be associated with other parts of the island.

Tobacco grows in many of the valleys, and coffee plants, once the preserve of Yauco and other towns in the island's arid southwest, can be seen growing on local hillsides.

Guajataca Forest

Northeast of San Sebastián, 7 miles (11 km) south of the coast at Quebradillas, is **Lago Guajataca** ⑬, a reservoir built in 1929 by US Army engineers. It offers a splendid natural retreat, with a recreational area for visitors and a wildlife reserve maintained by the Department of Natural Resources (DRNA). Fishing is popular, as the lake is stocked with freshwater fish, such as bass, tilapia and catfish, and small electric boats or kayaks are available for rental most days. The Río Guajataca, which runs from the mountains above Lares to the sea at Quebradillas, is as beautiful as it is forbidding, and pocked with a cave system which, although not completely charted, appears to be quite as extensive and awesome as that of the caves at Camuy.

The **Guajataca Forest Reserve** ⑭ (Information Center at Route 446, Km 9; tel: 787-999-2200; free) covers 2,350 acres northwest of the lake in the Montañas Aymamon. There are 25 miles (40km) of trails in total, but most visitors limit themselves to the circular Interpretive Trail and the Cueva del Viento Trail (Trail 1), which leads off it, starting from the Information Center. Staff at the center have trail maps (in Spanish) explaining what plant life you will see at 14 marked stations on the Interpretive Trail. There are also lots of birds and butterflies along the way. A spur off the Interpretive Trail leads steeply uphill to an observation tower, which

Whitewashed holiday homes dot the northern coast.

Exploring Cueva Clara.

TIP

If you happen to be in Quebradillas in the week of October 24, don't miss the town's Fiestas del Pueblo, which include a marathon and live music.

you can climb for a great view of the treetops and good birdwatching. When you reach the cave at the end of Trail 1, there are steep steps down to its mouth. Bring a good flashlight if you want to explore further than the entrance as the cave is not lit. There are lots of stalactites and stalagmites, bats which take flight when disturbed, and tree roots to trip over if you're not careful.

West of Arecibo

The town of **Hatillo**, on the north coast west of Arecibo, produces a third of the milk consumed on the island. Its biggest attraction, however, is in late December when **Día de las Máscaras**, one of the most popular mask festivals in Puerto Rico is held. Hundreds of people from around the island gather at the town's main square to enjoy the colorful festivities, which see locals dressing up with masks to enact King Herod's soldiers running after newborn boys, with murder on their minds. The festival was introduced by immigrants from the Canary Islands when they settled the area in 1823.

Quebradillas

Perhaps the single most stunning view in all of Puerto Rico is the approach to **Quebradillas** ⓖ continuing west from Hatillo on Route 2. As you drive up a hill that curves to the left you will see deep-blue sea and then a breathtaking coastline of cliffs and rolling sea. Make the approach slowly. Quebradillas itself adds to the appealing oddities you expect from the towns west of Arecibo – spiritualist herb shops, narrow streets, and houses sloping towards the water line – with some geological oddities that make it a town well worth going out of your way for.

A short drive or walk northwest of town, **Playa Guajataca**, described paradoxically by the local people as a "nice, dangerous beach," is to be taken with extreme care. Deep waters, white sands, and raging surf make it a highly attractive proposition for surfers and bathers, but highly dangerous for the average swimmer, virtually anyone incapable of swimming the English Channel. Even expert swimmers and surfers should exercise serious caution.

Karstic country.

Arecibo Observatory

Hidden among the mountains, where the stars shine undimmed by city lights, sits the most sensitive radio telescope on Earth.

The Arecibo Ionospheric Observatory is so huge that you can spot it from a jumbo jet at 33,000ft (10,000 meters). Yet on the ground, first-time visitors will need a detailed road map to find its guarded entrance. Located at the end of winding Route 625, in the heart of Puerto Rico's karst country, the observatory has been the focus of numerous astronomical breakthroughs over the years, ranging from Aleksander Wolszczan's 1992 discovery of planets outside our own solar system to NASA's $100 million Search for Extraterrestrial Intelligence.

US patronage

In 1993, the Arecibo Observatory dish gained world prominence when two American astronomers, Russell A. Hulse and Joseph H. Taylor Jr, won the Nobel Prize for Physics for work done using the powerful facility.

The observatory owes its existence largely to Puerto Rico's political status as a United States Commonwealth and to the island's geographic position 17° north of the equator. That makes it ideal for the observation of planets, quasars, pulsars, and other cosmic phenomena. The telescope is so sensitive that it can listen to emissions from places 13 billion light years away.

The Arecibo Observatory is funded by an annual $7.5 million grant from the National Science Foundation, though its day-to-day affairs are managed by Cornell University in Ithaca, New York.

The observatory counts some 140 full-time employees among its staff, and has hosted more than 200 visiting scientists from countries as diverse as Argentina, Bulgaria, Brazil, and Russia. Note that no military experiments of any kind are conducted here, and, despite the presence of security guards, there's absolutely nothing secretive about this place.

World's largest observatory dish

The dish itself, suspended over a huge natural sinkhole, is by far the largest of its kind in the world. Spanning 1,000ft (300 meters) in diameter, it covers 20 acres (8 hectares) and is composed of nearly 40,000 perforated aluminum mesh panels, each measuring 3ft by 6ft (1 meter by 2 meters). A 900-ton platform is suspended 425ft (130 meters) over the dish by 12 cables strung from three reinforced concrete towers. Underneath the dish lies a jungle of ferns, orchids, and begonias.

In 1997, Cornell University inaugurated the Angel Ramos Foundation Visitor Center (tel: 787-878-2612; www.naic.edu; June–July, Dec 15–Jan 15 9am–4pm, rest of the year Wed–Sun 9am–4pm), including a 120-seat auditorium, a 4,000-sq-ft (370-sq-meter) scientific museum, a gift shop, and a trail leading to a viewing platform from which the telescope can be seen at close range. Some 100,000 visitors are received here each year, of whom about 30 percent are school children.

The observatory has featured in several movies, including *Contact*, in which Jodie Foster plays an astronomer searching for extraterrestrial life, and the James Bond film *Goldeneye*. It was also used as a setting for the sci-fi television show *The X Files*.

The dish at the Arecibo Observatory is hidden in a natural sinkhole and is off-limits to visitors.

San Germán.

Guarding Playa Boquerón.

THE WEST

The west coast, known as "Porta del Sol" (Gate of the Sun) is brimming with great beaches, surfing, snorkelling, and diving and is the place *sanjuaneros* come for a weekend break.

San Juan

ll along the west coast there are spectacular beaches and surfing spots, from Aguadilla in the north to Boquerón in the south, with Rincón at the point furthest west. The towns range from gracefully colonial to beach blanket bingo, but all have glorious sunset watching. When *sanjuaneros* need a break from the busy metropolitan area, they plan a weekend on the west coast.

Just two hours from the capital by car, Porta del Sol offers a variety of adventure options, but also a serenity that islanders flock to year-round. It is also "the destination" for some of the finest seafood in Puerto Rico.

The town of Isabela

Isabela ❶, along the north coast, is an amalgam of all the charms of this corner of Puerto Rico, with a cluster of brilliant whitewashed houses tumbling down the hills to some of the island's most renowned surfing and swimming beaches.

The Taíno chief Mabodamaca ruled the region of the "Guajataca" (the Taíno name for the northeastern region of Puerto Rico) where Isabela was originally founded in the 18th century. The first Spanish settlement arrived by the end of the 17th century or beginning of the 18th century in what today includes Isabela, Camuy, and Quebradillas.

There are many small farms in the area, providing much of the produce available at local markets. Isabela is also known for *queso de hoja* (leaf cheese), a delicious small-production white cheese wrapped in banana leaves, which can be bought at local *panaderías* (bakeries) or at roadside stands. As well as dairy cattle, there are several ranches breeding the exquisite Paso Fino horses found on the island, particularly to the southwest, around Arenales (see page 55).

Main Attractions

Isabela
Aguadilla
Aguada
Rincón
Mayagüez
Cabo Rojo
Boquerón
San Germán

Plaza Colón in Mayagüez.

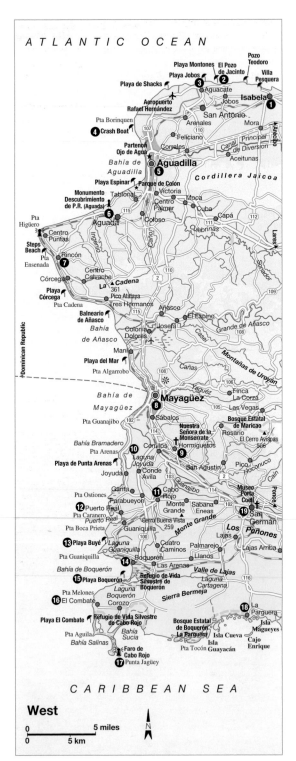

ATLANTIC OCEAN

West

0 _____ 5 miles
0 _____ 5 km

CARIBBEAN SEA

Beaches of the northwest

A string of beaches stretches west from Isabela, accessed from Route 466 and 4466. Although they all have names, not all of them are marked, so it is sometimes difficult to find the one you want and then tricky to find somewhere to park. **Villa Pesquera** has a group of *kioskos* by a small beach, which are good for local food and drinks. It can get busy at weekends with a consequent accumulation of trash, but the beach is clean. Following Route 466, look for the sign for **Pozo Teodoro** which you get to across the dunes. An attractive pool, sheltered by rocks from the waves, Pozo Teodoro is only a couple of feet deep, so it gets very warm and is ideal for small children.

Beautiful cliffs frame many of the beaches. One of these is home to **El Pozo de Jacinto ❷**, a spurting blowhole where waves meet cliff. The story goes that Jacinto was a farmer who had a favorite cow. He tied himself to the cow with a rope while he was pasturing his herd around the cliffs so he wouldn't lose her. Said bovine got too close to the edge and tumbled into the sea, taking poor, hapless Jacinto with him. Today, locals stand at the edge of the cliff and shout "*Jacinto! Dame la vaca!*" (Give me the cow!) as the spray comes up. It is said to bring good luck.

At **Playa Montones** there is good snorkeling and a blue hole to explore if the sea is not too rough. Always monitor surf conditions in this area and only swim in protected places or on calm days. **Playa Jobos ❸**, is the place everybody heads for and is known worldwide for great surfing. However, there is a rip tide and lethal undertow near the rocks and this beach has the unfortunate record of the greatest number of drownings in Puerto Rico. There are no warning signs and bathers are taken unawares, even when only thigh deep. Surfers find they are rescuing swimmers almost daily in high tourist seasons. It is, however, a great place to hang out and surf, or watch the surfers. Hire an umbrella from the beach bar and stay there, close to shore.

Further west, **Playa de Shacks** is an all-purpose destination: diving, snorkeling, and swimming among underwater caves and exploring a blue hole are favorite activities, while windsurfers and kiteboarders from around the world skim across the waves with their colorful sails. You will also see horses being ridden along the beautiful sand. Just a short walk from the beach is Tropical Trail Rides (tel: 787-872-9256; www. tropicaltrailrides.com) offering horse-back excursions along the beach and through an almond grove, with stops for caves and swimming or just photo opportunities.

There are a dozen pretty little beaches tucked among the coves of the northwest. **Crash Boat Beach ❹** (Route 2 to Route 107 to Route 458) is one of the best known and best serviced; it is frequented by ebullient locals at the weekends, when you can go for a look at how Puerto Ricans celebrate the natural gifts of their island.

Aguadilla and Aguada

The two lovely seaside towns of **Aguadilla ❺** and **Aguada ❻** have a running rivalry over the exact spot of Columbus's first landing on Puerto Rico in 1493. **Parque de Colón**, a mile (1.6km) northeast of Aguada on Route 441, dead center of **Playa Espinar**, a 2,500ft (760-meter) stretch of golden beach, is Aguada's monument to its Columbus claim. Aguadilla's believed site is at **Parque El Parterre**, where a freshwater spring gives historical backing to the belief that Columbus and his sailors stopped here for refreshment on their second voyage of discovery to the West Indies.

Aguadilla, the home of the former **Ramey Airforce Base**, is the more prosperous of the towns. The base is no longer in service, but **Rafael Hernández Airport** is operated from there and has the longest runway, at 11,000ft (3,350 meters), in

FACT

Whale-watchers are becoming increasingly attracted to the Rincón shores; a bit farther out is a wintering place for humpback whales. (See page 191.)

Crash Boat Beach in Aguadilla.

FACT

A big attraction in Rincón has nothing to do with the surf: the Horned Dorset Primavera Hotel here is considered one of the best hotels in the whole of the Caribbean (tel: 787-823-4030; www.horneddorset.com).

the Caribbean. The airport is mainly used by JetBlue and Spirit Airlines for flights to the US eastern seaboard. In 2011 it was used to test the new Boeing 787 Dreamliner, taking off here at sea level and flying to the highest commercial airport in the world, in Bolivia.

Rincón

Rincón ❼, southwest of Aguadilla, has become an escape destination for locals and visitors. A peninsula that becomes the westernmost point of the island and is separated from the rest by green mountains, Rincón's relative isolation makes it seem like an island unto itself. Its community, made up of farmers and fishermen who have lived there for generations, and gringos there for the surf and the ecology, creates a friendly environment more like the tiny islands of the Eastern Caribbean than bustling Puerto Rico. *Rincón* means corner in Spanish and is an apt moniker for the town, but it actually got its name from a Spanish aristocrat called Rincón who

deeded this hillside village to the laborers who worked for him.

Visitors mostly come for the beaches. The Atlantic north side of the point is the Caribbean's stellar surf strip where you can find huge waves, particularly in the winter months. The south side is a dead-flat bathing beach, with the quietest sea from April to October. Even here, however, you should watch out for currents. If the sea is good for surfing, it will be dangerous for swimming. Look and see if anyone else is in the water and exercise caution. The Tres Palmas Marine Reserve has excellent snorkeling on a coral reef which runs parallel to the shore for about 0.75 mile (1km). At Steps Beach in the reserve (turn off Route 413 at Km 1.7), the coral and the colorful small fish that live off it are particularly fine and you can often see turtles. Winter tends to be high season, because of the waves and whales but any time of year is good for the romantic sunsets and photo opportunities at the **Punta Higüero Lighthouse**, set in the charming El

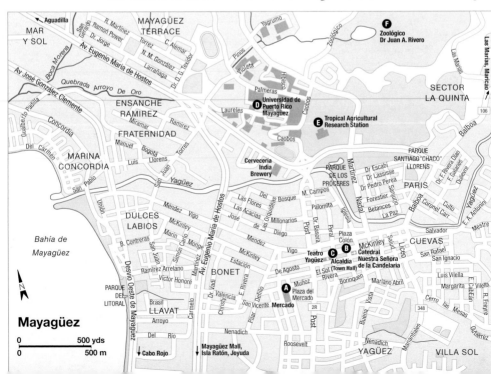

Mayagüez

0   500 yds

0   500 m

Faro Park overlooking the sea with Domes Beach to the right and Indicators Beach to the left. **Domes Beach** is good for surfing all year round but in winter the waves are enormous. It gets its name from the green dome of a nuclear facility which was never activated.

Favorite activities include horseback riding (Pintos 'R' Us, Route 413; Km 1; tel: 787-516-7090; www. pintosrus.com) on the beach, across fields and through forests; drives over the mountains to photograph panoramic views, and collecting sea glass on Sandy Beach. For the energetic, there is an excellent 4.5-mile (7km) mountain bike trail known as **Domes**, starting from the Lighthouse. Used for the 2010 Central American Games, it has some steep climbs and a couple of very fast downhills, with some technical challenges, lots of roots and some rocky parts. In June, dozens of lush mango trees that line the south end of Route 115 drop ripe fruit all over the road. Pull over and harvest some; they are delicious.

Mayagüez – looking forward

Mayagüez ❽, a one-time colonial gem, is the third-largest city in Puerto Rico, southeast of Rincón on Route 2. Once a flourishing port with tuna canning factories and industries benefiting from Section 936 tax breaks, it is past its heyday although it still benefits from the ferry service to the Dominican Republic.

But Mayagüez has survived devastating blows before. The earthquake of 1918 practically swallowed up the town; a fire took out the imposing Teatro Yagüez in 1919; and then Hurricane San Cipriano almost blew away the city and the surrounding farms in 1932.

Mayagüez is a modern city, but you can still find wooden homes with gingerbread trim dating back to the 19th century, which somehow survived the disasters, and colonial mansions among the mixed-up cityscape.

The **Plaza del Mercado ❹** (Market Square) is one of the most active and traditional around, despite modernization. Once an open-air covered market

EAT

While in Mayagüez, try the local gastronomic specialty: traditional *mofongo* (big meatball) stuffed with shrimps.

The Teatro Yagüez.

DRINK

Mayagüez is home to Compañía Cervecería de Puerto Rico, the largest Puerto Rican brewery, known for its flagship beer called Medalla Light.

filled with the sounds of chickens, it is now positively deluxe, with air conditioning and no more livestock. Although many of the exotic fruits and vegetables come from the Dominican Republic and Costa Rica, you can still buy *productos del país* (local products) such as bananas, plantains and the prized, small, round, yellow Mayagüez mangoes. Mayagüez is also famous for its *brazo gitanos*, a jelly-roll-style cake, and the family-made Sangría de Fido.

The beautiful **Plaza Colón** Ⓑ commemorates Christopher Columbus with a large statue and a fountain flanked by an avenue of trees often attractively lit by fairy lights at night. He is surrounded by a court of 16 aristocratic bronze ladies brought from Barcelona. He is also often surrounded by transvestites: Mayagüez is well known for its coterie of exclusive cross-dressers who have made Plaza Colón their weekend evening catwalk for the past 50 years.

At one end of the plaza, the restored Corinthian **Alcaldía** Ⓒ (Town Hall) is an experience in

Contemplation on the beach.

filigree. At the other, the long-suffering cathedral of **Nuestra Señora de la Candelaria** underwent a multimillion-dollar restoration, completed in 2003, which was paid for by generous parishioners who raised funds through extra collections; even the two towers that fell in the 1918 earthquake were finally replaced.

Around the corner from the plaza, the historic **Teatro Yagüez** (Calle McKinley; tel: 787-834-0523; Mon–Fri 8am–4.30pm) has also been totally restored; its colorful dome is a beloved Mayagüez landmark.

The **Universidad de Puerto Rico Mayagüez** Ⓓ campus on Route 108 is an engineering and agricultural powerhouse that draws students from neighboring islands and Latin American countries. The campus is hilly and green and has some notable buildings, as well as a noisy flock of emerald-green parrots. The adjoining **Tropical Agricultural Research Station** Ⓔ (tel: 787-831-3435; Mon–Fri 7am–4pm; free), run by the US Department of Agriculture, offers wonderful grounds for strolling and learning about the many tropical trees and plants brought here from around the world.

Across the street, **Parque de los Próceres** (Patriots Park) is a riverside park with walkways and fountains and gazebos popular with families and early-morning walkers. And on the northeastern outskirts of the city is the **Zoológico Dr Juan A Rivero** Ⓕ (tel: 787-834-8110; Wed–Sun and public holidays 8.30am–4pm), the island's premier collection of African animals, which roam freely in an environment as close to their natural habitat as possible.

Hormigueros

Just 5 miles (8km) south of Mayagüez, inland off Route 2, is the tiny *municipio* of **Hormigueros** ❾. This is a city with the slow pace of the northwest and the layout of a Cordillera town, with narrow winding streets and one of the finest cathedrals on the island. The **Basílica Santuario Nuestra Señora de la Montserrate (Our Lady of Montserrat)** is at once breathtaking and unassuming. Bone-white towers of varying dimensions rise to silver domes, topped with austere white crucifixes of wood. Its hilltop position gives the impression that it is soaring into the sky, and it makes a useful landmark for finding your way around. The redbrick stairs up to the cathedral are a workout, but the view from the top is worth it.

The word *hormiguero* means anthill or ant trail. It has been speculated that the name of the town could derive from the Taíno word *horomico*, for the Horomico River, which was once a source of gold. Archeological finds have established there were tribes already settled here around 820 BC. Spanish colonists moved into the area at the beginning of the 16th century.

Laguna Joyuda

Heading back toward the coast via Cerrillos you'll reach **Laguna** **Joyuda** ⑩, a mangrove swamp that is a sanctuary for native birds. Mangroves, in addition to being the nursery for all the delicious crustaceans and fish served in the local restaurants, are hotbeds for semi-tropical bird life, and this 300-acre (120-hectare) expanse is one of the most populated. Herons, martins, and pelicans, including the lovely maroon pelican, make their home here, and the lagoon itself is full of fish. On moonless nights, it is reputed to be phosphorescent, due to a concentration of the marine dinoflagellate organism *Pyrodinium bahamense*. **Joyuda**, a strip of seaside restaurants along Route 102, is one of the few places in Puerto Rico which specializes in seafood. The community gets very busy at weekends when locals come for a rustic, slap-up seafood lunch or sunset dinner overlooking tiny **Isla Ratón** (Mouse Island).

Cabo Rojo

Washed by coral-studded Caribbean waters, bathed in dry tropical heat year-round and sculpted into

The green hills of Cabo Rojo.

*White sand and
turquoise waters at El
Combate Beach.*

an odd network of cliffs, lagoons, promontories, and swamps by fickle surf and tides, the district of **Cabo Rojo**, to the south, shows Puerto Rico's landscape at its most alluring. Stretching along 18 miles (29km) of coast from Mayagüez, this region is among the most remote on the island; whether approaching from Ponce or Mayagüez, you notice the landscape becoming drier, the population more sparse, and the scenery more beautiful.

But for those to whom the name "Cabo Rojo" has become synonymous with isolated retreats and breathtaking vistas, the town of **Cabo Rojo ⓫** is worth exploring to see provincial life reminiscent of the 1950s. The town is honored to be the birthplace and last resting place of Dr Ramón Emeterio Betances (see page 172), whose ashes rest in a monument to him in the plaza. It was in front of the 18th-century Iglesia San Miguel Arcángel that the doctor gave liberty to children who were slaves when they were brought to be baptized. Children ride their

bikes and men play dominoes in the plaza outside the church, site of all the *fiestas patronales*. Other notable people whose roots were in Cabo Rojo are documented in the Museo de los Próceres (Route 312, Km 0.4; tel: 787-255 1560; Mon–Sat 8am– 4.30pm; free), which also includes a display on the local indigenous heritage, and a small theater.

Beaches and fishing villages

Back on the coast, you come to **Puerto Real ⓬**, perhaps the last authentic fishing village in the region, tucked into a sheltered cove. When it comes to picking a favorite beach along the Cabo Rojo coastline, there are plenty to choose from, but mention **Playa Buyé ⓭** to a Puerto Rican and you are sure to receive a nostalgic sigh for an answer. The houses in tiny Buyé, just southwest of Cabo Rojo town on Route 307, come down close to the water's edge, and there is something magical about its half-moon curved beach with its warm, calm water. The landscape

changes with shocking suddenness just south of Buyé, as the cliffs of **Punta Guaniquilla** give way to the swamps and mangroves of tiny **Laguna Guaniquilla**.

The cliffs and lagoon are best reached by making the 0.75-mile (1km) walk south out of Buyé or by taking the dirt road that leads out of the tiny settlement of **Boca Prieta**.

Just 7 miles (11km) south of the town of Cabo Rojo on Routes 4 and 101 lies **Boquerón** ⓮, a one-time fishing port turned recreational beach town. It is blessed with a mangrove forest which shelters some of Puerto Rico's loveliest birds – the Laguna Rincón and surrounding forests have been designated a bird sanctuary as one of three parts of the **Refugio de Vida Silvestre de Boquerón** (Boquerón Nature Reserve). But what really brings visitors to the town is the 3-mile (5km) -long curving bay whose placid coral-flecked waters and sands backed by a palm grove make **Playa Boquerón** ⓯ almost without question one of the finest beaches on the island. It is

a government-run *Balneario*, meaning that restrooms, showers, lifeguards, and other services are available and it is a Blue Flag beach, ensuring good water quality. However, Boquerón at the weekends is often a frenzied, crowded and noisy place, and it is impossible to get into the small town at night because of the wild revelries. To enjoy its wooden shacks, fried snacks, and tranquil waters in peace, go on a weekday.

At the end of Route 301, a circuitous 6 miles (10km) south of Boquerón, **El Combate** ⓰ is another remarkable stretch of beach along the Cabo Rojo coastline with lots of bars and restaurants which get busy at weekends. Nevertheless if you walk far enough along the narrow strip of sand you can find a private spot.

Salt mining center and bird reserve

The salt flats at the dirt-road end of Route 301 give a view into Puerto Rico's past which continues as you hike over the promontory to reach **El Faro de Cabo Rojo**, one of the island's

Fisherman and anglers also enjoy the calm waters of Playa Boquéron.

historic lighthouses, it overlooks another of the island's most beautiful crescent beaches.

Punta Jagüey , a kidney-shaped rock outcrop, supporting the lighthouse, is connected to the land by a narrow isthmus which is flanked by two lovely bays – **Bahía Salinas** and **Bahía Sucia**, also called **La Playuela**.

If you have never seen how sea salt is harvested, now is your chance. On the east of the isthmus that connects to the lighthouse you can see the grid for the evaporation system as well as piles of harvested salt. An **Interpretive Center** (tel: 787-851-2999; Thu–Sat 8.30am–4.30pm, Sun 9.30am–5.30pm; donation) gives information on salt mining and you can view the process from an observation tower. The salt flats are considered very important for migratory birds in the Caribbean. Around 40,000 birds visit this place every year. Here too is the Refugio de Vida Silvestre de Cabo Rojo, a reserve covering 1,800 acres (728 hectares): the peninsula and the surrounding waters are protected as well as land stretching

San Germán is an architectural gem.

back from the coast. Hiking and biking trails take you through several ecosystems, including dry forests, saltwater lagoons, mangroves, sea grass, and coral reefs. Birdwatching is excellent and there is even a butterfly trail, but take sunscreen and insect repellent, a hat, water, and wear long pants and trainers.

The **Faro de Cabo Rojo** is a breathtaking specimen of Spanish colonial architecture, with a low-lying, pale-sided main building and squat, hexagonal light tower. It perches atop dun-colored cliffs at the very extremity of the peninsula and commands views of almost 300 degrees of the Caribbean. The *faro* was built in 1881 over limestone cliffs that drop 200ft (61 meters) into the sea and is also known as "Faro de Los Morrillos." This old lighthouse was automated and electrically charged in 1967. The structure is at its most awe-inspiring when given a faint blush of color by either sunrise or sunset. A trail leads from the lighthouse to La Playuela, a curve of white sand enclosing perfect blue water. Its high salinity leaves

your skin feeling as though you've had a spa treatment.

The southwest corner

La Parguera  , on the southern coast, due east of Boquerón and south of San Germán on Route 116, leads a dual life as a quiet coastal town and – on summer nights and weekends – a party town alive with young *sanjuaneros* and thrill-seeking tourists. This is not to say the place is spoiled; it serves a useful function of diverting crowds from the area's more delicate attractions.

Offshore there is a string of some 30 mangrove islets, breeding grounds for fish and a haven for birds, while you might also see dolphin, turtles, and even manatee. A kayak tour is the best way of experiencing the area as you can paddle quietly in the channels between the islets. One of the cays, **Isla Magueyes**, is home to a colony of lizards. Sunset snorkeling trips are also popular.

La Parguera is also the starting point for a night-time 20-minute boat trip to one of Puerto Rico's biobays, where phosphorescence is produced by billions of micro-organisms belonging to the family of dinoflagellates known as *Pyrodinium bahamense*. Try to see this unique phenomenon on a cloudy night with a light breeze, when no other light sources muddle the brilliance of the waters, and wavelets make ever-changing patterns on the surface. Some companies allow you to get into the water and swim with the pixie dust, which is fun, but bear in mind that such activities have polluted the water and reduced the effect in recent years.

San Germán

San Germán  , Puerto Rico's second-oldest town, is a well-preserved and attractive Spanish colonial town known as "the city of the hills," about halfway between Ponce and Mayagüez on pretty Route 119.

Founded in 1510 by the second wave of Spanish colonists, San Germán was San Juan's only rival for prominence on the island until the 19th century. Forces invading or retreating from San Juan, notably the English, French,

One of the many santos displayed in the Porta Coeli Church, now a museum.

José Campeche's Virgen de la Leche, inside Porta Coeli Church.

THE ART OF JOSÉ CAMPECHE

It is no surprise that the work of José Campeche adorns San Germán's Porta Coeli, one of Puerto Rico's most architecturally important churches. Many of the island's churches – as well as the cathedral in Old San Juan – feature paintings by Campeche, Puerto Rico's first native painter and its first artistic genius. He was born José de Rivafrecha y Jordán in 1751; his father, Tomás Rivafrecha y Campeche, was a black freeman and his mother, María Jordán y Marques, was a Spaniard from the Canary Islands. Campeche, like his brothers, learned about art and painting through Tomás, who was a master gilder and carver, a painter, and an ornamentalist.

But José excelled at more than art: he was also a professional musician, sculptor, surveyor, and decorator, as well as an architect. Well educated and a devout Catholic, he was considered a gentleman. He was fortunate to live after Puerto Rico's towns and cities were established: before that, not much emphasis had been given to the arts.

Through his approximately 400 paintings of religious themes and historical events, and portraits of prominent politicians and local landed gentry, he gained a deserved reputation as "the most gifted of Latin American rococo artists." Campeche died in 1809 and is buried in San Juan Cathedral.

and Dutch, often stopped here to arm themselves or lick their wounds. In the 19th century it became one of Puerto Rico's great coffee towns, with magnates building some of the truly unique homes on the island. San Germán's historic district in the western part of town includes more than 100 significant buildings, most of them domestic properties, although you can visit the Museo de Arte y Casa de Estudio (tel: 787-892-8870; Wed–Sun 10am–noon, 1–3pm; free) on Calle Esperanza and a couple are now restaurants. Although you cannot enter private homes, a walking tour of the town reveals a wide variety of architectural styles from Spanish colonial to Victorian and Art Deco.

The **Museo de Arte Religioso Porta Coeli** (tel: 787-892-5845; Wed–Sun 8.30am–4.20pm; free) was founded in 1606 as part of a Dominican convent, but only this small, simple chapel now remains. *Porta coeli* means "heaven's gate" and, indeed, it could be interpreted as such, standing as it does at the top of a broad, spreading, brick stairway. Its large doors are of beautiful *ausubo*, a once-common Puerto Rican hardwood.

Inside, the pews and altar are all original, with embellishments. The altarpiece was painted by the first great Puerto Rican artist, José Campeche, in the late 18th century. Today the church is a small religious art museum containing some ancient *santos* (see page 70). Porta Coeli overlooks pretty **Plazuela de Santo Domingo**, with its two rows of benches and trees.

San Germán, like Ponce, is a two-plaza town, and its second, the **Plaza Francisco Mariano Quiñones**, is no less impressive, with the same lovely walks, period lamplights, and marvelous topiary. It is overlooked by the church of **San Germán de Auxerre**, first built in 1688 and repaired several times since then due to earthquake damage, lastly in 1920 when the tower was rebuilt. The interior is lavishly decorated with a trompe l'oeil painting on the ceiling to imitate wood. It dominates the town, and is particularly impressive when viewed from the surrounding hills on a bright and sunny day.

The nave in San Germán de Auxerre Church.

Making Waves and Watching Whales

In winter weather, the northwestern coast of Puerto Rico becomes heaven on earth for the Hang Ten set and whale-watchers.

The cold fronts blowing southeast from Canada may drop unwelcome snow and ice on New England, but those same weather systems push wind toward the Caribbean. That wind ruffles the Atlantic into waves – big waves – that hit the northwest corner of Puerto Rico and produce the Caribbean's best surf.

The first place on the island to become a surf mecca was the town of Rincón, a pointy peninsula at the western tip of the island which held its first World Amateur Surfing Competition in 1968. This tropical corner was rapidly colonized by serious surfers, who began opening campsites and bunk-bed accommodations especially for fellow big-wave seekers. Rincón has continued evolving into a guesthouse and resort town where surfers are still the main – but not the only – avid repeat guests. Several high-end resorts, including the Horned Dorset Primavera (see page 182), pamper the wealthy, while beach bungalows cater to the bargain hunters among us.

Tourists from the north are not the only ones escaping winter in Rincón. Humpback whales *(ballenas corcovadas)* are regular visitors from January through March, calving and frolicking in the warm waters. While there is at least one tour operator taking whale-watchers out on boats to get close to the magnificent mammals, most locals prefer not to disturb the animals; they limit themselves to lookout towers along Route 115, to afternoon observations with binoculars at the Punta Higüero Lighthouse or hope for random sightings along Sandy Beach.

Whale migration

Around the first half of November each year, thousands of humpback whales make their way from the North Pole to Atlantic waters north of the Dominican Republic to practice their mating rituals. At times they also cross into the Caribbean Sea through Canal de la Mona (La Mona Channel), the deep trench that separates the Dominican Republic from Puerto Rico.

North of Rincón, the towns of Aguadilla and Isabela are following the surf town's lead. They also have superior surf locations and now more enterprising surfers and hoteliers are opening up businesses to service the growing interest in water sports.

Among the best northwestern surf spots are Tres Palmas (the heaviest spot in the Caribbean), Domes (next to a closed nuclear facility and the lighthouse), and Sandy Beach (beginners) in Rincón; Hawaiian-style Table Rock in Aguada; Gas Chambers, Wilderness, and Pressure Point in Aguadilla; and world-famous Jobos (heavily territorial), left-breaking Golondrines and Salsipuedes (which means "get out if you can") and not-so-Secret Spot in Isabela. Lock your car and leave nothing attractive inside; these are often isolated places and break-ins do happen.

And all of the towns are playing up their year-round aquatic attributes: windsurfing and kiteboarding are world-class and attract adventurous Europeans who do not mind simple amenities. Reefs just offshore create tranquil pools for swimming, snorkeling, and diving, perfect for beginners – manatees are frequently spotted – while the more expert divers can scuba in the underwater karst caves.

Although there are ever more upscale hotels and restaurants popping up, Puerto Rico's northwest remains a more rugged destination, with rough winding roads and deserted beaches with few, if any, amenities.

Humpback whales are seasonal visitors.

PUERTO RICO'S FANTASTIC FLORA

One would expect luxuriant flora on a tropical island, but Puerto Rico's exceeds all expectations, and much of it is protected in the forest reserves.

Everything seems to grow in Puerto Rico – and in abundance. This lush, green island produces a vast array of flora which ranges from myriad varieties of orchid to a cornucopia of trees, many of them bearing fruit, including coconuts, limes, pineapples, and the exotic starfruit.

Puerto Rico's flora is as colorful as the many other aspects of the country. Visitors will at once notice the exotic splashes of bougainvillea that adorn homes, businesses, and even bridges. Gardenias and jasmine fill the air with their fragrance, while pink oleander and red hibiscus dot the countryside and towns.

The forests of Puerto Rico are home to more than 500 species of trees. Bamboo, mahogany, and *lignum vitae*, the hardest wood in the world, are cultivated for local use as well as international export.

The 200-acre (80-hectare) Botanical Garden in Río Piedras (see page 129) is a particularly good place to see much of the island's tropical plant life in one location. Along similar lines, the Tropical Agricultural Research Station in Mayagüez (see page 184) has one of the largest collections of tropical and semi-tropical plants in the world.

Although various hurricanes have taken their toll, Puerto Rico also provides ample locales to explore the island's flora in its natural state, including El Yunque National Forest (see page 142).

There are also well-kept hiking trails in the Guánica Forest Reserve, which is known for its bird life as well as for its endangered plant species. Puerto Rico's wild karst country (see page 143) can also be discovered via the trails running through that area's four national forests – Cambalache, Guajataca, Rio Abajo, and Vega Alta.

Bright-red blossoms of the flaming royal poinciana, known locally as the flamboyant tree, light up the Puerto Rican countryside in June and July.

The Caribbean National Forest (El Yunque) is home to 240 species of tropical trees, flowers, and wildlife, including more than 20 kinds of orchid.

Carambola or starfruit grow wild in Puerto Rico. The fruit is entirely edible, including the slightly waxy skin.

The University of Puerto Rico's Botanical Gardens at Río Piedras are considered to be one of the best in the Caribbean.

Cassia Polyphylla at the University of Puerto Rico's Botanical Garden at Río Piedras. This tree can be seen throughout the island.

Breadfruit is one of the highest-yielding food plants, with a single tree producing up to 200 or more fruits per season.

FRUITS OF A FERTILE LAND

It would probably come as no surprise to a Puerto Rican if a planted toothpick took root, so fertile is the soil on the island. Fruit-bearing trees are a prime example: oranges, lemons, mangoes, papaya, and guava grow wild on the island, although many fruits are also cultivated. Pineapple, *parcha* (passion fruit), and *quenapa* (Spanish lime) are also abundant on the island.

The country's most unusual fruit has to be the weird, head-sized breadfruit, from a flowering tree of the mulberry family, which islanders prepare in a number of ways but most commonly as *tostones* – fried green-breadfruit slices – that accompany many main courses. When cooked, the taste is described as potato-like or similar to fresh baked bread (hence the name).

More familiar to visitors is the banana, which grows in abundance here, alongside its close relative, the plantain, which cannot be eaten raw. You'll see plantains on menus everywhere, most commonly in the form of appetizer *tostones* or fried up in *mofongo*, a particular island favorite.

The rich and fertile fields of Puerto Rico produce a wide variety of vegetables. A favorite is the chayote, a pear-shaped vegetable called christophone throughout most of the English-speaking Caribbean. Its delicately flavored flesh is often compared to that of summer squash.

The island's beautiful flora isn't limited to reserves – in nearly every garden and around every corner are brilliant tropical blossoms.

The fishing port of Playa Guayanilla.

THE SOUTH

Ponce, Pearl of the South, lies on the southern coastal plain flanked by fishing villages, forest reserves, and mangroves. Igneri ball courts, sugar haciendas, and a US war zone are historical attractions.

When the Las Américas Expressway, or the Autopista Luis A. Ferré, between San Juan and Ponce, was completed in 1975, it cut travel time in half between the traditionally separated north and south of the island. The toll road, Expressway 52, which goes through mountains and valleys and is big on scenery, makes the 90-minute trip a treat. As you descend from the central mountain range, you discover more arid, sweeping vistas with the clear, blue Caribbean Sea opening out in front of you. The flat plains of the south were once covered with sugar cane as far as the eye could see, but now the fields lie empty, evidence of a collapsed industry.

The city of Ponce, is at the epicenter of the southern region, driving the economy and culture. There are waterside towns nestled at the foot of mountain ranges and valleys that offer visitors the chance to explore off the beaten path, although there are fewer beaches than in other parts of the island, and consequently fewer tourists. Nature reserves protect mangroves and dry forest both east and west of Ponce and the birds, animals and marine life that depend on them.

Ponce

During the 19th century, **Ponce ❶**, a natural harbor, flourished, fuelled by the arrival of skilled or moneyed immigrants. Some were French, fleeing the revolution in Haiti with their slaves, capital and plantation know-how. Others came from Latin America when those countries broke away from the Spanish Crown, many of them merchants looking for trading opportunities. Still more came from Europe, seeking their fortunes. In 1848 the hamlet was proclaimed a villa and in 1877 it became a city. By 1898 and the Spanish-American War, Ponce was the island's main financial

Main Attractions

Plaza las Delicias
Parque de Bombas
Centro Ceremonial Indígena de Tibes
Reserva Natural de Caja de Muertos
Yauco
Guánica
Jobos Bay National Estuarine Research Reserve
Coamo

Salinas is famed for its seafood restaurants.

center, based on the fortunes made by these immigrants in sugar cane, rum, coffee and trade, bringing in industrial machinery and exporting their produce. It was also the largest city on the island with a population of 22,000 and some spectacular residences built by the wealthy. Not surprisingly, its thriving port facilities, its telegraph cable communication with other islands and a good road to San Juan made it attractive to the Americans and the taking of Ponce was a turning point in the war.

Ponceños have always been a breed apart from other Puerto Ricans because of this 19th century self-sufficiency. Their insularity is legendary, and some Puerto Ricans claim that even the dialect here differs slightly from that spoken on the rest of the island. They are also racially different: you'll see more people of African descent here than anywhere else on the island except Loíza Aldea, because of slavery on the plantations, and a great deal of African and other regional customs live on in the city.

The honors for most fabulous city in Puerto Rico is a theme that *sanjuaneros* and *ponceños* have fierce and passionate arguments about. But even the *capitalinos* from the northern coast admit to what *ponceños* proudly claim as the sobriquet of their city. **Ponce** is indeed *La Perla del Sur* or "The Pearl of the South."

Ponce has the best weather on the island. It is located in a "rain shadow"; the afternoon storms which beleaguer the north coast are stopped dead by the peaks of the Cordillera Central. You can see the rain from Ponce – it's in those purple clouds pulsing above the hills 10 miles (16km) north – but you're not going to feel any of it.

The landscape surrounding the city is a typical southwestern palette of tumbling grasslands, much of it derelict sugar cane land, parched to gold by the Caribbean sun, against purple-and-lavender skies.

From the hills above the town, the view across Ponce shows the coral and white of the town's stately houses, the turquoise waters of its Caribbean harbor, and the stripes of green mangrove

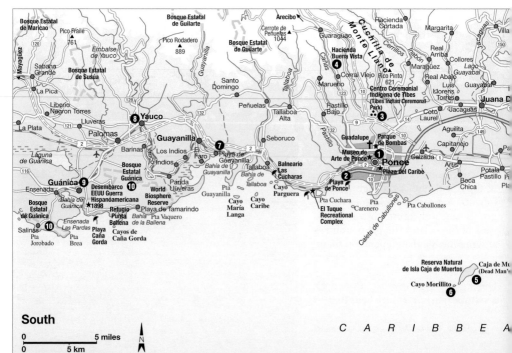

South

0   5 miles
0   5 km

C A R I B B E A

and travertine coral formations of the archipelago that surrounds the isle of Caja de Muertos.

Playa de Ponce

Ponce has an enviable natural harbor and a busy port away from the inland city center. Coming from San Juan, a left turn off the *autopista* will take you to the interesting outpost at **Playa de Ponce ❷** – a collection of old brick warehouses and more modern storage areas – and the wharf at **Muelle de Ponce. La Guancha Board Walk** is a popular gathering place, where there are plenty of *kioskos* selling fried food, craft stalls, an open-air stage and live music. You can buy a bag of sardines to feed the fish and pelicans by the Fisherman's Club, climb the observational tower for a good view or just chill with a sunset cocktail and watch people out for a stroll.

Alternatively, leave the *autopista* at the Ponce/Route 1 exit and head into the historical district, which has earned Ponce the epithet Museum City, where you can take advantage of the trolley system.

Here, you'll see the results of the "Ponce en Marcha" program, begun in 1986 by former Puerto Rican Governor Rafael Hernández Colón, himself a *ponceño*, and Rafael "Churumba" Cordero, Ponce mayor from 1989 until his death in 2004. The massive beautification effort resulted in the burying of unsightly phone and electric cables, the repaving of streets, and the renovation of nearly every structure in the downtown district.

Plaza las Delicias

The main commercial street is **Calle F.P. Duperán**, also known as Calle Comercio (Route 133), a major access road to Route 1 and Route 52, running east to west. At the end of Calle Duperán is the cluster of architectural beauties which gives Ponce its reputation as being one of the most Spanish of Puerto Rican cities. Here the magnificent **Plaza las Delicias ❹**, lush and beautifully landscaped, sits pounded by sunlight amid a pinwheel of old streets. Huge fig trees stand in lozenge-shaped topiary, and large, shady islands of grass are punctuated by dramatic

TIP

Island Venture (www.islandventurepr.com) offers private day trips to Caja de Muertos (by appointment only). For more information, tel: 787-842-8546.

Enjoying a piña colada.

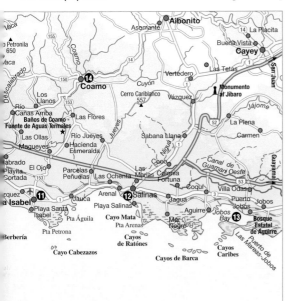

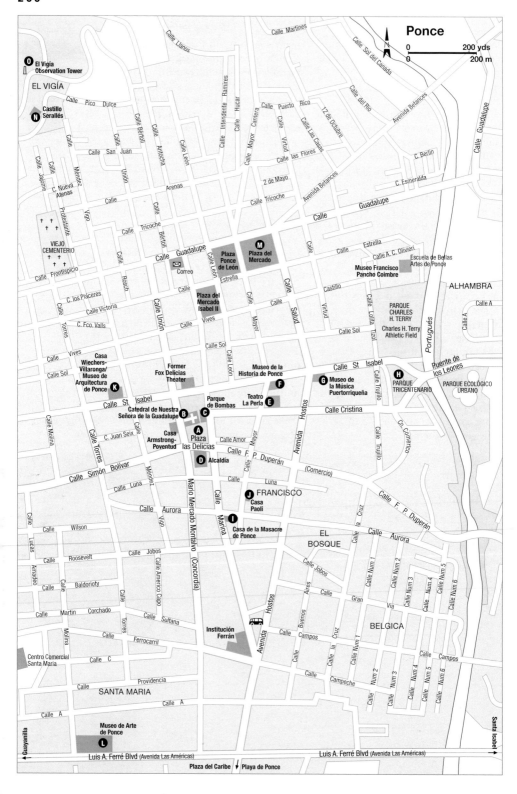

Ponce

0 — 200 yds
0 — 200 m

El Vigía Observation Tower

EL VIGÍA

Calle Llanos

Calle Martines

Calle Sol del Canada

Calle del Río

Calle Guadalupe

Castillo Serallés

Calle Pico Dulce

Calle Bértoli

Calle San Juan

Calle Antocha

Calle León

Calle Mayor

Calle Intendente Ramires

Calle Huear

Calle Puerto Rico

Calle Virtud

Calle Las Casas

1/2 de Octubre

Avenida Betances

C. Berlin

C. Esmeralda

Calle Jágone

C. Nueva Atenas

Calle Méndez

Calle Unión

Calle Vigo

Arenas

Calle Tricoche

Calle las Flores

2 de Mayo

Calle Tricoche

Avenida Betances

Calle

Guadalupe

Calle

VIEJO CEMENTERIO

Protestante

Calle Frontispicio

Calle Rosch

Calle Guadalupe

Calle León

Calle Bértoli

Correo

Plaza Ponce de León

M Plaza del Mercado

Calle Estrella

Calle A. C. Olivieri

Calle Estrella

Castillo

Museo Francisco Pancho Coimbre

Escuela de Bellas Artes de Ponde

ALHAMBRA

Calle A

C. los Pláceres

Calle Victoria

C. Fco. Valls

Calle Unión

Calle

Plaza del Mercado Isabel II

Calle

Vives

Calle Salud

Calle Virtud

Calle Lolita Tizal

PARQUE CHARLES H. TERRY

Charles H. Terry Athletic Field

Calle A

Calle Torres

Vives

Calle Sol

Casa Wiechers-Villaronga/ Museo de Arquitectura de Ponce K

Calle Sol

Calle León

Calle Mayor

Calle Sol

Calle Sol

Former Fox Delicias Theater

Museo de la Historia de Ponce F

Calle St Isabel

Calle Trujillo

H Parque TRICENTENARIO

Portugués

Puente de los Leones

PARQUE ECOLÓGICO URBANO

Calle Molina

Calle St Isabel

C. Juan Seix

Catedral de Nuestra Señora de la Guadalupe B

C

Parque de Bombas

Teatro La Perla E

G Museo de la Música Puertorriqueña

Avenida Hostos

Calle Cristina

Cn. Comercio

Calle Torres

Casa Armstrong-Poventud

A

Plaza las Delicias

Calle Amor

Calle Mayor

Calle F. P. Duperán

Calle Simón Bolívar

Méndez

D Alcaldía

(Comercio)

Calle F. P. Duperán

Calle Luna

Luna

Calle

Calle Aurora

Calle Vigo

Mario Mercado Montalvo (Concordia)

Calle Marina

J FRANCISCO

Casa Paoli

Calle la Cruz

Calle Aurora

EL BOSQUE

Calle Wilson

Calle Lucas

I

Casa de la Masacre de Ponce

Calle Num 1

Calle Num 2

Calle Num 5

Calle Roosevelt

Calle Jobos

Amadeo

Calle Jobos

Aires

Calle

Gran

Via

Calle Num 3

Calle Num 4

Calle Num 6

Calle Baldorioty

Calle

Calle Martin

Corchado

Calle Sultana

Calle Americo Capo

Torres

Hostos

Cruz

Calle la

Calle Num 1

BELGICA

Molina

Calle

Ferrocarril

Institución Ferrán

Avenida

Calle Campos

Buenos

Calle Campos

Centro Comercial Santa Maria

Calle C

Providencia

Campeche

Num 2

Num 3

Num 4

Num 5

Num 6

SANTA MARIA

Calle A

Calle A

Calle

Calle

Calle

Calle

Guayanilla

Museo de Arte de Ponce L

Santa Isabel

Luis A. Ferré Blvd (Avenida Las Américas)

Luis A. Ferré Blvd (Avenida Las Américas)

Plaza del Caribe ↓ Playa de Ponce

fountains. Broad paths of rose-colored granite weave through the squares, bordered by slender old lamp posts which make the plaza both attractive and accessible in the evening.

Plaza las Delicias is dominated by the pretty **Catedral de Nuestra Señora de la Guadalupe** Ⓑ (Our Lady of Guadalupe; daily with limited hours, so call first, tel: 787-842-0134) which splits the plaza in two. The northern, smaller part is called Plaza Luis Muñoz Rivera, with two fountains and a bronze statue to the poet-politician. The southern part is Plaza Federico Degetau, which includes the impressive Fuente de los Leones (Lions Fountain), where the water is enhanced by colored lights.

Though not as old as San Juan's, built in the late 17th century and remodeled several times since, Ponce's cathedral makes ample use of the reflected sunlight from the plaza. Its silvery twin towers – a characteristically Puerto Rican touch in religious architecture – are shaped like little hydrants, and glow oddly at midday. This gives the building a bright and inviting look, against which the eerie stillness of its lofty interior creates a startling contrast. Every February, at the Festival of Our Lady of Guadalupe, *ponceños* parade around the city in colorful and carnivalesque masks made of local gourds.

Our Lady of Guadalupe may hold the religious high ground, but the fancy-looking red-and-black-striped building behind it cuts more ice with the tourist crowd. This is the **Parque de Bombas** (tel: 787-284-4141; Wed–Mon 9.30am–6pm; free), Ponce's unmissable red and black Victorian Gothic-cum-Moorish fire station and perhaps the most photographed building in all of Puerto Rico. Across from the fire station, King Cream ice cream shop sells some of the island's best homemade ice cream. Delicious flavors to try are coconut, guanabana, passion fruit, tamarind, mango, and almond. The neoclassical **Alcaldía** Ⓓ, at the southern end of the plaza, was built in the 1840s as a prerequisite for Ponce becoming a *villa*. All Spanish colonial towns had to have a central

Ponce's week-long Carnival in February is the oldest in the country and where the vejigante masks were first created.

Plaza las Delicias at dusk.

square with a church and a city hall. An architectural landmark at the northern end of the plaza is the old **Fox Delicias Theater**, a movie theater from 1931 to 1980, then a shopping mall in the 1990s and then a hotel, now sadly closed.

There are plenty of peaceful perambulations to be made around Plaza las Delicias. **Calle Cristina** and **Calle Mayor** are particularly renowned for the wrought-iron grilles and balcony work which evoke in Ponce, as in San Juan, the spirit of European cities. Even the highly commercialized Calle Duperán has a number of quaint shops and a shady marketplace.

The Pearl Theater

About a block away from the cathedral, at the corner of *calles* Cristina and Mayor, is the stately **Teatro La Perla** Ⓔ (tel: 787-843-4080; Mon–Fri 8am–4.30pm; free), where plays are performed by local theater companies. On occasion, productions shown in San Juan go on the road to Ponce. Built in 1864 but partially destroyed in the 1918 earthquake, it is

also the home of Ponce's annual Luis Torres Nadal Theater Festival.

Around the corner on Calle Isabel, history comes to life at the **Museo de la Historia de Ponce** Ⓕ (tel: 787-844-7071; Tue–Sun 8am–4.30pm). A fascinating feature outside is a 1,500lb (680kg) marble bathtub, built by Samuel B. Morse, inventor of the telegraph. The museum was inaugurated on December 12, 1992 – Ponce's 300th anniversary – and is considered Puerto Rico's best civic museum, with some lovely, original stained glass.

Two hours here and you will emerge an expert on all aspects of Ponce's history: economic, political, racial, medical, educational, and industrial. This is also the starting point for a walking (or trolley) tour of the historical area.

Close by on the corner of *calles* Isabel and Salud is the **Museo de la Música Puertorriqueña** Ⓖ (tel: 787-290-6617; Tue–Sun 8.30am–4.20pm; free), which describes the history of the island's music, (evolved from African, European, and native traditions), runs videos of it in action, and exhibits some of the instruments. Also well worth a visit is the **Parque Tricentenario** Ⓗ and the Puente de los Leones (called the Lion Bridge because of its twin lions) at the eastern end of Calle Isabel. South of the Alcaldía at the corner of Calle Marina with Calle Aurora, is the **Casa de la Masacre de Ponce** Ⓘ (tel: 787-844-9722; Tue–Sun 8.30am–4.20pm; free). This museum commemorates a tragic moment in Ponce's more recent history. On 21 March 1937, a march was organized by the Puerto Rican Nationalist Party to celebrate the anniversary of the abolition of slavery and to protest against the imprisonment of their leader, Dr. Pedro Albizu Campos on charges of sedition. Things went badly wrong when police opened fire on unarmed demonstrators and bystanders, killing 19 and wounding over 200 others, many of whom were running away at the time and were shot in the back, including a seven-year old girl. The

La Perla del Sur Restaurant on Calle Cristina, Ponce.

event has been known ever since as the Ponce Massacre.

Famous homes

On Calle Mayor, **Casa Paoli** ❶ (tel: 787-840-4115; Tue–Thu, Sat 8am–noon; free) is the home of the renowned tenor Antonio Paoli (1871–1946), heralded as the "King of Tenors" in the early 20th century in competition with Enrico Caruso. It is now a research center belonging to the Centro de Investigaciones Folklóricas de Puerto Rico.

Approximately four blocks westward from the History Museum stands the pink confection of the **Casa Wiechers-Villaronga/Museo de Arquitectura de Ponce** ❶ (tel: 787-848-7016; Tue–Sun 8.30am–4.20pm; free). This beautiful colonial home was built by the architect Alfredo Wiechers for himself in 1912 and illustrates life at around that time, when Ponce was enjoying its heyday.

Museo de Arte de Ponce

The jewel in the city's crown is the **Museo de Arte de Ponce** ❶ (tel: 787-848-0505, 1-855-600-1510 [toll-free];

www.museoarteponce.org; Wed–Sat and Mon 10am–5pm, Sun noon–5pm), farther south on Avenida Las Américas 2325, across from the Catholic University. Mostly dedicated to Western art, with contemporary and classical works, the museum houses more than 4,500 pieces of art, including paintings, sculptures, and works on paper.

Designed by world-renowned architect Edward Durell Stone and established in 1959 with just 71 paintings, MAP was the brainchild of *ponceño* founder of the pro-statehood New Progressive Party and former governor Luis A. Ferré, who wanted to broaden the understanding of the arts in Puerto Rico and who, until he died in 2003 at the grand old age of 99, was still one of the island's most vigorous supporters of the arts.

The Italian Baroque School and 19th-century Pre-Raphaelite paintings are among its greatest strengths. However, Lord Frederick Leighton's *The Flaming June* (1894) is its most treasured work of art, which has become iconic on the island, inspiring local theater and dance performers.

Some beautiful architectural touches grace the homes of the inhabitants of Yauco.

A fire station like no other in the world.

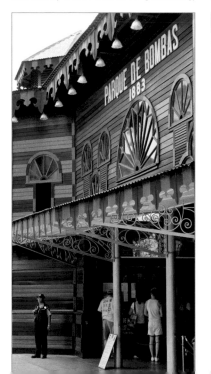

FANTASY FIRE STATION

What must be the oddest – and certainly most whimsical – fire station ever built, Ponce's Parque de Bombas was originally erected as an exhibit for the 1882 Trade Fair. It was one of two structures built in Arabic architectural style for the fair; the other, known as the Quiosco Arabe, was destroyed in 1914, although a glassed-in scale model of it can be viewed in the Industry Room at the Museo de la Historia de Ponce. The Parque de Bombas was put into use as a fire station the year after the fair, and it remained the headquarters of the Ponce Fire Corps for over a century, until 1989.

The following year the remarkable red-and-black wooden structure was restored and reopened as a museum featuring fire-department memorabilia. The old fire-fighting equipment on display includes antique fire trucks and hand-pulled tanks, which needed the movement of rushing to the scene of a fire to build up the pressure.

The exhibits in the upstairs museum also detail fire-fighting techniques of the late 19th century and provide interesting information on the Great Fire of 1906. With its playful collection of poles, sideboards, crenellations, and cornices, the Parque de Bombas is a gaudy and riotous building with a playful, truly *ponceño* spirit – and has come to symbolize Ponce itself.

Shopping experiences

Continuing south on the road to Playa de Ponce, shopaholics may wish to experience Ponce's **Plaza del Caribe**, a vast shopping center. The more traditional shopper may prefer the buzz of the finest market in town, in the **Plaza del Mercado Ⓜ**, which spreads across several blocks north of the Plaza las Delicias. Here, the merchants haggle with the customers over anything that can be worn, ogled or eaten, in an atmosphere as charged with excitement as any world market.

El Vigía

There's no better way to take in all the beauty and diversity of this city than to stroll north of Plaza las Delicias for several hundred yards to the hilly neighborhood of **El Vigía**.

From the winding road to the top you can see the mansions of Ponce's great families, the roofs of its townhouses and the turquoise glint of the Caribbean below.

The most important of these mansions is the magnificent **Castillo Serrallés Ⓝ** (tel: 787-259-1774; www.

Carnival dancers in Ponce.

castilloserralles.org; Thu–Sun 9.30am–5.30pm, last tour 5.15pm), located right next to the huge, 100ft (30-meter) -high cross-shaped **El Vigía Observation Tower Ⓞ**. You can buy a combination ticket to visit Castillo Serrallés, the tower and, just downhill, the Japanese Gardens.

Castillo Serrallés was formerly the home of Don Juan Serrallés, whose family became rich and powerful during the rum- and sugar-boom years of the early 20th century. The "castle" itself was designed by architect Don Pedro Adolfo de Castro y Besosa in the Spanish Revival style popular throughout the 1930s. The Serrallés family moved in around 1934 and stayed until 1979. In 1986, the City of Ponce bought it from the estate for $500,000 – an unbelievable bargain – and spent the next three years restoring it in painstaking detail.

Among the mansion's highlights are a formal dining room with the table set for 12; a vestibule decorated with furniture of the era; an 1865 rum-distilling unit in the central interior patio; and an octagonal fountain with

PONCE CARNIVAL

The Ponce Carnival is a true expression of the town's Caribbean culture, blending Catholic, African, and Taíno rites with sun, rum, and a sense of fun. As is traditional, it is held in the week before Ash Wednesday and attracts some 100,000 people out on to the streets. The *vejigantes* are the stars of the show, symbolizing demons in their mishmash of folklore. A traditional costume comprises an elaborate mask with a colorful conflagration of teeth and horns, making the wearer look huge and terrifying. A suit and flowing cape complete the outfit. *Vejigantes*' role is to chase away evil spirits and this involves arming themselves with *vejigas* (originally inflated cow bladders, but now substitutes are often used), and bombarding children and innocents to drive off lingering evil.

Carnival is a week-long party, a loud, noisy, boisterous family event accompanied by *bomba y plena* music, plenty of eating and drinking, parades, and competitions. On the Wednesday is the *Vejigantes* Party, Thursday is the King Momo Entrance Parade, Friday the Child Queen is crowned, Saturday the Carnival Queen is crowned, Sunday is the Main Parade, Monday sees the Carnival's Ball Dance, and on Tuesday the festival ends with the *Entierra de la Sardina*, the Burial of the Sardine. This mock funeral, with a dummy in a coffin, symbolizes the burning away of the sins of the flesh prior to the coming period of Lent.

tiles imported from Spain. Even the kitchen is preserved with its original stove and refrigerator made of metal and porcelain. An upstairs terrace offers a spectacular view of Ponce and the Caribbean.

Tibes Ceremonial Park

Just outside Ponce are two other interesting sites. The **Centro Ceremonial Indígena de Tibes** ❸ (Tibes Indian Ceremonial Park; Route 503, Km 2.2; tel: 787-840-2255; Tue–Sun 9am–4pm) is the first. It is a 10-minute drive north of the city and one of the most important archeological discoveries made in the Antilles, found by a farmer in 1975 after flooding. The discovery provides an insight as to how the indigenous tribes of the Igneri and later the Taíno lived and played before the arrival of Christopher Columbus in the New World. Radiocarbon dating and pottery styles point to occupation of the site from AD 400–1000, but further work is likely to reveal that people lived here even earlier.

An archeological treasure, it features rectangular and U-shaped ball courts and ceremonial plazas with petroglyphs. There is also the largest indigenous cemetery yet discovered, with 186 bodies, most from the Igneri period and all pre-Taíno. So far, archeologists have concentrated on uncovering the bateyes but it is expected that they will find plenty more between them, such as postholes, indicating remains of houses, shell middens and refuse sites. Artifacts from the site are displayed in a small museum here and at the Ponce Museum of Art. Reproduction *bohíos*, cottages, and the *cacique*'s larger *caney* show how the Igneri lived. Note that you can only visit the site with a guide (free of charge).

The second is **Hacienda Buena Vista** ❹ (Route 123, Km 16.8; tel: 787-722-5882; Sat–Sun, by reservation, tours at 8.30am, 10.30am, 1.30pm, 3.30pm, only the last in English; group tours can be arranged Wed and Thu), about 7 miles (11km) north of Ponce, off Route 10 up in the humid sub-tropical forest in the hills. This is an 80-acre (932-hectare) restored coffee-and-corn plantation from the mid19th century, complete with working original machinery, that details every step in the coffee-harvesting process. Reservations are required because you need a guided tour to explain the waterway system, to open the sluices and to operate the equipment. Water is diverted from the river through channels to drive water-wheels to power a coffee depulper and a corn grinder as well as other equipment. The hydraulic turbine has been declared an historic monument and is believed to be the only one of its kind in the world to have survived to this day. The diverted water is cleaned, aerated and returned to the river under an agreement reached with the government in the 19th century. You can also see the plantation house where the family lived and follow a riverside trail to a waterfall in the forest.

Southern isles

It's almost true that it never rains in Ponce, but at times the weather on

TIP

Free internet access is widely available thanks to the City of Ponce. This is the latest initiative to bring wireless public-access zones to citizens and visitors. These Wi-fi zones are: Plaza las Delicias at the heart of the city; La Guancha – Ponce's low-key seaside recreational, cultural, and food zone, and the Julio Enrique Monagas Recreational Park.

El Vigía Observation Tower.

Puerto Rico's sun-bombarded south coast can get so hot and steamy that you may wish that some of those hanging clouds would make it over the Cordillera Central.

Fortunately, however, the environs of Ponce offer strategies for cooling off as diverse as they are effective. Nautical enthusiasts head their boats into the breezy waters for a trip to the fascinating archipelago that is located 8 miles (13km) south. You can charter a boat at the Ponce Yacht and Fishing Club (see page 257) or take a ferry (Island Venture Water Tours; tel: 787-842-8546; www.islandventurepr.com) to the three islets that make up the **Reserva Natural de Isla Caja de Muertos**.

The largest of this string of Caribbean islets is **Caja de Muertos** ❺ (Dead Men's Coffin), 2 miles (3km) long and 1 mile (1.6km) wide, as popular with birdwatchers and botanists as it is with sailors and once was with pirates.

This being one of Puerto Rico's driest regions, the majority of Caja de Muertos' flora resembles that of the Guánica Dry Forest Reserve (see page 208). Some of the more prevalent plant species include certain herbs, some dwarf forests of white mangrove, and great quantities of bindweed.

Four of the plant species on Caja de Muertos are extinct on the Puerto Rican mainland and classified as endangered. This is also a haven for endangered reptiles: iguanas and lizards abound, and two species of Culebra lizard live here. Most spectacular is a type of whiptail lizard, Whetmore's ameiva (*Ameiva wetmorei*), or blue-tailed ameiva, which has a long, brilliantly blue tail. Leatherback and green turtles nest on the beaches and manatee have been seen here.

Cayo Morillito ❻, just a few hundred yards across flat sea, is the smallest cay, with only a few acres of territory, but is home to more endangered birds than the other two combined. Among these are boobies, pelicans, and sea eagles. **Cayo Berbería**, which is the closest of the cays to the mainland at 3 miles (5km), is mostly mangrove but blessed with a fauna no less extensive and no less idiosyncratic.

West of Ponce

Though the charms of the rippling, brown-green, semi-arid landscapes of Puerto Rico's southwest are well known to those who love the island, few travelers get this far. Its towns are small, but surrounded by natural preserves that Unesco has recognized as World Heritage sites.

Route 2 moves westward out of Ponce and hugs the shore for about 2 miles (3km). It meets the coast at popular **El Tuque Recreational Complex**, which houses a hotel and a speedway racetrack complex.

Continue westward and you will find **Balneario Las Cucharas**, a tiny bathing beach more notable for the excellent seafood restaurants that overlook the bay. Another 6 miles (9km) on is the **Guayanilla** exit. This pretty town was founded in 1833, but its history goes back to one of the Taínos' most important *caciques*, Agüeybaná. A mile away, at the mouth of the Río

Lottery tickets for sale.

Guayanilla, is the desolate and hushed fishing port at **Playa de Guayanilla** ❼ tucked away in a beautiful bay formed by Punta Gotay and Punta Verraco, with mangroves sheltering hundreds of species of wild birds and small creatures.

The town of Yauco

The attractive town of **Yauco** ❽ lies 3 miles (5km) west of Guayanilla on routes 2 and 127. By the late 19th century, Puerto Rico had developed the most advanced coffee industry in the world. In the coffee houses of late-colonial Europe – in Vienna, London, Paris, and Madrid – Puerto Rican coffee was considered the very best that one could drink. "Yauco" was that coffee's name.

Whatever can be said about its other effects, the 20th-century presence of Americans on the island removed Yauco from this position of pre-eminence, as emphasis shifted to manufacturing and cane production, while traditional markets were lost with the change from Spain to the US. Coffee is no longer grown here (Café Yauco sources its beans from *haciendas* at higher altitudes), although there is still some production and export. Fortunately, vestiges of that halcyon era remain – the stately homes of Yauco's coffee barons. Yauco shares with San Germán and Mayagüez an architecture that is distinctively Puerto Rican and among the best Spanish-influenced work of its day.

Some of these old residences are open to the public: **El Centro de Arte Alejandro Franceschi** (corner of Calle Betances and 25 de Julio; tel: 787-267-0350 at the Yauco Tourism Office; Tue–Sun 8am–3pm; free) is one such treasure. The house was commissioned in 1907 by one of the wealthiest men in town and because it was on a corner plot, the French architect Fernando Troublard designed it with an entrance on each street. Ionic columns adorn the facade and the interior was decorated with murals and paintings. The Casa Museo de la Música Amaury Veray Torregrosa (Calle Santiago Vivaldi Pacheco 15; tel: 787-856-4400; Mon–Fri 8am–4pm) is the birthplace of a locally renowned composer who died in 1995. Built

View towards the Caja de Muertos from Ponce.

by his father, a dentist, in 1919, the wooden house, now owned by the municipality, has been restored as a museum and performance space, also housing a *trova* music school.

Historic Guánica

Guánica , 5.5 miles (9km) past Yauco on Route 116, has historical significance which draws many travelers and historians. In the midsummer of 1898, at the height of the Spanish-American War, General Nelson Miles, having had no success in a month-long attempt to break the Spanish defenses around San Juan, landed in Guánica with some troops before traveling on to Ponce. He had come, he said, "to bring you protection, not only to yourselves but to your property, to promote your prosperity, and to bestow upon you the immunities and blessings of the liberal institutions of our government."

Out of this promise came American Puerto Rico, and the degree to which the promise has been kept or breached has defined almost all political arguments on the island for the past century.

There is a commemorative stone placed at the edge of Guánica harbor.

Guánica's reserves

Guánica is the ornithological capital of Puerto Rico. Covering 1,570 acres (635 hectares) of subtropical dry forest, the **Guánica Dry Forest Reserve** ❿ (tel: 787-821-5706; 8am or 9am–4pm or 5pm; information center closed noon–1pm; free) is the largest remaining tract of dry tropical coastal forest in the world and home to half of Puerto Rico's bird species. Most treasured among these is the highly endangered Puerto Rican whippoor-will (found here in the 1950s, some 80 years after it was thought to be extinct).

This low-lying area also has 48 endangered plant species, 16 of which are endemic to the forest. Well-kept hiking trails and a pleasant beach make the reserve a good respite in a hectic sightseeing schedule. Unesco has designated the area a World Biosphere Reserve, and it is also part of the US National Forest network. The **Punta Ballena Reserve** next to the

Yauco Town Hall.

Guánica Forest is included in the Biosphere Reserve because of its coastal ecosystem. It contains mangrove forest, manatees, nesting sites for hawksbill turtles, and crested toads.

The reserve also has several miles of cycling tracks designed in loops so you can choose how far you want to push yourself. The trails are mostly rocky, uphill and downhill, inland and beside the beach, out to Punta Ballena and back to the Ranger Station. Staff at the gate can give you maps and advice and will come looking for you if you are not back by closing time, 5pm. It is very hot here, so take lots of water and puncture repair kits and be prepared to be scratched by thorns and scrub. The views are lovely, though, and make the effort worthwhile.

Some of the best bathing, snorkeling, and diving can be found here. **Caña Gorda** balneario acts as a springboard for the popular **Cayos de Caña Gorda** – a string of mangrove cays dotting a large and shallow bay protected by an extensive reef – the best known of which is Gilligan's Island. Small launches leave from a tiny dock on the beach several times a day, costing $4–5, or you can rent a kayak and paddle your own way there. The bay area gets extremely crowded and noisy at weekends, so try to visit there during the week.

Toward Jobos Bay

Route 1 heads east along the coast from Ponce to **Santa Isabel** ⓫. The town center features the typical layout of a 19th-century square plaza, Plaza de los Fundadores, fronted by the church, Iglesia Santiago Apóstol. As with most Puerto Rican towns, it is well endowed with festivals: the Mango Festival in May, the Crab Carnival in June, its patron saint celebrations in July, and the Cemí Carnival in October. One of the folk-art specialties of Santa Isabelinos is producing a type of drum used to play *bomba* music.

South of the town at a *villa pesquera* (fishing village) neighborhood

eateries offer fresh seafood options like crab *empanadillas* (fritters) and other delights. Locals and visitors alike enjoy the waters at either Jauca Beach or Punta Águila, wading pools gentle enough for the children and lined with palm trees and mangroves.

Route 1 then hugs the coast as far as **Salinas** ⓬, a lip-smacking destination, famed across the island for its seafood restaurants, which can be found tucked behind a beautiful bay edged with mangroves. This small town, crisscrossed by narrow roads, is considered the birthplace of *mojo isleño*, the sautéed onion, pepper, and tomato sauce that all Puerto Ricans love to smear on their fish.

Salinas is also home to the **Albergue Olímpico Germán Rieckehoff** (Olympic Training Center; tel: 787-824-2200; www.albergueolimpico.com; daily 10am–5pm) where so many of Puerto Rico's world-class athletes come to train before international events. Automotive sports are also big in this area, and the **Puerto Rico International Speedway** on Route 3, Km 155.2, is one of the largest (tel:

Pastel-colored houses vie for space on this Yauco hillside.

787-824-0020; Mon, Wed, and Sat 1–11.30pm).

Southeast of Salinas is **Aguirre**, the site of a former sugar mill where many of the old buildings still stand. A nine-hole public golf course, built here in 1926, is claimed to be the oldest one on the island (tel: 787-853-4052; www.prga.org/-aguirre). Aguirre is framed by the **Jobos Bay National Estuarine Research Reserve**, a research site encompassing mangrove forests, a series of cays, and salt flats, where you can rent a kayak, birdwatch, and hike. **Jobos Bay** (Visitor Center on Route 705, Aguirre; calling ahead is recommended, tel: 787-853-4617; www.nerrs.noaa.gov; daily 7.30am–4pm), one of the finest protected shallow water areas on the island, is close by. Popular with ichthyologists (fish enthusiasts) and ornithologists, the reserve has several species of rare Puerto Rican birds, and fish are well served by the bay's healthy quantity of microorganisms.

Driving around the area, you will come across seafood kiosks such as La Casa del Pastelillo, a waterfront deck with hammocks and seafood-stuffed pastries of every description. If you see an inviting beach, ask around first before stopping for a dip, as some parts along here have dangerous currents.

Thermal springs of Coamo

Northeast of Ponce, Route 14 goes directly to **Coamo** ⑭. Its thermal springs – known to the Taíno Indians, who considered them sacred – were discovered by the Spanish in 1571 and the city itself founded in 1579, making it one of the oldest cities in Puerto Rico. Some say that the springs are the Fountain of Youth that Ponce de León was looking so hard for. In the early part of the 20th century, the springs (located at the end of Route 546) grew into a major Caribbean resort and attracted an international clientele. After World War II, however, the resort fell into decay.

Today, a resort stands on the ruins of the old one and once again visitors join locals in taking to the waters at the pool, staying at the atmospheric Parador Baños de Coamo. There is an adjacent golf course, Coamo Springs (tel: 787-825-1370; www.coamosprings.com).

Wooden boats in Guánica Bay.

A Museum City

The town of Ponce showcases some of the most eccentric architecture of the 19th and early 20th centuries.

While the center of Ponce is a modern, busy and technologically advanced city, it is also a living museum of unusual architecture that has been well preserved and, these days, celebrated on a national scale.

This town, established in the late 17th century, was first populated by Spanish farmers and ranchers, but the city is unrecognizable from those days. It was only in the 19th century that a booming plantation economy brought growth of the population and a boom in construction of architectural merit. Spanish policies of encouraging immigration to boost coffee and sugar cane production brought many adventurers from Spain, particularly Catalonia. There were also refugees fleeing revolution in Haiti and independence in Latin America, who had already made one fortune and brought their capital and slaves with them to make another.

As *ponceños* became wealthier, they began to visit the countries of Europe, bringing back architectural ideas and fancies that they applied to their own homes. The result is an almost whimsical blend of neoclassical, Spanish Revival, Creole, and even Moorish styles that change from house to house and block to block.

It is no wonder that the US National Endowment for the Humanities and Puerto Rican Foundations for the Humanities have singled out 45 sites, dating from the end of the 19th century and the beginning of the 20th, for their architectural beauty and historical importance.

Self-guided tour

Of course, you can just wander around on your own, but with a deposit of $20, you can borrow a guidebook (in English and Spanish) for two days to take you through the historical and architectural importance of the city. The book is available from the Museo de la Historia de Ponce, the first stop on the museum trail. Built in 1911 for the Salazar family in an eclectic neoclassical style, some lovely stained glass has been carefully preserved.

From there, you can walk or take the free trolleys that leave from Plaza las Delicias. The first stops on the plaza are the Parque de Bombas and the Cathedral of Our Lady of Guadalupe. Overlooking the cathedral is the imposing Casa Armstrong-Poventud, a two-story former family home built in the 1890s in an ornate Victorian style incorporating columns and statues into the facade. The interior is adorned with highly decorated ceilings, chandeliers and some very pretty stained glass as well as the family's original furnishings.

The neoclassical Museo de la Música Puertorriqueña, which has some magnificent stained-glass panels, is next. This was designed by an Italian architect for the wealthy Serrallés family who made their fortune from rum. You can see Catalan-styled furniture and curious bathroom fixtures at the Casa Weichers-Villaronga, a wedding cake of a house designed by a recently graduated architect for himself in 1911. This is now a museum of architecture.

The home of the late renowned tenor Antonio Paoli is now a cherished museum. Currently on exhibit are documents and memorabilia that belonged to this well-known singer.

Further away from the center, and modern rather than historical but no less important to Ponce or to the Caribbean, stands the impressive Museo de Arte de Ponce, an important center of European art.

Ponce policewoman guarding the Parque de Bombas.

Flower nursery in Aibonito.

CORDILLERA CENTRAL

This remote heart of the island features characterful villages, forest-covered mountains, and spectacular scenic views. The landscape is ideal for hiking, cycling, and canyoning, or gentler activities such as birdwatching.

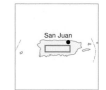

San Juan

The Cordillera Central or "central spine" towers over the middle of the island, its peaks and valleys stretching 60 miles (96km) from east to west. It is a region of superlatives and extremes – the highest, the deepest, the roughest, the coldest. And also the remotest: most visitors to the island choose to ignore its allure, staying on the beaches or in San Juan.

The Cordillera offers cool mountain lakes and streams, isolated green spots, and remote country inns. The temperature in the mountains drops one degree for every 500ft (150-meter) increase in elevation. This means that when San Juan is broiling, you just might need a sweater on Cerro de Punta. The contrast between Puerto Rico's urban industrial character and its countryside is both delightful and thought-provoking.

The best way to see the Cordillera is by car. Allow at least two full days, and find a good road map of the island. Getting around in the mountains is half the fun.

Roads are two lanes and paved, although some turn into dirt tracks halfway up deserted hillsides. Be prepared for some arduous driving on hairpin and switchback curves. The roads connecting most mountain towns run from plaza to plaza, making navigation easy. Here, you are never more than a few minutes away from the next *colmado* – a roadside store selling cold drinks, essential groceries, and perhaps a sandwich or two.

Jíbaro country

The Cordillera was the last retreat of the once-ubiquitous *jíbaro*, the hardy Puerto Rican mountain peasant, whose exploits had been the stuff of legend and literature from the chronicles of the early settlers to the stories of Emilio Belaval. The virtually extinct *jíbaros* are to Puerto Ricans what cowboys are to the Americans,

Main Attractions

Caguas
Cidra
Cayey
Cañón San Cristóbal
Bosque Estatal de Toro Negro
Bosque Estatal de Guilarte

The aptly named Aibonito.

or bushrangers to the Australians. The *jíbaro*, frequently the butt of jokes by more sophisticated city slickers, was nevertheless shaped by an exacting landscape and possessed of pride, resourcefulness, and a wry pessimism.

Along Route 52, just after the Cayey turn-off on the way to Ponce, stands the Monumento al Jíbaro Puertorriqueño – a huge white statue dedicated to these machete-swinging philosophers who today live on in songs, paintings, and the memories of their descendants.

Eastern Cordillera

Two roads connect San Juan with **Caguas** ❶, 20 miles (32km) to the south: Route 52, the fast modern tollway that runs all the way to Ponce, and the older and slower Route 1, with no toll collectors. Caguas, a large city but with a declining population, lies in the broad and fertile **Turabo Valley**. Three different mountain ranges make up the valley's walls, accounting for its unusual expanse. To the north and east rises the **Sierra de Luquillo**, which runs almost to the coast. To the south, the **Sierra de Cayey** climbs rapidly, blotting out the horizon. And to the west, the Cordillera Central stretches up and across the island.

Caguas is named after the Taíno *cacique* Caguax, who ruled the people of the Turabo Valley area at the time of the Spanish Conquest. Caguax was one of the two *caciques* who made peace during the Indian uprisings of 1511 and converted to Christianity. The Indians, fearing reprisal after drowning a Spanish boy, revolted. Several *caciques* led guerrilla bands on raids in the following weeks, but Ponce de León, with the help of peaceful *caciques*, soon restored order.

Plaza Palmer

Plaza Palmer, one of the most appealing plazas in Puerto Rico, is the center of Caguas civic and spiritual life. Almost as large as the one at Ponce, it is dominated by two ancient rubber trees with benches built into their huge trunks. Pigeons inhabit the plaza, some in an aviary and others flocking freely. In the middle, a solemn statue of the 19th-century poet José Gautier Benítez, Caguas's most famous son, stands on a pedestal. Goldfish sun themselves in a mossy pond, and, on weekends, musicians bring salsa rhythms to a small bandstand. There

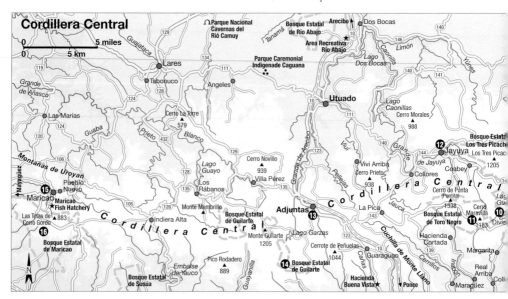

is also the Daliesque **Reloj Florido**, a giant clock face planted with flowers.

The imposing cathedral of the **Dulce Nombre de Jesús** (Sweet Name of Jesus) faces one side of the plaza. The church has been rebuilt and enlarged several times as hurricanes destroyed the original building. The first Puerto Rican (and only the second layperson in the Western Hemisphere) to be beatified, namely Charlie Rodríguez (1918–63), is buried here. The day he died, July 13, is his feast day.

On any afternoon the plaza attracts a good number of people: couples sit quietly holding hands; old men move from bench to bench, following the shade; and kids plan mayhem while their mothers shop. Every city or town in Puerto Rico has its plaza, but few as lively or picturesque as this.

On the other side of the plaza is the **Alcaldía**, which boasts an 1856 facade. The **Museo Histórico de Caguas** (Calle Luis Muñoz Rivera; tel: 787-744-8833 ext. 1847; Tue–Sat 9am–noon, 1–5pm; free) traces the history of the area from the times of Caguax and the Taíno, through the prosperous times of the 19th century and developments under US rule up to the present day. Just round the corner on Calle Betances 87, is the small tobacco museum, **Museo del Tabaco Herminio Torres Grillo** (tel: 787-744-2960; Tue–Sat 9am–noon, 1–5pm; free). Several craftsmen roll and sell cigars here. **Museo de Arte** (corner Calle Ruiz Belviz and Padial; tel. 787-744-8833 ext. 1838; Tue–Sat 9am–noon, 1–5pm; free) has two temporary exhibition galleries exhibiting paintings, sculptures and other artworks of local artists and a permanent showroom. It also offers workshops for local children.

A walk down Calle Ruiz Belviz reveals a tiny 19th-century **Baptist church**. Farther along, on a side street, the historic **Piedra de Polanco** can be found. This large rock was once used to mount and dismount from horses. Today it is part of a jewelry store. For lovers of traditional music, the **Casa del Trovador** (Calle Alejandro Tapia y Rivera 10; tel: 787-744-8833 ext. 1843; Tue–Sat 9am–noon, 1–5pm; free) is worth a visit, dedicated to several local musicians and the history of the music of the *jíbaro*. Many local literary figures are honored at the **Casa Rosada** (Calle Intendente Ramírez 12; tel: 787-286-7640; Tue–Sat 9am–noon, 1–5pm;

FACT

Economic activity in Caguas includes diamond-cutting, tobacco processing, and manufacturing. Caguas is also the island headquarters for US retail giant Wal-Mart and Sam's Club, which is Puerto Rico's largest private employer.

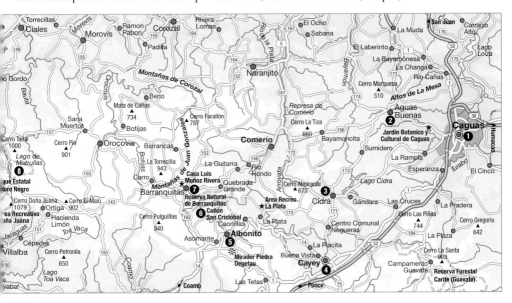

free), including Abelardo Días Alfaro (1916–99). The 19th century house is used for writers' get-togethers as well as a museum.

Botanical Gardens

The **Jardín Botánico y Cultural de Caguas** (tel: 787-653-8990; Thu–Sun 10am–4pm) lie in the Cañabón region. The 58-acre (23-hectare) gardens cover what was once Hacienda San José, a sugar plantation of the 19th and early 20th centuries, and grounds inhabited by pre-Columbian Taínos.

Among the attractions are the Taíno arboretum – with over 50 species of indigenous trees, an artistic recreation of a Taíno ceremonial *batey*, and authentic Taíno petroglyphs lining the river.

The African arboretum houses a 14ft (4-meter) bronze statue of Osaín, the Yoruba nature god, by Puerto Rican artist Samuel Lind, 40 species of trees, and plants from different regions of Africa.

The gardens also feature a butterfly house, a flowering tree arboretum, and a *manigua* (Taíno word for marsh),

used as an education and research center and home for various species of birds. One trail over a bridge leads to a typical 19th-century farmhouse with a working vegetable-and-herb garden.

The facilities include a greenhouse, a cafeteria, an artisans' shop, an amphitheater, and a lakeside recreational spot. Tours of the ruins and the gardens are available in English or Spanish.

The southern tip of **Lago Loíza** may be reached by taking Route 796 northeast out of town. The road skirts the lake's banks, with several likely picnic or fishing spots, before circling back to join Route 1 north of Caguas.

Caguas to Aguas Buenas

The 6 miles (10km) between Caguas and **Aguas Buenas ❷** to the west mark a profound change in the landscape. Route 156 begins to climb as soon as it leaves the city behind. Aguas Buenas is perched on a hill that is part of the far northeastern extension of the Cordillera Central.

Mountain palms and bamboo start to line the roadside. The lush green

Food kiosk in Caguas.

miniature valleys glimpsed through the breaks in these trees are a rugged preview of the contours of the Cordillera, and the hills and curves of Route 156 serve as a beginner's course in Cordillera driving.

Aguas Buenas is dashed across the hillside as if with one hurried stroke of a paintbrush. A modern church and a school struggle for space on the small plaza, which often fills with children.

The Department of Natural Resources used to run tours at weekends to the nearby **Aguas Buenas Caves**, but the caves have been closed for some time. It is, however, possible to enter them off Route 794, but only experienced spelunkers should attempt serious exploration. The road, at any rate, has some interesting views as it leads down out of the town and then up to rougher country.

Cidra and the Turabo Valley

Nine miles (14km) southwest of Aguas Buenas is **Cidra ❸**, which can also be reached from Caguas on Route 172. This road offers excellent panoramic views of the entire **Turabo Valley**, including Caguas. Known as the "city of eternal spring," Cidra is famous for the endangered blue-eyed pigeons (*palomas sabaneras*) which live here and which even have their own festival in November. Cidra is a larger town than it seems and has several manufacturing plants including factories making the top-secret flavoring concentrates for Coca Cola and PepsiCo.

Lago Cidra, 5 miles (8km) long, supplies water to San Juan, Cataño, and other cities. The lake, an artificial one, was dammed in the 1940s. While there is no boating, residents claim that the fishing is well worth a try. The houses around the lakeshore, with their serene views, give quiet testimony to the gracious lifestyle of their lucky inhabitants. A restaurant on the shore with outdoor tables shares the view.

Between Cidra and Las Cruces on Route 787, **Rancho Pepón** provides a pleasant family *pasadía* (picnic ground), a large covered patio,

SHOP

Look for the roadside fruit stands along Route 172 between Caguas and Cidra, where you can pick up some delicious local fruits and vegetables (some varieties of which are never seen in San Juan), or a bunch of fresh flowers for your hotel room.

Mountains in the mist.

a swimming pool, and a restaurant open on weekends.

Cayey

Whether you follow either the tollway or the lesser Route 1 south of Caguas, the next major town is **Cayey** ❹, 12 miles (19km) away. The first view of Cayey is of a modern strip-cum-shopping center at the highway exit. Founded in 1773, Cayey is a city of nearly 50,000 people, with a university campus and growing industry. The city sits on the northern slope of the Sierra de Cayey; from the *autopista* you can see the huge AT&T earth stations that carry most of Puerto Rico's long-distance telephone calls.

Southeastern Puerto Rico is a tobacco-growing region, and Consolidated Cigars has a large plant in Cayey. Here popular brands like Muriel and Dutch Masters are manufactured.

Cayey's **plaza** features a large church, built in 1813, with an extremely long nave, a single square tower, and a dome overlooking the transept. Anyone interested in

Going for a stroll in Cayey.

the works of Ramón Frade (1875–1954) should visit the **Museo de Arte Dr. Pío López Martínez** (tel: 787-738-2161, ext. 2209; Mon–Fri 8am–4.30pm, Sat–Sun and holidays 11am–5pm), at the university, where the works and papers of this prolific artist, photographer, architect and engineer are preserved and exhibited in rooms designed to look like Frade's house.

Ruta Panorámica

The Ruta Panorámica avoids Cayey, passing several miles to the south, but Cayey is a good place to pick up the Ruta Panorámica from San Juan, little more than 30 minutes' drive from Condado. Route 1 becomes the Panorámica about 2 miles (3km) past the town. Care should be taken, for the Panorámica shifts to Route 772 after another 3 miles (5km).

The Ruta Panorámica, as its name suggests, is rich with vistas. Remember, though: Cordillera driving is no picnic. Do not forget the essential map for winding road navigation, and pack some motion-sickness pills – you never know.

Aibonito to Barranquitas

Set in a narrow valley, **Aibonito** ❺, at 2,400ft (730 meters), has the highest altitude of any town in Puerto Rico, and the lowest average temperature. The Ruta Panorámica narrowly misses the town, which can be reached from Cayey via Route 14, a road rivalling the Panorámica for both valley viewing and for its great number of curves.

Aibonito is a traffic-choked town famous for its flower and nursery industry. The **Flower Festival**, which takes place in late June and early July, is one of the most popular events on the island. For a panoramic view, visit the **Mirador Piedra Degetau** observation tower on Route 7718. On a clear day you can even see San Juan. The restaurant alongside also has a good view.

Near Aibonito is the **Cañón San Cristóbal** ❻ (San Cristóbal Canyon), the deepest gorge on the island. Formed by the Río Usabón, this canyon, with walls up to 700ft (210 meters) high, is so deep and narrow that from the air it looks like a slit in the hills. From the ground, the only way to see it is to stand on the very rim or to get down inside it. The river has formed several spectacular waterfalls, the largest being El Juicio, about 250ft (80 meters) high, which crashes down over the rocks in times of plentiful rainfall.

To approach the canyon, follow Route 725 to the north. In this area, businesses tend to call themselves El Cañón, Tienda el Cañón, Ferrenta el Cañón, and so on. One of the most *simpático* of these establishments is the **Bar el Cañón**, at Km 4 on Route 725. Among its attributes are a jukebox and canned beer at country prices. The canyon can be reached from here, but it is a rough hike, so it's better to go on to Km 5.5, where a narrow unmarked side road comes a little closer to the edge. From there it is a short hike down to the canyon and a 100ft (30-meter) waterfall.

Four miles (6km) north as the crow flies, but double that by car, is the town of **Barranquitas** ❼ on the other side of San Cristóbal Canyon. The canyon is managed and preserved by by the Para La Naturaleza, part of the Conservation Trust of Puerto Rico (tel: 787-722-5882; www.paranaturaleza.org), who were instrumental in cleaning up the garbage and waste metal that had been dumped and burned there over many years. Their native tree nursery, part of their Árboles, más Árboles (Trees, More Trees) reforestation program, is outside Barranquitas.

Barranquitas is known as the birthplace of Luis Muñoz Rivera, the autonomy-minded statesman. His birthplace, an unprepossessing timber house with a veranda typical of the colonial style, is now a museum, Casa Natal de Luis Muñoz Rivera (Calle Muñoz Rivera 10, corner Calle Torres; tel: 787-857-0230; Tue–Sun 8.30am–4.20pm; free). Muñoz Rivera and his son Luis Muñoz Marín, governor of the island from 1948 to 1964, are both buried near the plaza in a small complex, **Mausoleo Luis Muñoz Rivera** (Calle El Parque; daily 8.30am–4.20pm) that includes a museum full of Muñoz Rivera memorabilia.

This "Birthplace of Patriots" has a beautiful church in the plaza with an impressive wooden ceiling and glowing stained glass all around. Another attraction in Barranquitas is the annual Artisans' Fair in July, when some 130 Puerto Rican artisans sell their work at reasonable prices – the perfect time to buy a painting, a flute, or jewelry made from local stones. Traditional music and food are also a major part of the fair, which began in 1964.

Hill country drives

There is a more direct route from San Juan to Aibonito and Barranquitas, a pleasant drive through hilly country.

Aibonito locals chatting away on the main square.

Barranquitas' superb Art Deco bandstand.

TIP

If you're interested in Puerto Rican political history, you may want to visit the small museum in the Barranquitas house where Luis Muñoz Rivera was born.

Take Route 2 from San Juan to Bayamón, and from there take Route 167 south until it intersects Route 156, which goes to Barranquitas. This route looks less taxing on the odometer; in reality, it involves nearly 30 miles (48km) of demanding two-lane roads. If you plan any mountain driving beyond Aibonito or Barranquitas, it is probably better to take the *autopista* to Caycy.

Route 167, though, is worth a trip in itself, especially on a Sunday afternoon. Immediately south of Bayamón, the road begins playing a game of peek-a-boo with the **Río de la Plata**, named after the mighty South American river, and its subsidiary streams. The streams jump back and forth across the road until at last, near **El Ocho**, a panorama of the broad river unfolds.

Route 167 passes through or near settlements with rustic names, such as Pájaro Puertorriqueño, Sabana, and Naranjito (Puerto Rican Bird, Savannah, and Little Orange). On Sunday afternoons in nearly every one of these little towns, musicians will be tuning up in bandstands and *colmados*. They will start to play as the sun's rays stretch out, singing to audiences of 20, 30, or 50. If there are no musicians around, a group of men in a bar will begin to sing and keep singing until long after sunset. Thus the country people – and the city visitors – squeeze every moment out of the weekend.

Toro Negro

The **Bosque Estatal de Toro Negro** ❽ (Toro Negro Forest Reserve) is at the intersection of Routes 149 and 143. Route 143 is an east–west road that follows the backbone of the Cordillera Central from Adjuntas to a point near Barranquitas. This 30-mile (48km) section of road is the longest continuous stretch of the Ruta Panorámica; views along this section pan north and south to both coastlines. If you are coming from the south, it is 14 tortuous mountain miles (22km) on Route 150 from Coamo to Villalba, from where Route 149 begins to climb in earnest.

To the east of the intersection of Routes 149 and 143 is the **Area Recreativa de Doña Juana** ❾, a *pasadía* viewpoint that features a large freshwater swimming pool and several trails through dense forests of large mountain palms. There is a campground, and a ranger station for the forest reserve at Km 32.4 on the north side of the road. Trail maps are available. A trail leads from the pool to a deserted lookout tower about 2 miles (3km) away; the first quarter of the trail is paved with uneven, mossy stones, and moss turns very slippery with the smallest amount of water, so make sure you take care on wet days. The **Doña Juana Falls**, a 200ft (60-meter) waterfall, is nearby.

Climbing the peaks

West of the intersection, the road climbs into the silent peaks. **Lago Guineo** ❿ (Banana Lake), the highest lake on the entire island, hides at the

The annual Aibonito Flower Festival is a popular summer event in this area.

end of a gravel road marked only by a wooden sign reading *Prohibido Tirar Basura (Do not drop litter)*.

A dam across the Toro Negro River keeps the lake full. It's difficult to find, walled about by steep red clay banks choked with bamboo. Only the high-pitched chatter of the *coquí* disturbs the perfect isolation of this little round lake. The clay banks demand caution; clay is another surface that gets very slippery when wet.

Farther west (and higher up), the road passes **Cerro Maravilla ⑪**, a lofty peak that bristles with antennae and relay towers. This mountain, at 3,970ft (1,183 meters) one of the island's highest, occupies a tragic place in 20th-century history: on July 25, 1978, two young independence supporters planning to blow up the WRIK-TV transmitter atop the mountain were killed by policemen who had been tipped off. The deaths triggered an investigation and political controversy.

Oddly, no sign directs visitors to the spot where it all happened, and the gravel road leading to Cerro Maravilla

– Route 577 – does not appear on the official highway map. If you make a left turn at 577 and ascend the hill for half a mile, however, you'll see two stone crosses marking the graves of the two revolutionaries murdered there – Arnaldo Darío Rosado and Carlos Soto Arriví.

The men's graves are surrounded by flowers and Puerto Rican flags. Don't be surprised to find several people at the site. Since the events of 1978, it has become a shrine for those who support the cause of Puerto Rican independence.

Cerro de Punta

Across the road from the peak, a grassy picnic area overlooks the entire south coast. A gravel parking lot on the north side of the road at Km 16.5 marks the base of **Cerro de Punta**, at 4,390ft (1,338 meters) the island's highest peak. The summit can be reached on foot or by car up a treacherously steep paved road considerably less than one lane wide.

On top, the solitude is shared by more antennae and a shed. On a clear

TIP

A good view of Villalba, Lago Toa Vaca and down to the Caribbean Sea can be had from the *colmado* (grocery store) La Collaloma on Route 149 by the intersection with Route 514.

The Cañón San Cristóbal attracts thrill-seekers.

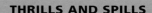

THRILLS AND SPILLS

There are countless opportunities for adventure tourism in the area around Barranquitas. The **Cañón San Cristóbal**, a deep gorge with the Río Usabón at the bottom, has waterfalls, boulders, rocks, and caverns, lending themselves naturally as a playground for those who like to push themselves to the limit. For guided tours of the area, call Go Hiking Puerto Rico (tel: 787-857-2094), who also offer ziplining in the canyon, swimming, rappelling, and rock climbing. Another company offering rappeling, canyoning, and scrambling along the river, over boulders, behind waterfalls, between rocks and caverns and generally getting soaked, exhilarated, and exhausted, is Montaña Explora (tel: 787-516-6194; www.elyunquedaytrips.com).

Another option is the **Toro Verde Nature Adventure Park** (787-867-7020; www.toroverdepr.com). Head west of Barranquitas on Route 157, then turn north on Route 155 just after Orocovis. This forested playground in the mountains has the latest methods of taking you beyond your comfort zone while offering something for everyone in the family, subject to height and weight restrictions. Ziplining is the core activity, with an added feature of a line where you lie horizontal in a harness and fly like a bird for nearly a mile high across the valley. There is also an 8-mile (13km) mountain bike trail, rappelling and hiking across swaying wooden suspension bridges.

Even the smallest buildings in the Cordillera – like this barber shop – are splashed with color.

day you can see for 50 or 60 miles (80 to 100km). The view includes San Juan, unless of course a stray cloud happens to get in the way. To be on Cerro de Punta when the mists roll in is a powerful experience.

A few miles directly north of the mountain, **Jayuya** nestles in its valley; unfortunately for the driver, no road connects the two points. Take Route 144 to the town from either the east or the west.

The hidden treasure of Jayuya, a Taíno stronghold, is *La Piedra Escrita* (The Written Rock). A large boulder that forms a natural pool in Río Saliente, it features petroglyphs from prehistoric inhabitants and is located off Route 144 at Km 2.3.

In Jayuya, a short stay in the stately **Hacienda Gripiñas**, a *parador* situated on an old coffee plantation, might be tempting. A wide porch on the restored 200-year-old house overlooks a cool valley, atmospheric at sunset when the *coquí* begin singing. A trail connects the *parador* with Cerro de Punta just a short distance away.

The Doña Juana Falls.

The Western Cordillera

West of Toro Negro, the mountains start to change character once again. The stately peaks give way to rougher, lusher country. The valleys are smaller, shallower, and more numerous. The tall mountain palms yield to bamboo, ferns, and hardwood trees like teak. Flowering bushes intermittently line the roadsides.

The town of **Adjuntas** marks this area of transition. It is a rugged town filled with no-nonsense hardware stores and lumberyards; local produce includes coffee, bananas, oranges, and other fruits. Attractions include the **Mariposario** (Butterfly Garden, Casa Pueblo; tel: 787-829-4842; donation), and there's now easier access via Route 10 from Ponce. Casa Pueblo is a local museum and cultural institution founded by a group of activists who fought against the copper mine exploitation of the area for decades. Casa Pueblo is responsible for many environmental projects, namely the preservation of forests and lakes.

Guilarte Forest Reserve

The **Bosque Estatal de Guilarte** ⓮ (Guilarte Forest Reserve) west of Adjuntas is another good place to get back to nature. A hillside *pasadía* is set near a eucalyptus grove whose fragrant, blade-shaped leaves litter the ground. A few hundred feet up the road, a well-marked trail leads to the top of 3,900ft (1,205-meter) **Monte Guilarte**. Watch out for any slippery clay on the trail.

Between Adjuntas and Monte Guilarte are many small farms, tended by the last of the *jíbaros* (mountain smallholders). This area is one of the few places on the island with such a concentrated population of these legendary people. The Ruta Panorámica passes right through their farmland, and they enjoy the opportunity to talk to travelers in a Spanish that is nasal, twangy, and high-pitched.

North of Adjuntas toward **Utuado**, the Cordillera begins its descent to the coastal plain. But that does not mean the land gets flat. The haystack karstic hills north of Utuado march all the way to the Atlantic.

Maricao

On the far western edge of the Cordillera, not far from Mayagüez, is **Maricao** ⓯, one of the smallest *municipios* in Puerto Rico. Route 120 approaches the town from the south through the **Bosque Estatal de Maricao** ⓰ (Maricao Forest Reserve), or you can take Route 105 out of downtown Mayagüez. By the roadside in the middle of the forest is a castle-like stone tower, four stories tall, which overlooks the entire western half of the island from 2,600ft (800 meters), giving you a breathtaking view from Ponce to Cabo Rojo to Mayagüez to Guajataca. There is also a campground, parking, picnic benches, toilets and trails, but no map – ask the ranger for directions.

Maricao's tiny plaza features a rustic cream-and-brick-colored church. Just outside the town is the **Maricao Fish Hatchery**, where many species of freshwater fish are hatched and raised, then relocated to 26 lakes around the island to replenish their indigenous stocks. On the road to the fish hatchery is a mountainside shrine, a haven of serenity and dignity.

TIP

A good time to visit Jayuya is in November during the Jayuya Indian Festival, which focuses on the Taínos' culture and traditions, including their music, food, and games.

Bust of Don Luis Muñoz Rivera in Washington Park, Newark, New Jersey.

A MAN WHO MADE A DIFFERENCE

Luis Muñoz Rivera, one of the most famous men in the political history of Puerto Rico, devoted his life to the struggle for his country's autonomy. Born in Barranquitas on July 17, 1859, he attended a local private school and later worked in his father's store. Muñoz Rivera was one of the founders of the Autonomist Party and its newspaper "voice," *La Democracia*. In 1897, he was appointed Secretary of State and Chief of the Cabinet of the newly independent Government of Puerto Rico. After the Americans arrived on the scene in 1898, he again turned to journalism, founding the newspaper *El Territorio* and later, while living in New York, the *Puerto Rican Herald*.

After returning to Puerto Rico in 1904, Muñoz Rivera became one of the founders of the Unionist Party and served in the House of Delegates until 1910, when he was elected Resident Commissioner to the US House of Representatives. Here, he pushed to amend the Foraker Act. His work led to the passing of the Jones Act, which, among other things, gave Puerto Rico more autonomy and granted United States citizenship to Puerto Ricans. He did not live to see the bill signed into law by President Wilson in 1917; Muñoz Rivera returned to Puerto Rico in September 1916, ill with cancer, and died on November 15 of that year.

Punta Mulas lighthouse, Vieques.

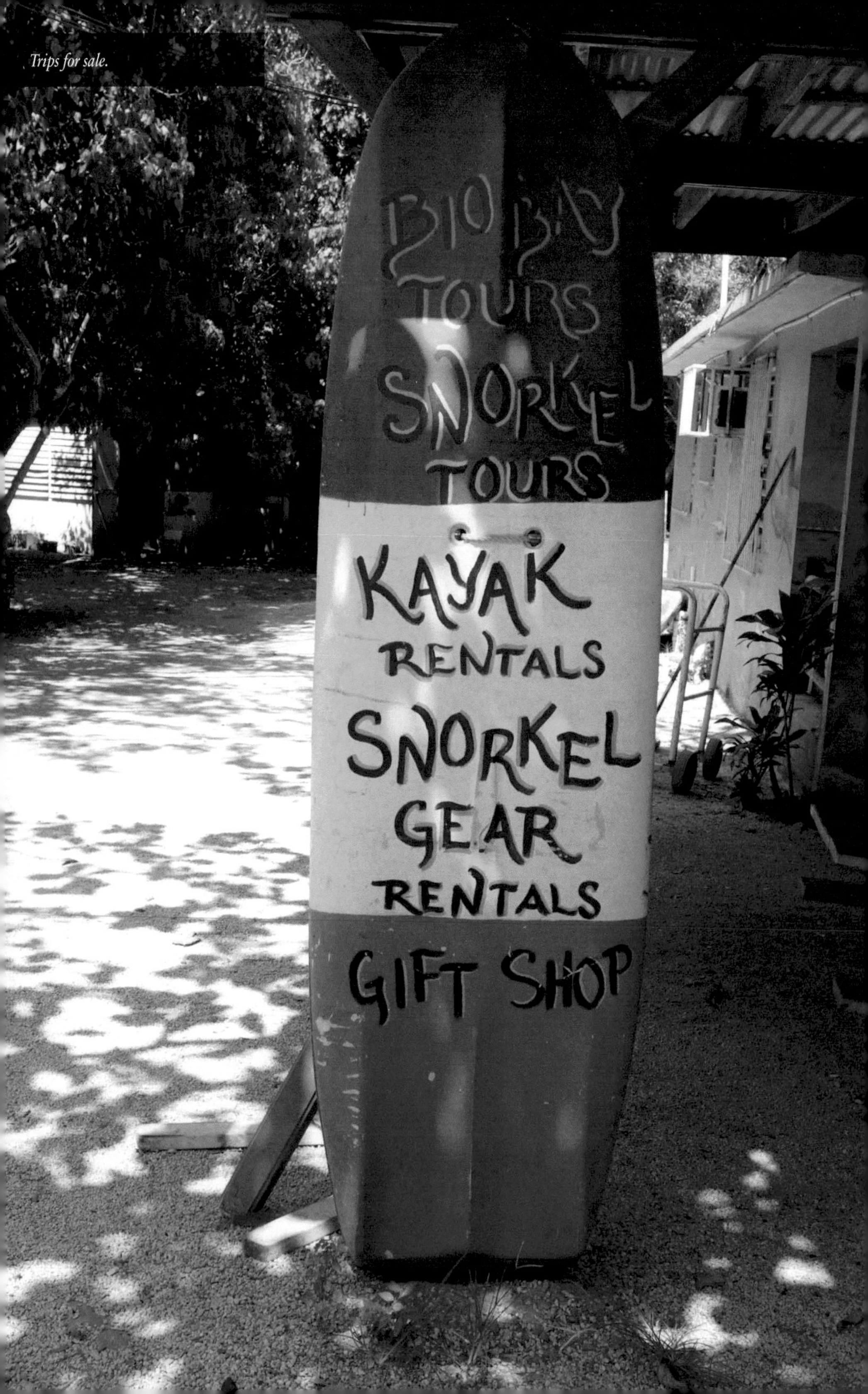
BIO BAY
TOURS
SNORKEL
TOURS
KAYAK
RENTALS
SNORKEL
GEAR
RENTALS
GIFT SHOP

Trips for sale.

OUTER ISLANDS

Off the east coast of Puerto Rico, Culebra and Vieques beckon with their pristine beaches and wild horses, while untouched Mona, far off the west coast, has unique charms of its own.

San Juan

S ix miles (10km) off the east coast of Puerto Rico lies **Vieques**, with twice the acreage of Manhattan and twice the charm of some islands many times its size. Like Culebra, Vieques belongs geologically to the Virgin Islands, but this is not all that separates it from mainland Puerto Rico. The island has grown in popularity among expatriates, although traditional ways live on. Islanders still refer to crossing the sound as "going to Puerto Rico," and the more formal *usted* form of second-person address, which is extinct on the mainland, is still heard in everyday conversation here.

Vieques's varied terrain

Much of Vieques looks like Californian cattle country: dry, rolling hills, scattered lazy herds and flocks of white egrets. But the island also enjoys scores of beaches, a small rainforest, exotic wild flowers, and a healthy population of tree frogs, mongoose and horses. A hundred or so beautiful *Paso Fino* (fine-gaited) horses, descended from 16th-century Spanish steeds, roam wild over the island (see page 55).

The Taíno Indians who first settled the island called it *Bieques*, or "small island"; Columbus named it *Graciosa* (gracious). English pirates called it Crab Island for the still-common land crabs they depended on for a tasty dinner. And the Spanish (who built the lighthouse and an unfinished fort) called Vieques and Culebra *las islas inútiles* – the "useless islands" – because neither had gold.

The US Navy had a base on the island for more than 50 years and the military occupied about 70 percent of the island, east and west, leaving only the central corridor from Isabel Segunda to Esperanza inhabited. After years of protests at the pollution and degradation of the environment and the loss of civil liberties caused by land and sea exercises, the navy moved

Main Attractions

Vieques
Isabel Segunda
Esperanza
Reserva Natural Bahía
  Bioluminiscente
Sun Bay
Culebra
Dewey
Playa Flamenco
Isla Mona

Eating out in Esperanza.

Exotic Caribbean flora on the island of Vieques.

out in 2003. The land they occupied is now a wildlife refuge. The western part covers 3,100 acres (1,255 hectares) of what was mostly used for storage on the island, while the eastern end, at 14,700 acres (5,950 hectares), still has a section that is off limits because it was formerly a live firing range.

Tucked into various spots on the island are some first-rate inns and hotels, such as the eco-friendly Hix Island House, built on 13 acres (5.25 hectares) mid-island, and the Inn on the Blue Horizon perched on a bluff overlooking the Caribbean Sea. There are also lots of rental villas and apartments for those who prefer to self cater, or the luxury W Retreat and Spa for those who want to be pampered.

Isabel Segunda

Vieques is accessible by air from San Juan and Ceiba or by sea from Fajardo for an 18-mile/29km journey. Flights from Ceiba with Vieques Air Link or Air Flamenco are the cheapest and quickest option. If you want to travel by sea, be prepared to get to Fajardo early to be sure of getting on a boat.

Note that locals refer to the cargo ship that takes cars (hired cars prohibited) as the "ferry" and the passenger-only boat as the lancha. The crossing provides great views but it can be rough and you should take precautions for sea sickness. The ferry is heavier, slower and more stable than the *lancha*.

Near the ferry landing, **Isabel Segunda ❶**, Vieques's only town, has the staples of any modest Puerto Rican municipality. Many of the island's 9,300 residents live here or nearby. Some work in factories, but unemployment remains relatively high. Young people who leave the island to study rarely return except on vacation. Agriculture has been in decline for many years. In spite of its problems, the town is dotted with trendy restaurants, upscale bakeries, and real estate offices, and the sound of construction is in the air as mansions and small developments are built.

The town has the distinction of having the last fort built by the Spaniards in the New World, **El Fortín Conde de Mirasol**. Constructed between 1845 and 1855, it was never used for defense

Isla de Vieques and Isla de Culebra

but it housed the military and served as a jail for a while before being abandoned in the 1940s. Although it was never completed, what was there has been well restored and it has an excellent historical museum (tel: 787-741-1717; Wed–Sun 10am–4pm; free) with information on the island's archeology and temporary art exhibitions. There is also another small museum at the **Punta Mulas Lighthouse** (tel: 787-741-0060; Mon–Fri 8am–3pm; free) to the north of town. The squat, square building was constructed in 1896 and now has exhibits on local history as well as marine and natural history.

Esperanza

A 10-minute drive across the 25- by 4-mile (40- by 6km) island is **Esperanza** ❷, a small fishing village consisting of little more than The Strip – a string of guesthouses and restaurants overlooking the water. Do not be fooled: this is *the* place to eat well, sleep well, sunbathe, and explore. At weekends local food is sold from *kioskos* or from the restaurants so you can indulge in fried delights such as *pastelillos* (fried dough stuffed with meat or seafood), *alcapurrías* (mashed plantain stuffed with meat or seafood) or arepas. People from Vieques like their *arepas* (fried dough usually served with fish) so much that they are nicknamed *areperas*. If it's nightlife you're after, try Banana's, Tradewinds and (Saturdays) Cerromar. Saturday nights are especially lively, when pretty much the entire town turns out along the seafront to promenade in their finest, talk, and flirt. During the *Fiesta Patronal* (Patron Saint's Festival), which takes place in the last two weeks of July, things really hop.

The **Vieques Historical and Conservation Trust**, founded in 1984 initially to save the island's biobay but now with a much wider remit, has a small **Archeological Museum** (Calle Flamboyan 138; tel: 787-741-8850; www.vcht.org; Tue–Sun 11am–4pm; free), gift shop and information center on The Strip. On display are a few artifacts from pre-ceramic inhabitants of the island up to the Taíno period including pottery fragments from Sorcé (La Hueca) on Vieques (AD

The site of the discovery of the Puerto Ferro Man.

PUERTO FERRO MAN

Vieques was first inhabited by hunter-gatherers between 3000 BC and 2000 BC. They were known as Archaic people of a Stone Age culture who depended on what they could harvest from the sea and the forest for their subsistence. Archeological evidence of their existence is mostly of shells and bones left in piles after they had eaten.

In 1991, excavations by archeologists from the University of Puerto Rico at a site in Puerto Ferro uncovered a fragmented human skeleton buried in a hearth area at the center of a group of large boulders. The site is just under a mile (1.6km) north of Mosquito Bay, off Route 997. This skeleton, now known as *El Hombre de Puerto Ferro*, is believed to be about 4000 years old by the radiocarbon dating of shells found in the hearth, which indicated a burial date of 1900 BC. Rows of smaller stones radiate from the central boulders, but it is not clear what their significance is. Puerto Ferro Man is now on display at the Museo El Fortín Conde de Mirasol and his age makes him one of the most important discoveries in Caribbean history. His burial site, marked only by two huge boulders, can be visited, but there is no security or organization. The area is frequently vandalized, while trucks pass through on their way illegally to mine sand from a dry river bed. Volunteer brigades clean it up from time to time but lack of funds mean there is no official maintenance or protection for this most valuable site.

35–490). They also have an aquarium where you can see tiny turtles and other small creatures from the waters around the island in temporary captivity before being released back into the wild. Guided tours are offered Wednesday to Sunday, 1–3pm. The gift shop is stocked with local arts and crafts, reference books, and identification cards as well as toys for children.

Just outside Esperanza, **Sun Bay** ❸ (Sombé to locals) glistens with a popular crescent-shaped beach. Camping is permitted here, as long as campers have the free permit. Beyond Sun Bay, and more secluded, lie **Media Luna** and **Navio** beaches. Final scenes from Peter Brook's classic 1963 movie *Lord of the Flies* were shot at Navio, a favorite spot for locals. The other good beaches to visit are not far away, within former **US Navy land**, now a wildlife reserve, **Refugio de Vida Silvestre de Vieques.** As an impediment to development, the Navy was partly responsible for the island's charm. Though the inhabitants protested at the military presence, the Navy built roads, let cattle owners use Navy land,

and left reserves open for public access to beaches.

Colorful beaches

With characteristic imagination, the Navy named three of the island's beaches Red, Blue, and Green, although the color designations have now mostly been dropped in favor of local, Spanish names. Merely getting to these places is a small adventure; rocky approach roads wind through thick seagrape overbrush. **Red** (Playa Corcho) and **Blue** (Bahía de la Chiva) beaches are ideal for swimming, snorkeling, and scuba diving. Just 75yds/meters off Blue Beach lies a cay (Isla Chiva) to swim to and explore for helmet shells and coral. The way to **Green Beach** (Punta Arena) is long, bumpy, and tortuous. If you make the trek, stop to see **Mosquito Pier** ❹, a mile-long dock which is a relic of World War II.

Phosphorescent Bay

Vieques' major attraction is the **Reserva Natural Bahía Bioluminiscente** ❺ (**Phosphorescent Bay**) in Mosquito Bay, considered to have the best phosphorescent display in the world. Billions of dinoflagellates, the microscopic organisms that inhabit Mosquito Bay, emit a neon blue-green fluorescent light when the water stirs, bright enough to read a book by. The best time to come here is on a moonless night. Contact Island Adventures (tel: 787-741-0720, www.biobay.com) for tours on their electric pontoon boats with bilingual guides who explain the ecology of the bay as well as the stars in the sky. Swimming in the bay is no longer allowed, to prevent pollution destroying the organisms.

A decaying sugar mill

Under Spanish colonial rule, Vieques was a sugar economy, with plantations and five mills (*centrales*) owned by wealthy families. The average worker was desperately poor and downtrodden and conditions deteriorated under the US administration. Even

Riding through the surf on Vieques.

in the 1930s, per capita income was as little as $22 a year. Not much of this history can be seen today, but with guidance you can get a glimpse of the past. Every two weeks on Thursday at 9am in the winter season, visitors meet at the Conservation and Historical Trust for a short talk and then car pool with a guide to the west of the island to explore the ruins of the **Central Playa Grande ❻**. This old sugar mill dates from around 1860 until it was expropriated by the US Navy in 1941, milling sugar for the last time in 1942. Built of bricks, concrete and iron, the mill's fascinating ruins are being swallowed up by vegetation and, despite being on the Register of Historic Places, it is gradually deteriorating. Wear long trousers, sturdy shoes and take insect repellent.

Or climb to the cave atop **Mount Pirata ❼**, where the ancient *cacique* Bieque allegedly hid his tribe's treasure once he realized the conquistadors' murderous intentions. Islanders say the sound of the cave's ceaseless roar attests that the great chief's ghost still rages. And while on the subject of superstitions, on Vieques's north coast near **Roca Cucaracha** (Cockroach Rock) is **Puerto Diablo** (Port Devil), said to be the third point of the notorious Bermuda Triangle, but off limits because of military contamination.

Culebra

From Isla Grande Airport, the short flight to isolated **Culebra** to the north of Vieques overlooks dramatic coastline, dozens of varied cays, and a turquoise-green Caribbean Sea. Columbus reportedly discovered this island on his second voyage in 1493. The first known inhabitants, the Taíno Indians, sought refuge on Culebra after the Spanish started colonizing the Puerto Rican mainland. Before long, pirates and privateers began to use Culebra's Pirate's Cay as a hiding place and supply base before sailing off to raid ships in the Virgin Islands. Infamous corsairs, including the Welshman Sir Henry Morgan, may have buried their treasure on and around Culebra; according to local legend, a road near Punta del Soledado, a bend on Los Vacos Beach, a clump of large trees near Resaca Beach,

Playa Esperanza is popular with families.

FACT

Income for most of Culebra's 1,818 inhabitants comes from tourism, construction, and a pharmaceutical plant in Dewey. Grazing livestock and fishing are two subsidiary activities.

and a rocky mound at the end of Flamenco Beach might be good spots to start looking for the 17th- and 18th-century fortunes.

By 1880, settlers from Puerto Rico and Vieques were braving severe droughts and swarms of mosquitoes to build a colony which grew tamarind, mango, cashew, and coconut trees. Then, a few years after the Spanish-American War of 1898, the US Navy opened facilities on Culebra, making Ensenada Honda its principal Caribbean anchorage. About this time, the island's town moved from what is now Campamento to Dewey. In 1909, one of President Theodore Roosevelt's last executive orders established parts of Culebra as a National Wildlife Refuge, one of the oldest in the US.

By the end of World War II, the US Navy had begun to use Culebra for gunnery and bombing practice. Sea vessels and fighter planes from the United States and its allies pummeled target areas; islanders recall days and nights of constant bomb bursts.

The Culebrans protested bitterly for many years. In 1971, Navy personnel and Culebrans exchanged tear gas and Molotov cocktails, for which some islanders were imprisoned. Finally, President Nixon decided that all weapons training on Culebra should be terminated. President Ford's National Security Council reaffirmed the decision, and Culebra was left alone in 1975.

Exploring Culebra's arid environment

Probably the most important feature of Culebra is its arid climate; with only 35 inches (89cm) of rain a year, there is always some sunshine here. Its 24 islands comprise 7,700 acres (3,100 hectares) of irregular topography and intricate coastline. Most of the terrain is good only for pasture, forest, or wildlife. Much of the land is administered by the US Fish and Wildlife Service, which aims to maintain the diverse fauna and flora of the islands. Culebra's cays provide flourishing nesting colonies for a dozen marine bird species, including brown boobies, laughing gulls, sooty terns, and Bahama ducks. The brown pelican, an endangered species, can often be spotted in mangrove areas.

Rare leatherback turtles nest on three of Culebra's beaches from April through early June: Zoni, Resaca, and Brava. The Department of Natural Resources uses volunteers to help in identifying and monitoring the turtles. Volunteers meet at happy landings at 5pm before heading to the beach, where they take turns from 6pm to 6am to watch for the large, lumbering reptiles delivering and protecting their eggs. Do not approach the female until she has prepared her nest. Once she starts to lay, she goes into a trance and will not notice if you gather round to watch and count the eggs. Large eggs are fertile, small ones are not. They hatch in 60 to 65 days and make their perilous way to the sea, braving predators, midday heat and obstacles. Only one in a thousand hatchlings makes it to adulthood. Call 1-877-772-6725 to make reservations with a qualified guide.

Poster advertising Conga music at Mamacita's Restaurant, Culebra.

As a result of the island having no freshwater streams, sedimentation is low, and Culebra enjoys one of the healthiest coral ecosystems in the Caribbean. Remarkable reefs make for an abundance of fish species and clear water.

According to the 2010 census, only 1,818 people live on Culebra, many in pastel-colored houses amid scrubby hills. Roads and front yards abound with jeeps and chickens. Time passes slowly; the atmosphere is one of tranquillity and bonhomie.

Dewey

The town of **Dewey** ❽ (which locals defiantly call **Puebla**), a 10-minute walk from the airport, covers only several blocks. (Be sure to remember Culebran law – no walking around town without a shirt!) At one end of town is the Fajardo ferry dock, known as the waterfront. Nearby you will find a dive shop, guesthouses, gift shops, a deli, and the highly recommended **Mamacita's Restaurant**. Down the road are two markets, the bank, the post office, and, across the bridge,

you'll find Dinghy Dock Restaurant & BBQ for a lively bar crowd and American and Creole seafood dishes.

Just beyond town is one of the few drawbridges in the Caribbean. Nearby is **Ensenada Honda** ❾ (Deep Bay), surrounded by mangrove forests and one of the most secure hurricane harbors in the area, not to mention a nice spot for windsurfing. Smack in the middle of the bay is **Pirate's Cay**.

Much to the dismay of locals, who prefer to keep tourism to a minimum in Culebra, several boutique hotels have opened here, among them Club Seaborne and Bahía Marina.

Flamenco Beach

While on Culebra, make a point of seeing **Playa Flamenco** ❿. A *público* (bus) can take you there, or you can make the long walk from Dewey. This is the sort of beach you have always heard about – soft white sand, clear blue water, and no one to kick sand in your face. A few hundred yards down the beach rest two archaic US Marine Corps tanks. Another fine beach is **Zoni Beach**, on the island's

Relaxing on Bahia de la Chiva, Vieques.

TIP

If you are making the long journey to Mona, make sure to take everything you need (including water); there are no facilities.

northeastern edge, some 7 miles (11km) from Dewey.

Half a mile uphill and east of Flamenco Beach stands **Mount Resaca**, the highest summit on Culebra, with a formidable 360-degree view of cays and some of the Virgin Islands, but off limits to visitors. Resaca hosts a dry subtropical "rock forest" where exotic Caribbean flora thrives amid thousands of large boulders. Last officially sighted in 1932, the Culebra giant anole, an extremely rare lizard, is still believed to survive in the forested areas of the mountain.

Of the north coast beaches of Culebra, **Playa Resaca** is perhaps the least visited. A long arc of white sand, it is usually empty except for the occasional group of surfers, perhaps because of the steep hike down to the beach.

The best way to see Culebra is by packing a picnic and hiring a boat for the day. Do some snorkeling or scuba diving from the boat as you travel to otherwise inaccessible beaches, lagoons, forests, and rocky bluffs on **Cayo de Luis Peña** and the mile-long

White sand and azure-blue sea at Playa Flamenco.

Culebrita. Here you will find the most exuberant wildlife on the island. On Culebrita, you can also see tidal pools and more spectacular, virtually deserted snow-white beaches.

Isla Mona

Throughout the Caribbean it is hard not to feel that, however breathtakingly beautiful the landscape may be, it must *really* have been heart-stopping before the European settlers arrived. There are still a few places that the reckless hand of civilization has not reached, though, and one of them, the tiny **Isla Mona**, belongs to Puerto Rico. Stuck 45 miles (72km) out to sea, in the Mona Passage half-way to the Dominican Republic to the west, this rugged island of 25 sq miles (65 sq km) is a haven for some of the oddest and most interesting wildlife in the Antilles.

Mona is protected by the Department of Natural Resources, which also supervises the use of Cabo Rojo and other spots of great scenic beauty on the mainland's west coast. Nobody lives there now, but Mona has had a

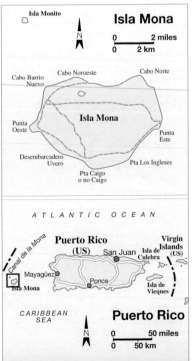

long history of habitation. Christopher Columbus found Taíno Indians there when he landed on the island, and Spanish settlers visited for many years in hopes of finding habitable and pleasant spots to settle. For centuries it was the stronghold for some of the most notorious of European and Puerto Rican pirates. Only a few naturalists and illegal immigrants visit the place now.

Except for an isolated lighthouse on a remote promontory, Mona is much as the Taínos left it. Cliffs 200ft (61 meters) high ring the tiny island, and are laced with a cave network which some say rivals that of the Camuy. Much of the island's ground is covered by small cacti that resemble a miniature version of Arizona's organ-pipe cactus, and tiny barrel cacti are common here as well.

Some of the vegetation on the island is known nowhere else in the world, while the fauna is even more astounding. Here are found the biggest lizards in Puerto Rico, as well as three species of endangered sea turtle. Naturally there are a large number of seabirds, including brown boobies (*Sula leucogaster*) and red-footed boobies (*Sula sula*).

Discarded island

In the Mona Passage, 14 miles (22.5km) off the west coast of Puerto Rico, is the uninhabited, 360-acre (145-hectare) island of **Desecheo**, a National Wildlife Refuge. *Desechar* in Spanish means to throw away, and this little island indeed seems to have been discarded. There are no signs that the Taíno bothered to live there and it has at times been used as for bombing practice by the US military. At one time home to the largest breeding colony of Brown boobies, now no seabirds nest there. The US Fish and Wildlife Service is attempting to eradicate introduced species such as rats, goats, and monkeys, which have eliminated birdlife and severely degraded the natural

forest, and protect and restore the island ecosystems. Dry tropical forest covers much of the rocky terrain, including large gumbo limbo trees in the valleys and the endangered higo chumbo cactus. Desecheo is much prized by divers because of its healthy reef and excellent visibility, with no rivers or people to pollute it, but you are not allowed to land on the refuge.

Traveling to Mona

There are those who would claim that anyone who wished to visit Mona could be called a booby as well. Cubans, Dominicans, Chinese, Filipinos, and North Koreans have been found here, trying to gain illegal entry to the US. Tourists, however, would be best advised to charter a boat or private plane in Mayagüez. Planes can be chartered from San Juan's Isla Grande Airport as well. Official information on hiking trails and on the island's topography is hard to come by, but try contacting the Department of Natural and Environmental Resources (tel: 787-999-2200).

Trailing for shellfish.

Playa de Morillos.

INSIGHT GUIDES TRAVEL TIPS
PUERTO RICO

TRANSPORTATION

GETTING THERE AND GETTING AROUND

GETTING THERE

By Air

Luis Muñoz Marín International Airport (SJU; www.aeropuertosju.com/en; tel: 787-791-1014/787-721-2400, ext. 5216), just to the west of San Juan in Isla Verde, is one of the largest and busiest airports in the Caribbean. It serves not only as Puerto Rico's main port of entry and a hub for several regional airlines, but also as a stopping point for most American, and some European, flights to the Caribbean.

There are also airports at Aguadilla (BQN), Ceiba (RVR), Culebra (CPX), Mayagüez (MAZ), Ponce (PSE), San Juan Miramar (SIG), and Vieques (VQS).

From the US

American Airlines
www.aa.com, tel: 800-433-7300; 800-981-4757 (toll-free)
Delta
www.delta.com, tel: 800-221-1212 (toll-free); 404-765-5000
Jet Blue
www.jetblue.com, tel: 800-538-2583 (toll-free)
Spirit
www.spiritair.com, tel: 801-401-2200 (toll-free)
United Airlines
www.united.com, tel: 800-426-5561 (toll-free)
US Airways
www.usairways.com, tel: 800-428-4322 (US and Canada)

From Canada

Air Canada
www.aircanada.com, tel: 888-247-2262 (toll-free)

From Europe

British Airways
www.britishairways.com, tel: 0844-381-6305
Condor
www.condor.com, tel: 0180-5-707202
Iberia
www.iberia.com, tel: 901-111-500
Virgin Atlantic
www.virgin-atlantic.com, tel: 800-862-8621

From the Caribbean:

American Eagle
www.aa.com, tel: 1-800-433-7300
Cape Air
www.flycapeair.com, tel: 1-800-227-3247
LIAT
www.liatairline.com, tel: 1-888-844-5428

On Arrival

Be sure to keep the ticket for your checked-in luggage because airport officials in the baggage claim area at the Luis Muñoz Marín International Airport will require this to verify ownership of your bags before allowing you to exit.

Porters or *maleteros* from the Operativa de Servicio de Equipaje are available in all baggage claim areas and will help carry bags for a fee of $1 per bag, regardless of size. The *maleteros* can be identified by their light blue shirts and dark blue pants and an ID tag with *Operativa de Servicio de Equipaje*.

If you arrive between 9am and 7pm, stop by the Tourism Company Information Center (tel: 787-791-1014) in concourse C at street level. Pick up a copy of *¡Qué Pasa!*, *Bienvenidos*, or *Places To Go* magazines.

By Sea

San Juan is the most popular cruise port in the Caribbean, receiving over 1 million visitors annually. Several modern "tourism piers" have been constructed at the harborside in Old San Juan, with the result that most cruise companies plying the South Atlantic make at least an afternoon stop in San Juan.

There is an international overnight ferry, America Cruise Ferries from Santo Domingo (tel: 809-688-4400) in the Dominican Republic to San Juan (tel: 787-622-4800) Sunday, Tuesday, and Thursday, returning the following night.

GETTING AROUND

Puerto Rico has one of the highest per capita rates of car ownership in the Americas, and Puerto Ricans drive everywhere. Public transport is not well developed and is difficult for an outsider to fathom. There are buses for urban transport, but longer distances are served by *públicos*, privately run minibuses or vans, which carry only about 10 people and often leave at inconvenient times for a visitor.

If you want to see anything of the island, a rental car is a necessity. Even guided tours expect you to rendezvous with the guide at the venue and transportation to the site is not included except for tours designed for cruise ship passengers. As a result of everyone using their cars all the time, traffic is horrendous and at busy times you should expect serious congestion in urban areas. Driving in the San Juan metropolitan area should be avoided if possible.

On the bus to El Morro, San Juan.

To and From the Airport

A free shuttle bus service operates between the airport and each car rental agency is located in or close to the airport. The Metropolitan Bus Authority (AMA) runs to various parts of the city, 9 miles (14km) away, for a small charge, but you can only take carry-on luggage on the buses. Taxis from the airport operate on a fixed-rate zone system for tourist areas; meter charges apply to places outside tourist locations. To take a cab, you must stand in line and obtain a transportation voucher from the Ground Transportation stand (orange with the Tourism Company's logo), located at street level and on the second (first) floor of all terminal exits. The voucher indicates the price and address of your destination. The best way to get to and from the airport if your hotel is in the San Juan tourist areas, such as Condado, Isla Verde, and Ocean Park, is by taxi.

By Air

There are airports around the main island and on the outer islands of Vieques, Culebra and Mona. Most international and many domestic flights (including those from the United States) to San Juan land at Luis Muñoz Marín International Airport in Isla Verde, while others use San Juan's second airport, Isla Grande, just across the estuary south of Puerta de Tierra. Ponce and Mayagüez have modern, small

Road Safety

Slow down if you see a sign indicating any of the following:
Desprendimiento **Landslide**
Desvío **Detour**
Carretera Cerrada **Road Closed**

airports that provide access to the capital in 20 minutes. Ponce receives regular flights from the US. Aguadilla and Ceiba Airports were formerly military bases and have exceedingly long runways. Vieques has a good airport, and the **Vieques Air Link** (tel: 787-741-8331; www.viequesairlink. com), which leaves Isla Grande daily is a pleasant way of getting to and from that lovely island, although flights from Ceiba are quicker and cheaper.

By Boat

A ferry operates from the tourist piers of San Juan to Cataño, a mile across San Juan Bay, is a time-saver (less than 10 minutes) and a bargain at $0.50 per ride. The ferry runs every 15 minutes from 6am to 10pm Monday to Friday and every 30 minutes at weekends and holidays.

Ferries also run from Fajardo to Vieques and Culebra and vice versa. They are scheduled to leave the docks at Fajardo for Vieques at 9am, 1pm, 4.45pm and 8.15pm each day, and 4am Mon–Fri. Ferries leave Vieques for Fajardo daily at 11am, 3pm, and 6pm; Mon–Fri 6am; and Sat–Sun 6.30am. Ferries from Fajardo to Culebra leave at 9.30am. Ferries from Culebra to Fajardo depart at 1pm. A one-way journey takes approximately 1 hour 15 minutes and costs $2.25 per adult from Fajardo to Culebra or $2 per person to Vieques. Children and seniors under 75 pay $1 to either island, seniors over 75 travel free. Seats can be reserved, but it's best to arrive an hour early. Ferries don't always stick to the schedule, so call to confirm and leave extra time if making connections.
For information and reservations:
Culebra, tel: 787-741-3161
Fajardo Port, tel: 800-981-2005 (toll-free)
Vieques, tel: 787-741-4761

By Rail

Puerto Rico's commuter rail system (Tren Urbano, tel: 1-800-981-3021) has 16 modern stations, connecting downtown Bayamón with eastern Santurce near Sagrado Corazón University, passing through the Torrimar neighborhood, the Centro Médico (the island's main medical center), the University of Puerto Rico at Río Piedras, and the financial district of Hato Rey. Route expansions are planned to Old San Juan, Carolina, and Caguas. Tren Urbano operates daily between 5.30am and 11.30pm. The fare is $1.50 per ride. Students and seniors (60–74) pay $0.75. Children under six and people over seventy-five travel free. A stored-value multi-use farecard may be used for travel on Metrobus buses as well as on trains. You can get an unlimited use ticket of $5 for one day, $15 for a week, and $50 for 30 days. When you get off the train you have two hours in which you can transfer to a bus (AMA or Metrobus) for free.

By Bus/*Público*

Most towns have private bus services. The only public bus service is in the San Juan metropolitan area. The Metropolitan Bus Authority (AMA) has routes through Bayamón, Guaynabo, Río Piedras, San Juan, Carolina, and part of Trujillo Alto. Adults pay $0.75 per trip on AMA buses and Metrobus. Buses run daily from 4.30am to 10pm; they are air-conditioned but can get crowded and do not operate on a set schedule. Buses can be hailed where you see signs: *Parada de Guaguas.* For information about bus routes and terminals, tel: 787-250-6064. If you are staying in Condado it is easy to get the bus into Old San Juan for the day, and considerably cheaper than the $15 taxi fare. Old San Juan and some other city centers provide a free trolley bus service for tourists, which you can hop on and off all day.

Puerto Rico's major cities are linked by *públicos*, independently owned small vans which run from the plaza of one town to the plaza of the next. They tend to travel out in the early morning and back in the evening and are used mostly by commuters. *Públicos* are good value but not particularly comfortable and can really only be recommended for specific routes, such as from San Juan to Mayagüez or San Juan to Ponce.

Blue Line
Tel: 787-765-7733
Río Piedras, Aguadilla, Aguada, Moca, Isabela, and others.
Choferes Unidos de Ponce
Tel: 787-764-0540
Ponce and others.
Línea Caborrojeña
Tel: 787-723-9155
Cabo Rojo, San Germán, and others.
Línea Sultana
Tel: 787-765-9377
Mayagüez and others.
Terminal de Transportación Pública
Tel: 787-250-0717
Fajardo and others.

By Road/Car Rental

Puerto Rico has many car rental companies. Avis, Budget, Hertz, and National have offices in the baggage claim area of terminal E at the Luis Muñoz Marín International Airport, while others are a short shuttle-bus trip away. Most have unlimited mileage. Smaller companies often have excellent automobiles and are less expensive. Even though insurance usually costs extra you would be advised to purchase it. And always carefully check the terms and conditions of the rental agreement detailing insurance coverage.

To rent a car, visitors must be fully qualified drivers of at least 25. Some allow drivers under 25, requiring an extra insurance fee. Agencies will usually require a deposit using a major credit card to secure the vehicle. However, some will accept a large cash deposit in lieu of the credit card. Foreign drivers must also produce either an International Driving Permit or a license from their home country. US licenses and international licenses are valid for use in Puerto Rico for up to three months.

Driving is on the right-hand side of the road. Speed limits are listed in miles, paradoxically – distance signs are in kilometers. The speed limit on the San Juan–Ponce highway and other expressways is 65mph (104kmh), although in some places the limit is 55mph (100kmh). Limits elsewhere are lower, especially in urban areas, where speed bumps (lomos) provide a natural barrier to excess.

Puerto Rico's older coastal highways are efficient routes but can be slow going, due to never-ending traffic lights. Roads in the interior are narrow, tortuous, poorly paved, and dangerous. Often, they run along dizzying cliffsides.

Hurricanes, too, take their toll on the roads, and traffic signals are regularly out of order, so drivers go at their own pace, which usually means too fast, weaving in and out of traffic. Also be aware that road signage is poor, and many of the smaller roads do not appear on any map. Be careful too with the many potholes you may encounter along the road.

By law, you must wear seat belts in Puerto Rico. As in some parts of the US, turning right on a red light when traffic allows is permitted – except at a few intersections, where a sign advising you not to do so is indicated. Be advised that hitchhiking and picking up hitchhikers can be dangerous.

In general, most Puerto Rican drivers tend to follow the rules of the road, but a formidable group do not, which can make driving hazardous. The best advice is to be aware of where you are at all times, drive defensively, and do not take anything for granted. Traffic signs and lights may not be heeded by other road users.

Be sure to carry change for the numerous tolls throughout the road network. There is a speed pass system, so check with the car rental company for availability.

Taxis

Taxis are plentiful, especially in tourist areas. Some metropolitan area taxi companies include:
Capetillo Taxi, tel: 787-758-7000
Major Taxi, tel: 787-723-1300
Ponce Taxi, tel: 787-842-3370

Fixed taxi rates apply under the Taxis Turísticos program, sponsored by the Puerto Rico Tourism Company, www.cabspr.com, tel: 787-969-3260. Participating taxis are white with the Taxis Turísticos logo on the door. Keep in mind that rush hour brings traffic jams, and heavy rain also slows things down.

Note that all tolls must be paid by the passenger. The Teodoro Moscoso Bridge toll is $3.25. A surcharge of $2 each applies to the sixth and seventh passenger in a vehicle, while $1 is charged for each piece of luggage and there is a $2 gas surcharge. Tips are not included in the set fare.

Metered taxi rates apply outside of the set San Juan tourism zones. The initial charge is $1.75, with $0.10 charged for every 19th of a mile or every 25 seconds of waiting time. The same luggage charges as in the transportation zones are applicable, as are the fees for the sixth and

seventh passenger. There is a $1 call charge, and the minimum charge for a trip is $3. Hourly rent charge is $36, and the night rate (from 10pm to 6am) is $1 over the meter charge.

If visitors wish to visit parts of the island outside the metropolitan area, ask for a metered journey or negotiate a flat price with the driver before setting off. However, such trips are expensive, so it is best to take a tour or rent a car for sightseeing trips around the island.

Travel Times

Estimated travel times by car from Luis Muñoz Marín International Airport when traffic is not heavy:
Airport to Aguadilla: 3hrs
Airport to Dorado: 30 mins
Airport to Fajardo: 1hr
Airport to Humacao: 1hr 20 mins
Airport to Isabela: 2hrs 30 mins
Airport to Mayagüez: 3hrs
Airport to Ponce: 1hr 15 mins
Airport to Rincón: 2hrs 30 mins
Airport to Río Grande: 45 mins

Cycling

Bicycles are not a common form of transport. There are cycle clubs who hold road races and group touring meets, while there are many keen mountain bikers who use trails in the forests, but as a means of getting around, cycling is rare. A nice place to take a bicycle ride is the Board Walk in Piñones state forest. Cars dominate the road and drivers squeeze past far too close and drive far too fast round mountain bends. The roads of the interior often have potholes – hurricanes can wreak havoc – and the surfaces become slippery in the rain. Never cycle after dark. Many resort hotels have bikes for hire, but for serious cycling you should bring your own or buy one from a specialist on the island.

On Foot

Old San Juan and town centers can easily be walked and this is often the quickest way of getting about if the traffic is heavy. Long distance walking is less successful. Places to stay are few and far between in the interior, which may mean walking further in a day than you planned and you may get soaked through in the rain. As with cycling, drivers are often not considerate of slower road users. Knowledge of Spanish is recommended.

EATING OUT

RECOMMENDED RESTAURANTS, CAFES, AND BARS

WHAT TO EAT

Aside from having a delectable and historic native cuisine, Puerto Rico benefits from its American and Caribbean connections in having just as many of the world's cuisines as you would find in the largest cities of the United States. Spanish, US, Mexican, Chinese, French, Italian, Swiss, Brazilian, Japanese, and other food is plentiful, especially in San Juan.

Puerto Rican cuisine (see page 59) has many similarities with its Spanish neighbors in the Caribbean. Relying heavily on rice, beans, starchy vegetables such as yuca, plantain, sweet potato, and pork or chicken, it is a mild, savory, style of cuisine, although Puerto Ricans are often criticized for their love of fried snacks.

WHERE TO EAT

Puerto Rican food can be found in all manner of spots: in the modest urban *fondas*, where a rich *asopao de camarones* will cost you under $8; in the rural *colmados* where delicious roast chicken is the order of the day; and in the upmarket restaurants of Old San Juan and Condado, such as La Mallorquina, the Caribbean's oldest restaurant.

The restaurants of San Juan tend to be concentrated in certain areas. While *fondas* are all over town, international cuisine tends to be concentrated in the trendier parts of Old San Juan and in the more expensive areas of Condado and Santurce, such as Ashford Avenue. There is also a high concentration of American fast-food and restaurant

chains in tourist areas and in shopping malls, whether it's the food court or in the vicinity of the mall.

Away from San Juan, there are fish restaurants all around the coast serving the freshest of seafood, beach bars catering to the surfing crowd, and local diners for the local market. In the Cordillera you will find places serving hearty fare with generous portions of meat and carbohydrate designed for the weekend trade when *sanjuaneros* escape the city to take a long lunch in the countryside. It can be difficult to find anywhere open to eat during the early part of the week.

SPECIALTY FOODS

For those who crave French breads, Japanese green tea, or curry paste, San Juan is home to Asian food markets and other international specialty stores. Also check out local supermarket chains, such as Pueblo,

Busy in the kitchen.

Grande, and SuperMax, as they expand their gourmet and organic food selections. The following stores are also recommended: Mother Earth (Plaza Las Américas, third level, tel: 787-754-1995) and Freshmart, an organic food supermarket with stores located in Carolina, Hato Rey, Aguadilla, Manatí, and Caguas.

For French goodies, stop in at Tradition Française or at La Boulangerie (174 Taft Street, Santurce, tel: 787-721-6272). This bakery and bistro offers an assortment of French pastries, soups, and sandwiches, as well as pastas and poultry dishes. For classic Spanish fare, such as paella, *jamón serrano*, wines, and more, visit La Ceiba (1239 Roosevelt Avenue in Puerto Nuevo, San Juan, tel: 787-782-0419, daily 6am–10pm) or Kasalta (1966 McLeary Avenue in Condado, tel: 787-727-7340), where President Barack Obama had lunch during his 2011 visit to Puerto Rico.

OLD SAN JUAN

311 Trois Cent Onze
311 Fortaleza Street
Tel: 787-725-7959
www.311restaurantpr.com
Provence was the inspiration for this formal French restaurant set in a landmark building and decorated with tradition and style. Meals are sophisticated yet simple. Two outdoor patios add to its charm. Reservations recommended. Tue–Sun 6am–10pm. **$$$**

Aguaviva
364 Fortaleza Street
Tel: 787-722-0665
www.oofrestaurants.com
Seaside Latino restaurant with chic and trendy decor. Mouthwatering seafood. Calling ahead to sign up on the waiting list is highly recommended. Dinner daily from 6pm, Dec–Apr Sat–Sun from 2pm. **$$$**

Café Berlin
407 San Francisco Street
Tel: 787-722-5205
www.cafeberlinpr.com
"Gourmet vegetarian" eatery offering fresh pastas, organic foods, and a delicious salad bar, but expect slow service. Daily 8am–10pm. **$$**

Café Manolín
201 San Justo Street
Tel: 787-723-9743
Puerto Rican restaurant with excellent authentic cuisine at reasonable prices. Breakfast and lunch Mon–Fri 6am–4.30pm, Sat 7am–4.30pm. **$**

Carli's Fine Bistro & Piano
206 Recinto Sur Street (Banco Popular Building), Plazoleta Rafael Carrión
Tel: 787-725-4927
www.carlisworld.com
For more than 10 years, a place where locals and international patrons gather to enjoy live jazz piano music from 7.15pm and fine dining in a relaxed atmosphere. Savor exotic assortments of gourmet tapas and exquisite local and international entrées. Reservations required for seven or more people. From 3.30pm Mon–Sat Sept–May, Tue–Sat June–Aug. **$$$**

La Cucina di Ivo
202 Cristo Street
Tel: 787-729-7070
Traditional Italian restaurant run by Ivo Bignami from Malzo, Italy. Try linguini di mare or mushroom risotto – both are excellent. Open from 1pm, closed Sun. **$$**

Dragonfly
364 Fortaleza Street
Tel: 787-977-3886
www.oofrestaurants.com
Sexy Asian-Latino fare in an intimate space. Small dishes to share. Calling ahead for reservations recommended. Dinner daily from 6pm until late. **$$$**

El Jibarito
280 Sol Street
Tel: 787-725-8375
Traditional criollo fare run for almost 30 years by the same family. Unpretentious fonda where you can try mofongo, tamales, and other local specialties. Open daily 10am–9pm. **$$**

La Mallorquina
207 San Justo Street
Tel: 787-722-3261
Puerto Rican cuisine in the oldest restaurant on the island, dating from 1848. House specialties: asopao de marisco and arroz con pollo. Worth a visit if only for the interior courtyard. Reservations required. Lunch and dinner Tue–Sun. **$$$**

Marmalade
317 Fortaleza Street
Tel: 787-724-3969
www.marmaladepr.com
This ultramodern restaurant, wine bar, and lounge is the place to be seen. It's also known for its vanguard cuisine. Reservations are recommended. Dinner Mon–Thu 6pm–midnight, Fri–Sat 6pm–2am, Sun 6–10pm. **$$$**

Il Nuovo Perugino
208 Ponce de Leon Avenue
Popular Center Atrium
Tel: 787-722-5481
www.ilnuovoperugino.com
Italian restaurant where chef-owner Franco Seccarelli prepares specialties such as pasta con vongole, carpaccio of Angus beef, and marinated salmon. Excellent wine list. Reservations required. Lunch Mon–Sat 11.30am–3pm, dinner Tue–Sat 6.30–10.30pm. **$$$**

Nuyorican Café
312 San Francisco Street
Tel: 787-977-1276
This music lounge features salsa, Spanish and local rock, jazz, and reggae, attracting an eclectic crowd. Excellent tapas, pizza, and seafood salads. Dinner Wed–Sun 9pm–4am. **$**

Old Harbor Brewery
202 Tizol Street, corner of Recinto Sur
Tel: 787-721-2100
www.oldharborbrewery.com
The only microbrewery on the island, it has seasonal hand-crafted beers in a family-friendly environment where old-world charms meet industrial chic. Top-quality steaks and local lobster. Lunch and dinner 11.30am–1am. **$$$**

Panza
329 Recinto Sur Street, Cervantes Hotel
Tel: 787-724-7722
www.cervantespr.com
Fine dining, with creative international cuisine. Reservations are required. Mon–Sat lunch noon–3pm and dinner 6pm–midnight. **$$–$$$**

The Parrot Club
363 Fortaleza Street
Tel: 787-725-7370
www.oofrestaurants.com
A contemporary Latin bistro and bar with live music at weekends. Call in advance for dinner reservations. Lunch and dinner daily, brunch Sat–Sun. **$$$**

El Patio de Sam
102 San Sebastián Street
Tel: 787-723-1149
Caribbean cuisine served in a casual setting. Sam's hamburgers are legendary. Reservations recommended. Daily 11am–2am. **$$$**

El Picoteo
100 Cristo Street, Hotel El Convento
Tel: 787-723 9020
www.elconvento.com
The perfect place to try a delicious paella, empanadilla, or tortilla accompanied by a glass of wine selected from the exceptional wine list. Also over 80 mouthwatering tapas to choose from. Daily lunch and dinner 11am–midnight. **$$$**

Raíces
315 Recinto Sur Street
Tel: 787-289-2121
www.restauranteraices.com
A spin-off of the original in Caguas, with 1940s rustic decor, this themed restaurant is a favorite for traditional local cuisine. Reservations required. Lunch and dinner Mon–Sat 11am–11pm, Sun 11am–10pm. **$$**

Toro Salao
367 Tetuán Street
Tel: 787-722-3330
www.oofrestaurants.com
Chef Hector Crespo creates his own artistic versions of Spanish tapas and raciones. Guests can dine inside or alfresco on a dog-friendly terrace. Nov–May daily from 11.30am, June–Oct Mon–Wed from 4pm and Thu–Sun from noon. **$$$**

PRICE CATEGORIES

Price categories are per person for three courses, with a half-bottle of wine:
$ = under $20
$$ = $20–40
$$$ = more than $40

METROPOLITAN SAN JUAN

Cataño

La Casita
27 Manuel Enrique Street, Palo Seco
Tel: 787-788-5080
Fancy restaurant in a poor neighborhood serving delicious fresh fish; specialties include a delicious octopus cocktail and *mofongo relleno* with lobster. Reservations recommended. Lunch and dinner daily. **$$$**

Condado

Antonio's Restaurant
1406 Magdalena Avenue
Tel: 787-331-1137
www.restauranteantonios.com
Spanish gourmet cuisine in an elegant atmosphere. Table settings are majestic, service impeccable. Steaks, chicken, and seafood complemented by Spanish wine. Reservations recommended. Mon–Fri noon–11pm, Sat 7–11pm, Sun noon–6pm. **$$$**

Bar Gitano/El Barril
1302 Ashford Avenue
Tel: 787-294-5513
www.ootwrestaurants.com/page.cgi
Across from the Marriott, Bar Gitano is a Spanish *tasca*, a bar and terrace with indoor or outdoor dining, serving tapas, Spanish cheese, and paellas, sometimes with live music and flamenco dancing. Mon–Wed 11.30am–11pm, Thu–Sat until midnight, Sun 11.30am–10pm. Next door is El Barril, a high-end sports bar serving comfort food, with live music or DJs. Mon–Sat 7pm–2am, Sun 5pm–2am. **$$–$$$**

Bodegas Compostela
106 Condado Avenue
Tel: 787-724-6088
Spanish restaurant serving authentic dishes and *pinchos* (tapas). The Galician chef-owner, José Rey, prepares the freshest seafood with a deft hand and a creative contemporary spirit. Reservations required. Mon–Fri noon–10pm, Sat 3–10pm. **$$–$$$**

Budatai
1056 Ashford Avenue
Tel: 787-725-6919
www.ootwrestaurants.com/page.cgi
Restaurant, bar, and terrace, above shops on two floors with sea view from huge windows. Chef Roberto Treviño serves a blend of Asian-inspired foods with subtle hints of Latin and Caribbean spices and flavors in an upmarket setting. One of the best restaurants on the island. Lunch and dinner daily. **$$$**

Buns Burger Shop
1214 Ashford Avenue
Tel: 787-725-7800
www.bunsburgershop.com
The juiciest burgers in town, fries, hot dogs, plus a great selection of craft beer. The focus is on fresh, never frozen ingredients. Mon–Wed and Sun 11.30am–10pm, Thu until 1am, Fri–Sat until 4am. **$**

Cielito Lindo
1108 Magdalena Avenue
Tel: 787-723-5597
Authentic Mexican cantina with casual decor and dining. The festive atmosphere appeals to both tourists and locals. Less formal than most Condado restaurants and good for children. Lunch and dinner Mon–Sun. **$$**

Green House
1200 Ashford Avenue, Diamond Palace Hotel
Tel: 787-725-4036
Short orders and full dinners at this popular place. Stop in after a hard night of clubbing. Breakfast, lunch, and dinner daily. Sun–Thu until 2am, Fri–Sat until 4am. **$$**

Oceano
2 Vendig Street
Tel: 787-724-6300
www.oceanopr.com
A trendy three-story venue with indoor and outdoor areas and breathtaking views of the ocean. Exquisite seafood dishes with a tropical twist. At night a popular place for cocktails. Live jazz on Sundays. Lunch and dinner Tue–Sun. **$$$**

Pikayo
999 Ashford Avenue, Conrad Condado Plaza Hotel
Tel: 787-721-6194
www.pikayo.com
The flagship restaurant for Chef Wilo Benet. Elegant fine dining, a creative fusion of Puerto Rican tradition with worldwide ingredients and flavors. Attentive service. Contemporary design, like the rest of the hotel, with a sea view. Reservations essential. Dinner only. **$$$**

Hato Rey

Metropol 3
244 F.D. Roosevelt Avenue
Tel: 787-751-4022
www.metropolpr.com
Cuban cuisine that is a long-time local favorite. Daily specials include meat, chicken, and fish dishes with rice and beans and fried plantain. Try *natilla* and Cuban coffee for dessert. One of six Metropols in Puerto Rico. Lunch and dinner daily. **$$**

Tierra Santa
284 F.D. Roosevelt Avenue
Tel: 787-754-6865
Hummus, tabbouleh, and shish kebab are favorites here. Entrées include *kustaleta* (lamb chops) and *gambary* (shrimps Arab-style). Belly-dancing Fri–Sat. Reservations recommended. Lunch and dinner daily. **$$$**

El Zipperle
352 F.D. Roosevelt Avenue
Tel: 787-751-4335
German/Spanish/Puerto Rican cuisine in an old-time eating and meeting place. Reservations recommended. Lunch and dinner daily. **$$$**

Isla Verde

Casa Dante
39 Isla Verde Avenue, Atlantic View sector
Tel: 787-726-7310
Unpretentious family-run restaurant serving local food and some international dishes. Excellent *mofongo* dishes, with every variety imaginable. Reservations recommended. Lunch and dinner daily. **$$$**

Lupi's Mexican Grill and Sports Cantina
Route 187, Km 1.3
Tel: 787-253-2198
Mexican bar/sports cantina with a Puerto Rican twist as you can have plantains instead of *tortillas* and *mofongo* is on the menu as well as the usual *burritos*, *fajitas*, and *nachos*. Eat inside or open air. Lunch and dinner daily, open until 3am. **$$**

Meat Market Miami
6063 Isla Verde Avenue, El San Juan Resort and Casino
Tel: 787-791-1000
www.elsanjuanhotel.com/dining
Excellent steaks and fresh seafood served in modern, energetic ambiance. Reservations recommended. Dinner Sun–Wed 5.30–10.30 pm, Thu–Sat until 11.30pm. **$$$**

La Piccola Fontana
6063 Isla Verde Avenue, El San Juan Hotel and Casino
Tel: 787-791-0966
Elegant northern Italian fare in classic surroundings. Good tasting menu and wine selection. Reservations recommended. Dinner only daily. **$$$**

Yamato
6063 Isla Verde Avenue, El San Juan Resort and Casino

Lobster at sunset.

Tel: 787-791-8152
www.yamatopr.com
Outstanding service in this teppanyaki and sushi restaurant. Reservations recommended. Lunch 11am–3pm. Dinner daily. **$$$**

Miramar

Augusto's Restaurant
801 Ponce de León Avenue, Courtyard by Marriott
Tel: 787-725-7700
The signature restaurant of chef Augusto Schreiner, now run by Ariel Rodriguez. Fine dining but not stuffy. Modern French cuisine with tried and tested favorites such as *escargots*, oxtail consommé, and chocolate soufflé. Reservations required. Lunch and dinner daily. **$$$**

Papillon
801 Ponce de León Avenue, Courtyard by Marriott
Tel: 787-919-0500
French bistro with a wide selection of house specialties like *escargots* or Provençal salad and local desserts, plus good coffee. Breakfast, lunch, and dinner daily. **$$**

Los Pinos Café
655 Ponce de León Avenue
Tel: 787-722-6862
Tasty contemporary local food and good sandwiches served in a relaxed and friendly ambience. Quick service; open 24/7. **$$**

Puerto Nuevo

Jinya's Restaurant
1009 Piñeiro Avenue
Tel: 787-783-2330
Delicious traditional sushi rolls and sashimi, as well as "Japanrican" rolls with *chicharrón* and *bacalao*. The freshest of fish draws a devoted clientele. This unpretentious restaurant also has steak and chicken teriyaki, tempura, and soft-shell crab, plus daily specials.

Reservations recommended on weekends. Lunch and dinner Tue–Sat, Sun 3–9pm. **$$$**

Margarita's
1013 F.D. Roosevelt Avenue
Tel: 787-792-0283
Mexican, well known for its margaritas, *enchiladas*, and *fajitas*. Mariachi band on weekends. Eat in or take out. Lunch and dinner daily. **$$**

Puerta de Tierra

El Hamburger
402 Muñoz Rivera Avenue
Tel: 787-721-4269
Before fast-food restaurants started to take over the island, El Hamburger was the place to go, and it still draws the crowds, despite plastic chairs and old furniture, because its burgers are nothing like you get in a chain. Build your own burger and pick your favorite jukebox song. Lunch and dinner daily, Sun–Thu until 1am, Fri–Sat until 4am. **$**

Lemongrass
Los Rosales, Caribe Hilton Hotel Gardens
Tel: 787-724-5888
www.lemongrasspr.com
A fusion of Indian, Thai, and Japanese flavors come together with Caribbean ingredients in this casual dining restaurant. Dinner daily 5.30–11.30pm. **$$$**

Marisquería Atlántica
7 Lugo Viñas Street
Tel: 787-728-5444
This Spanish seafood eatery prides itself on being the "friendliest fresh food and fish restaurant in town." Try daily specials. You can also buy fresh fish here. Lunch and dinner daily. **$$$**

Río Piedras

Café Valencia
1000 Muñoz Rivera Avenue
Tel: 787-764-4786
Traditional Spanish cuisine. Famous for its paella. Reservations

recommended. Sun–Thu 10.30am–10pm, Fri 11.30am–midnight, Sat 5pm–midnight. **$$–$$$**

Santurce/Ocean Park

Bebo's Café
1600 Loíza Street
Tel: 787-726-1008
With the casual ambience of a cafeteria, Bebo's offers cheap, filling, and tasty local dishes like *pastelones*, *mofongo*, and roasted *pernil*. There's also a full menu for breakfast, sandwiches, burgers, and local meals, and an extensive *menú del día*. Takeout meals available. CNN and sports on TV. Breakfast, lunch, and dinner daily, kitchen closes 12.30am.
$–$$

La Casona
609 San Jorge Street
Tel: 787-727-2717
www.lacasonainc.com
This Spanish restaurant, in an old Spanish-style home with a courtyard, has had the same chef for over 30 years. Lobster salad, stuffed rabbit loin, and the best paella in Puerto Rico. Immaculate service. Reservations recommended. Lunch and dinner Mon–Fri, dinner only Sat. **$$$**

Che's
35 Caoba Street, Punta Las Marías
Tel: 787-726-7202
www.chesrestaurant.com
Argentine restaurant in operation since the 1970s specializing in *parrilladas*, *churrasco*, and *chimichurri* as well as seafood and pasta. A casual, family-friendly place serving large portions. Reservations recommended. Lunch and dinner Sun–Thu 11.30am–10pm, Fri–Sat until 11pm. **$$$**

Pamela's Restaurant
1 Santa Ana Street
Tel: 787-726-5010
www.numero1guesthouse.com
This quaint little restaurant is at a guesthouse right on the beach. Casual fine dining at its best, the service is impeccable, and the Caribbean dishes are prepared with the freshest ingredients. Lunch noon–3pm, tapas 3–6pm, and dinner 6–10pm daily. **$$$**

Uvva
1 Tapia Street at Hostería del Mar
Tel: 787-727-3302
www.hosteriadelmarpr.com
Caribbean flavors mix with Mediterranean delights in this very romantic hotspot by the beach. Alfresco dining available. Breakfast, lunch, and dinner daily, 8am–10pm. **$$$**

THE NORTHEAST

Ceiba

Mi Terraza
Route 3, exit 2
Tel: 809-822-1347
Roadside dining on screened porch, friendly and cheerful service at this unprepossessing restaurant which serves up tasty, authentic local food such as pork chops, *mofongo*, fresh fish, and garlic shrimp. Lunch and dinner, except Wed. **$$**

Fajardo

La Estación
Route 987, Km 4, Las Croabas
Tel: 787-863-4481
www.laestacionpr.com
Casual, family-friendly restaurant with outdoor seating and a pool table. All food is cooked on charcoal, with a modern mix of local specialties, fresh fish, *mofongo*, and good daily specials. Generous portions. Reservations essential as it's always busy. Mon–Wed 5pm–midnight, Fri–

Sun 3pm–midnight. **$$–$$$**

Pasión por el Fogón
Route 987, Km 2.3, Barrio Sardinera
Tel: 787-863-3502
www.pasionporelfogon.net
Serves local and international dishes, seafood, and steak, with good flavor combinations for sauces and cocktails. Busy with locals and tourists; reservations essential. Lunch and dinner daily. **$$**

El Varadero Seaside Grill
Puerto Chico Marina, Route 924, Barrio Sardinera
Tel: 787-860-2662
www.elvaraderoseaside.com
Small, family-friendly restaurant serving great fish, conch salad, and ceviche. Or choose burgers and steak. Chef will prepare your catch for you if you've been fishing, with all the trimmings: *tostones*, salad, and rice. Live music at weekends. Lunch and dinner daily, breakfast Sat–Sun from 8am. **$$**

Friendly waitress.

THE SOUTHEAST

Daniel Seafood
Punta Santiago, Humacao
Tel: 787-852-1784
Casual, friendly, family-run restaurant by the beach serving fresh fish and other seafood, criollo-style. Lunch and dinner daily. **$$**

Paradise Seafood
Punta Santiago, Humacao
Tel: 787-852-1180
Typical seafood restaurant with marine memorabilia on the walls and

plastic tablecloths. Generous portions of fresh fish and good shrimp dishes, plus a wide choice of side dishes including *mofongo* and cassava puffs. Lunch and dinner daily. **$$**

Pura Vida
195 Palmas Inn Drive, Palmanova Plaza
Suite 119,
Palmas del Mar, Humacao
Tel: 787-531-8849
www.puravidapdm.com
Simple décor inside and a large

terrace outside. Pleasant staff serve up tasty, pretty criollo food, snacks, *asopao*, pasta, steak, and seafood. Lunch and dinner daily. **$$**

Zona Fresca Grill
122 Palmanova Plaza, Humacao
Tel: 787-636-5710
The *churrasco* with rice and beans served here is well worth trying, as are the hamburgers and steaks. Lunch and dinner Tue–Sat 11am–10pm. **$$**

THE NORTH

Menta Cuisine
171 José Cedeño Avenue, Arecibo
Tel: 787-642-3765
Small restaurant serving French Caribbean food with plenty of Puerto Rican favorites. Try the red *malanga* chips or *pastelillos* filled with mahi mahi. Excellent service from a chef who takes the time to greet customers and even catches his own fish for the table. Very popular with Puerto Ricans and tourists alike. Lunch and dinner daily. **$$–$$$**

Salitre Mesón Costero
Route 681, Km 3.8, Arecibo
Tel: 787-816-2020
www.salitre.com

White concrete greets you when you arrive at the parking lot, but the dining areas – indoors or on the terrace – are pleasant and rustic and right on the seafront. A wide range of menu items and prices offers something for everyone, and the lunch specials can be good value. The fish and lobster are fresh and portions are generous. Wheelchair-accessible. Open from 11am. **$$–$$$**

Salpicón
Route 681, Km 13.7, Arecibo
Tel: 787-408-0095
Dine inside or alfresco on the seafront with a stunning view of the coast between Arecibo and

Barceloneta. Good value and large portions of fresh fish, making it popular with both locals and tourists. Favorites are the fried red snapper with criolla sauce or the octopus salad, while the *tostones* and *mofongo* are of a high standard. Prompt service. Lunch and dinner daily. **$$–$$$**

PRICE CATEGORIES

Price categories are per person for three courses, with a half-bottle of wine:
$ = under $20
$$ = $20–40
$$$ = more than $40

THE WEST

Cabo Rojo

Tino's Restaurant
Route 102, Km 13.5
Tel: 787-851-2976
Typical Puerto Rican seafood restaurant, specializing in fish and *mofongo relleno*. Friendly, helpful service. Lunch and dinner Wed–Mon. **$$**

Vaivén Tasca en el Mar
Route 308 Km 4, Barrio Puerto Real
Tel: 787-717-3638
www.marinapescaderia.com
In the Marina Pescadería, this popular restaurant overlooks the water, with mostly outdoor dining. A Spanish chef prepares delicious seafood tapas and paella, as well as the catch of the day and kids' menus. Lunch and dinner Wed–Sun. **$$**

Isabela

El Carey Café
Route 4466, Km 5.6, Barrio Bajuras
Tel: 954-839-8356
Roadside, family-run café known for its breakfasts, from healthy berries and granola to *mangú* and scrambled eggs. Brunch and lunch on subs, burgers, wraps, *arepas*, fish dishes, and salads, all of which are tasty and filling. A surfers' spot for an energy boost. Free Wi-fi. **$–$$**

Ola Lola's Garden Bar
332 Barrio Bajuras
Tel: 787-872-1230
www.olalolaspr.com
Backyard bar and tables, very casual, two minutes' walk from Shacks Beach. Owners are keen photographers as well as water sports enthusiasts. Simple fare of burgers, wraps, dips, relishes, and salads,

plus calorie-laden desserts. Fri–Mon 3–9pm. **$–$$**

Pedro Fish – Sushi to Go
Jobos
www.pedrospescado.com
There are several informal small bars and restaurants in this area that have limited opening hours. This takeout sushi bar is only open Fri–Sat. Generous portions, delicious and all very fresh. **$$**

La Parguera

Moons Bar and Tapas
Route 304, Km 2.1
Tel: 787-362-0935
Extensive tapas menu, Puerto Rican style, or you can choose a huge burger. Lots of colorful cocktails and sangría. Friendly, fun atmosphere, all ages welcome. Thu–Sun 3pm–midnight. **$$**

El Turrumote
Route 304, Km 2.7, Club Nautico
Tel: 787-899-3361
The restaurant specializes in Caribbean meat and *frutti di mare* dishes. Lobster-stuffed *mofongo* is certainly worth a try. Wed–Sun noon–10pm. **$$**

Rincón

Rincón Tropical
Route 115
Tel: 787-823-2017
Casual, open-air dining, with plastic tables and chairs and canteen-type crockery. Huge portions of local food to fill any empty stomach after surfing. Good lunch specials. Popular with Puerto Ricans. Daily from early lunch to late dinner. **$–$$**

La Rosa Inglesa
Carr. Interior 413, Km 2, Barrio Ensenada
Tel: 787-823-4032
www.larosainglesa.com
The place to come for breakfast, run by an English couple. Full English breakfast, delicious French toasts, Mexican eggs, *burritos*, and eggs Benedict are just some of the delights on the extensive menu. Daily 8am–noon. **$**

Shipwreck Bar and Grill
564 Black Eagle Marina
Tel: 787-823-0578
www.rinconshipwreck.com
With outdoor seating under awnings and umbrellas, this casual, family-friendly place can accommodate large groups. The varied menu ranges from enormous burgers and *tacos* to fish meals and coconut shrimp. Cheap happy hour drinks. Lunch and dinner daily. **$$–$$$**

San Germán

Lechonera Figueroa
Route 102, Km 38.5
Tel: 787-873-1080
Spacious, family-run business with friendly ambiance, specializing in Caribbean cuisine. Daily 7am–7pm. **$**

Tapas
48 Dr Santiago Veve Street
Tel: 787-264-0610
In the old part of town, close to the Porto Coeli chapel, in a lovely old building. Spanish cuisine at its best, with serrano ham and cheeses, great meat balls, and shrimp. Wed–Fri 4.30–10pm, Fri–Sat 4.30–11pm, Sun 11am–9pm. **$$**

THE SOUTH

Ponce

El Ancla
805 Hostos Avenue
Tel: 787-840-2450
Both international and local cuisine, including prime steaks and seafood. Sun–Thu 11am–9pm, Fri–Sat 11am–10.30pm. **$$**

Café Cocina Criolla Espresso Bar
2638 Aurora Street, corner Mayor
Tel: 787-841-7185
www.cafecafeponce.com
The place to come for a mid-morning coffee break while touring the town. Locally grown beans are roasted on site and they do an excellent espressos – why not pair it with a yummy *flan*? There's a pretty garden

at the back of the old house and local art on the walls. Breakfast and lunch. Mon–Fri 11am–3pm. **$$**

Lola Eclectic Cuisine
Corner Reina and Unión streets, Ponce Plaza Hotel and Casino
Tel: 787-813-5033
Good food, a wide-ranging menu, and a pleasant environment. One of the few places in town open late. Mon–Fri from 11.30am, Sat–Sun from noon. **$$–$$$**

Pito's Seafood
Route 2, Km 2.18, Las Cucharas
Tel: 787-841-4977
www.pitosseafoodpr.com
Lovely location on the water's edge, the setting is worth a visit. Menu

of fish, seafood, and meat. Watch out for unexpected service charges. Lunch and dinner daily. **$$–$$$**

Yauco

La Guardarraya
Route 127, Km 6, Barrio Quebradas Guayanilla
Tel: 787-856-4222
www.laguardarraya.com
Family business offering hearty Puerto Rican food but famous for their pork chop Can Can, a huge, deep fried chop, with the rind scored so that it curls like a frilly cancan skirt. Finish with a coffee, roasted here. Tue–Sun 11am–7pm. **$$**

CORDILLERA CENTRAL

Aibonito

Tío Pepe
Route 723, Km 0.3, Barrio Asomante
Tel: 787-735-9615
Good criollo food. All the local favorites served in a pleasant setting with local art work on the walls and live music from a troubadour with a guitar. Up in the hills, surrounded by trees. Wed–Sun 10.30am–11pm. **$$**

Barranquitas

La Vecindad del Chavo
Route 771 Int. Km 4.1, Barrio Barrancas
Tel: 787-385-6417
Very popular place for families at weekends with waits of over an hour for their good *comida criolla*. It's named after a Mexican TV program. Music can be loud. Wed–Sun lunch and dinner. **$$–$$$**

Caguas

Angus Ranch
Jardines Shopping Center, Route 156
Tel: 787-258-8700
Steak house serving certified Angus beef. Extensive menu, large portions, tasty ribs, and 32oz (0.9kg) rib eye for the very hungry. Mon–Thu 11am–10pm, Fri 11am–11pm, Sat–Sun noon–10pm. **$$–$$$**

Cayey

El Mesón de Melquíades
Route 15, Ramal 741
Tel: 787-738-4083
Very popular local food of a high quality, much praised by Puerto Ricans. Try their renowned appetizers: corned beef *alcapurrías*. Thu–Sat 11am–8pm, Sun 11am–7pm. **$$–$$$**

OUTER ISLANDS

Culebra

The Homeless Dog Café
26 Feliciano Street
Tel: 939-452-9563
Not a restaurant, but a catering service, perfect if you want a meal in your rental villa but do not want to cook. Excellent quality delivered to your door when you want it – or even to the beach, whether for a romantic meal *à deux* or a wedding party. **$$–$$$**

Mamacita's
66 Castellar Street
Tel: 787-742-0090
www.mamacitasguesthouse.com
Long-established restaurant on the canal known for its Bushwacker cocktails, fun atmosphere, music, and dancing, as well as its good food. Daily breakfast, lunch, and dinner. **$$–$$$**

Susie's
Sardinas 2
Tel: 787-742-1141
www.susiesculebra.com
Fresh seafood, good *churrasco*, an interesting selection of appetizers, imaginative cooking, and great cocktails. Sit indoors or on the canalside. Reservations essential for this popular and friendly place. Fri–Mon from 6pm. **$$–$$$**

Vieques

Chez Shack
Route 995, Km 1.8
Tel: 787-741-2175
Caribbean seafood and steak. Go for the barbecue and steel band night when the rum punch flows, the atmosphere rocks and you can dance off your meal. Reservations essential if you want a table. Dinner only Wed–Sun, closed Sept and Oct. **$$**

Next Course
Route 201
Tel: 787-741-1028
Up in the hills, in an old house with wraparound balcony, this chic and pleasant restaurant has indoor and outdoor dining. Owned by New Yorkers, the service is faster than island style but still casual. Excellent food, with a wide-ranging menu of fusion cuisine. Dinner Fri–Wed 5.30–10pm. **$$$**

Sol Food
Route 997, at García Gate
www.solfoodvieques.com
On your way to or from the beaches of the southeast, stop at this food truck for a tasty lunch or snack. Great *empanadas*, pork sandwiches, shrimp skewers, hummus, and salads. There's a wide variety, but they sometimes run out of food by Sunday. Daily 11am–10pm. **$**

Taverna
453 Carlos Lebrum Street
Tel: 787-438-1100
www.tavernavieques.com
The only authentic Italian restaurant on the island. All the classic Italian dishes you would expect, including superb pizza and pasta, plus fresh salads and delicious desserts. Mon–Fri 5.30–9.30pm. **$$**

Guinea Hen and rice, washed down with a bottle of local Medalla beer.

PRICE CATEGORIES

Price categories are per person for three courses, with a half-bottle of wine:
$ = under $20
$$ = $20–40
$$$ = more than $40

ACTIVITIES

FESTIVALS, THE ARTS, NIGHTLIFE, SHOPPING, AND SPORTS

FESTIVALS

Annual Events

Almost every holiday is the occasion for a festival in Puerto Rico, many of them legislated, others informal. Every town has its patron saint, and every saint a festival. These, known as *fiestas patronales*, are the biggest events of the year in their respective towns and can last from one day to nine days. Usually held in the main plaza, they involve religious processions, parades, handicrafts, live music, dancing, food, and drink. At any of these festivals you are likely to see the mask-wearing *vejigantes*, the *cabezudos*, and the stilt-walking *gigantes*.

The most famous is probably Loíza's **Fiesta de Santiago Apóstol** in July. The largest is certainly San Juan's **Noche de San Juan Bautista** in late June, and a very popular one with islanders is the **San Sebastián Street Festival** in Old San Juan in mid-January. Juana Díaz comes to life on the Feast of the Epiphany or Three Kings Day on January 6, when an enormous street festival celebrates the African, Taíno, and European roots of modern-day Puerto Rico. Three Kings is celebrated all over the island and in many places there are children's activities, clowns, puppets, funfair rides, and presents distributed, although these children's festivals are not all on the same day and are spread around from January 5 to 8 in different towns.

Carnival is celebrated just before Lent and has similar festivities to a *fiesta patronal*. Ponce has a particularly exuberant carnival, which is one long party.

There are several food festivals during the year, celebrating local cuisine (see also page 61). In February, the **Puerto Rican Street Food Fest** is held at the Hiram Bithorn stadium, when mobile food trucks *(guagüitas)* line up to offer their wares and compete. Then there is the **Maricao Coffee Festival**, also in February, celebrating this local industry. In April, **Saborea Puerto Rico** (www.saboreapuertorico.com) is a culinary experience held over a weekend at Escambrón Beach, with demonstrations, tastings and parties. In May there are a clutch of food feasts, such as the Mango Festival in Santa Isabel, the Sugar Festival in Yabucoa, the Shrimp Festival in Moca or the Coconut Festival in Rincón. Once a year is not enough for the **SoFo Culinary Fest**, held in June and December in Old San Juan.

The Arts have several highly regarded events. The **Casals Music Festival** (www.festcasalspr.gobierno. pr) in February/March is world-renowned, held at the Performing Arts Center in Santurce. This is followed at the end of March by the **Puerto Rico Heineken Jazz Fest** held at the Puente Amphitheater in San Juan. In April, Rincón hosts an **International Film Festival** (www.rinconfilm.com), known as RIFF, where films from around the world are screened at outdoor beach-front venues, accompanied by themed dinner events. The **San Juan International Artisan's Festival** (www.ferinart.org) is held in May, featuring workshops, seminars, demonstrations, and sales. Salsa comes center stage in July with the **Puerto Rico Salsa Congress**, including competitions and workshops.

Sporting events are also worth looking out for, attracting athletes from the Caribbean, the US and from further afield. In January **La Vuelta Puerto Rico** (www.lavueltapr.com) is a three-day, 375-mile (603km) cycling marathon around the island. In February there is the **Annual Freefall Festival** (www. xtremedivers.com) held in Arecibo, followed In March by the **Puerto Rico Open**, a regular stop on the PGA Tour, and the **Ironman 70.3 San Juan** (www. ironmansanjuan.com), with a swim, cycle, and run totaling 70.3 miles

The modern facade of the Fine Arts Museum in Caguas.

Street music in Old San Juan.

(113.1km). The **San Juan International Billfish Tournament** (www.sanjuan international.com) draws keen deep-sea fishermen from around the world to the Club Náutica in Miramar in September. For further information on festivals, see page 78.

For further information on festivals, see page 78.

THE ARTS

Art Galleries

Almost all of Puerto Rico's cities sell local crafts and art, from Aguadillan lace to Loízan *vejigante* masks, but an art "scene" exists primarily in San Juan. Here, the combination of a radiant light and an active network of patronage draws most of the finest painters of Puerto Rico and many from North America and Europe. Sculpture thrives, as do the crafts of Puerto Rico and other Latin American nations. Many galleries are huddled together on a few of Old San Juan's streets, while Santurce has become the hub of contemporary art and design and the place to find experimental works and emerging artists. The following is a list of some of the galleries in the metropolitan area.

C787Studios
734 Cerra Street
Santurce
The gallery has changing exhibitions of contemporary Puerto Rican artists as well as some international artists. The shop attached sells art works as well as limited edition T-shirts and caps and other items designed by contemporary local artists.

Espacio 1414
1414 Ave Fernández Juncos
Santurce
Tel: 787-725-3899
www.espacio1414.org
This gallery houses the Berezdivin collection, built up since the 1970s by a Cuban couple whose core works initially came from Israel, Cuba and Puerto Rico but have now diversified into Latin American and international contemporary art, providing a platform for emerging artists. Visits by appointment only.

Galería Botello
208 Cristo Street
Old San Juan
Tel: 787-723-9987
www.botello.com
Fine international paintings, sculpture, *santos*, and graphic art. Mon–Sat 10am–6pm.

Galería W. Labiosa
200 Tetuán Street
Old San Juan
Tel: 787-721-2848
Email: galeriawlabiosa@hotmail.com
Prints, silk screens, and original paintings. Mon–Sat 9am–6pm.

Galería Petrus
726 Hoare Street
Santurce
Tel: 787-289-0505
www.petrusgallery.com
At the forefront of contemporary Puerto Rican art, look for the large steel spikes coming out of the ground, a sculpture making the entrance to the building.

Galería San Juan
204 Norzagaray Street
Old San Juan
Tel: 787-722-1808
www.thegalleryinn.com
A sizeable changing collection of fine paintings in an elegant old building that doubles as a hotel and is always open.

Liga de Arte de San Juan
Beneficencia Street
Old San Juan
Tel: 787-722-4468
A small, changing display of some of San Juan's up-and-coming art students, with a tendency towards the vanguard and the experimental. Mon–Sat 9am–5pm.

Viota Art Gallery
793 San Patricio Avenue
Puerto Nuevo, San Juan

Tel: 787-782-1752
The gallery features the work of contemporary Puerto Rican artists and foreign artists residing on the island. Mon–Sat 9am–6pm.

Concerts

Puerto Ricans are big fans of the arts, and there are plenty of venues that showcase local and international talent. The busiest venues are the Centro de Bellas Artes Luis A. Ferré in Santurce and the Coliseo de Puerto Rico José Miguel Agrelot.

The Centro de Bellas Artes Luis A. Ferré (tel: 787-620-4444) was founded in 1981 and quickly became the premier venue for musical and theatrical productions in Puerto Rico. It houses three performance halls, a *café teatro* and an outdoor pavilion. The arts center is also home to the Puerto Rico Symphony Orchestra and the annual **Casals Festival**.

The Puerto Rico Symphony Orchestra, founded in 1956, is the island's foremost musical ensemble, and one of the most eminent orchestras of the Americas. Sponsored by the government, its 76 regular musicians perform a 48-week season, which includes symphonic concerts, operas, ballets, pop, educational, and children's concerts. It also offers outdoor concerts throughout the island. The highlight of the classical music year comes during the **Casals Festival** in February/March, when the Puerto Rico Symphony's performances at Bellas Artes are complemented by guest appearances from musicians from around the world.

The Coliseo de Puerto Rico José Miguel Agrelot (tel: box office 787-294-0001, toll-free 1-866-994-0001; www.coliseodepuertorico.com; Mon–Fri 10am–6pm) is a multi-purpose arena, located in the heart of Hato Rey, accommodating any size of audience, from an intimate theater setting of 3,500 to center-stage concerts of 18,000. The venue hosts concerts, family shows, sporting events, trade shows, conferences, and theatrical performances, attracting people from all over the world. It also turns into a state-of-the-art ice-skating rink during the winter holidays.

Dance

There are plenty of opportunities to see ballet in San Juan. The San Juan Ballet periodically hosts performances at Bellas Artes. Ballet Concierto has a classic repertory. The San Juan

City Ballet performs regularly at the restored **Tapia Theater** in Old San Juan. Rounding out dance offerings are the modern dance shows given at the **Julia de Burgos Amphitheater** in Río Piedras as part of the University of Puerto Rico's cultural activities.

Movies

Independent movie theaters have gone the way of the movie multiplex. Santurce, once crowded with such theaters, currently has only one, as does Miramar, though they now belong to the biggest movie theater chain in Puerto Rico, Caribbean Cinemas. Cinemas within **shopping centers** are much more common today, most notably in **Plaza Las Américas**. The independently run Teatro Roosevelt survives in Hato Rey, as does the Caribbean's only drive-in, Auto Cine Santana in Arecibo. Check local newspapers for a complete list of theaters, current movie listings, and show times.

Museums

Puerto Rico's museums place great emphasis on the colorful history of the island and its people. The island's most famous museum, the **Museo de Arte de Ponce** (see page 203), is primarily devoted to classic paintings which represent schools from around the world. The **Museo de Arte de Puerto Rico** (see page 128) in Santurce houses masterpieces by Puerto Rican artists. San Juan's **Museo de San Juan** (see page 119) depicts the story of the city dating back to the 16th century, while the **Museo de las Américas** (see page 115) houses a collection of items from New England to Mexico, with a strong emphasis on Puerto Rican

life. Most of the island's museums are open daily. Try to plan a museum trip on a weekday, when there are usually fewer visitors.

NIGHTLIFE

The nightlife of Puerto Rico ranges from the tranquillity of coffee and conversation to the steamy, fastlane excesses of San Juan's clubs. On cool nights in the Cordillera, nightlife resembles what Puerto Ricans have probably enjoyed for decades, if not centuries. Townspeople gather round local plazas and sing with guitars, finding time between tunes for a couple of sips of Don Q or Medalla.

San Juan duplicates much of this rural nightlife – on weekends in the Old City, youths mill about the Plaza San José by the hundreds in bars, restaurants, and coffee houses. Note, however, that there is a ban on drinking in the streets in Old San Juan, so you can't enjoy a beer while chilling in the plazas. This is usually lifted during official fiestas and street parties. But in San Juan and other big cities, partying is generally taken with more reckless abandon. The whole city is crowded with bars and dancing establishments of every description.

Bars and Nightclubs

Old San Juan

Los 3 Cuernos
403 San Francisco Street
Tel: 787-242-8666
The name comes from the carnival horned masks adorning the wall. This bar specializes in many flavors of shots, *chichaítos*, and there is music on Wednesdays from 11pm.

What's On

Free publications such as *¡Qué Pasa!* and *Bienvenidos*, usually found at hotels and tourist offices, provide up-to-date information on local nightlife, while www. seepuertorico.com has listings.

Gay and lesbian travelers can check the websites www. puertorico.gaycities.com or www. babylonsanjuan.com for current listings.

Aquí Se Puede
50 San Justo Street
Tel: 787-724-4448
Great bar offering tapas with the drinks. Good music, occasionally live bands. The atmosphere is laid back and relaxed. Daily.

El Batey
101 Cristo Street
Tel: 787-723-7657
Small, loud dive. Great classic rock jukebox. Daily 24 hours.

Brickhaus Sports Bar and Grill
359 Tetuán Street
www.brickhaussportsbars.com
A sports bar with good burgers and delicious wings. Sit at the bar for entertainment from the bartender. They stock microbrewery draft beers, Kofresí (stout), and Old Harbor (pale ale). Daily.

Carli's Fine Bistro And Piano
Corner of Recinto Sur and San Justo streets, Plazoleta Rafael Carrión
Tel: 787-725-4927
www.carlisworld.com
Restaurant and bar with live jazz by former Beach Boys pianist Carli Muñoz. No cover charge except when there are visiting musicians. June–Aug Tue–Sat, Sept–May Mon–Sat; jazz from 7.15pm.

El Farolito
277 Sol Street
Tel: 787-644-0702
Small, local bar, popular with an arty crowd, intimate and welcoming to tourists. Daily.

Nuyorican Café
312 San Francisco Street, entrance through the alleyway
Tel: 787-977-1276
House band plays classic salsa on Wednesday and Friday. Other nights feature Latin jazz, rock, or Latin fusion. Poetry and theater as well. A casual bar and restaurant popular with a diverse crowd. Daily until late.

La Sombrilla Rosa
154 San Sebastián Street
Tel: 787-725-5656
A friendly spot with Medalla at good prices, known for its late-night live

A typical Friday night on Plaza Mercado in Old San Juan.

Ocarinas for sale.

reggae party on Thursdays. Daily.

La Taberna Lúpulo
Sol Street corner Cruz Street
Tel: 787-721-3772
The bar has a large assortment of beers, domestic and imported from around the world, and good music.

Santurce

La Hoja Eco-Bar
1412 Ponce de León Avenue
Tel: 787-403-1175
Good live music: salsa on Thu–Fri, *bomba* on Sat. Wed–Sat 6pm–2am.

La Placita
Historic open-air plaza, during the day a farmers' market; at night the square is filled with young professionals, *fondas*, restaurants, street food, and live music. Thu–Fri.

La Respuesta
1600 Fernández Juncos Avenue, corner Parque Street
Not only a club for hip hop, urban music, and experimental new bands, but also a space for Puerto Rico's underground artists, part of the movement which has put Santurce on the map as the place to come for what's new in artistic expression. Daily.

Tia Maria's
326 José de Diego Avenue, Stop 22
Tel: 787-724-4011
Casual pub with billiards. During business hours there is a mixed heterosexual crowd; after 7pm it attracts an older gay crowd and gets packed. Karaoke Tuesday and Sunday, mixed music Friday and Saturday. Daily, until late Sat–Sun.

Isla Verde

Brava
El San Juan Resort and Casino
6360 Isla Verde Avenue
Tel: 787-791-2781
www.bravapr.com
Elegant yet fun, an old-style disco for night owls aged 18 and over. Some nights are 21 (ladies) or 23

(gentlemen) and over only. Thu–Fri 10am–5am, Sat until 6am.

Brother Jimmy's
El San Juan Resort and Casino
6360 Isla Verde Avenue
Tel: 787-791-1000
Sports bar and grill, part of a New York chain, notable for its huge flat screen TV on the rooftop outdoor deck. Mon–Thu 5–11pm, Fri until 1.30am, Sat 1pm–1.30am, Sun 1–11pm.

The Lobby at El San Juan Resort & Casino
6360 Isla Verde Avenue
Tel: 787-791-1000
It feels as if all of San Juan heads for the lobby on Thursday and Friday nights for salsa and merengue. Dress to impress. Daily.

La Playita
Hotel La Playa
6 Amapola Street
Tel: 787-791-1115
www.hotellaplaya.com
Good wine and drinks at the oceanfront. Exclusive smokers lounge by the bar. Daily.

San Juan Water Beach Club Hotel
2 Tartak Street
Tel: 787-728-3666
www.waterbeachhotel.com
The rooftop bar and lounge, called Mist, features a swimming pool, a spectacular view, signature cocktails, unique decadent food, and music by local and international DJs. Daily.

Hato Rey

Downtown
Avenida Arterial B, Trocadero Diverplex
Tel: 787-523-6666
Nice place to listen to excellent live music and have a beer selected from a wide assortment they stock. Wed–Sun until 2am.

Taberna Boricua
418 Agueybana Street
Tel: 787-640-4499
Beer drinkers' heaven, with over 100 craft beers from around the world to

choose from. Friendly and comfortable with good music. Tue–Sat.

Casinos

Gambling is legal in Puerto Rico and there are over 20 casinos around the island, although mostly in the Metropolitan area. Casinos have blackjack, roulette, poker, slots, and games of chance.

Casinos are permitted only in hotels and usually tend to open from noon until the early hours although several are open daily, round the clock.

Casino del Mar
La Concha Resort
1077 Ashford Avenue, Condado, San Juan
Tel: 787-977-3210
www.laconcharesort.com
A 24-hour lobby-level casino, with high-tech slot machines, gaming tables, and poker daily starting at 6pm.

Casino Metro
Sheraton Puerto Rico Hotel & Casino
200 Convention Boulevard, San Juan
Tel: 787-993-3500
www.sheratonpuertoricohotelcasino.com
Open 24 hours, this is the largest casino in Puerto Rico, where servers ply you with complimentary snacks and drinks (for a tip) and there is live music and entertainment on the Mezzanine Stage.

Casino del Sol
Courtyard by Marriott Isla Verde Beach Resort
7012 Boca de Cangrejos Avenue
Isla Verde, San Juan
Tel: 787-791-0404
www.sjcourtyard.com
Over 400 slot machines, table games, race book, and lottery station. Open 24 hours.

Hilton Ponce Golf & Casino Resort
1150 Ave Caribe, Ponce
Tel: 787-259-7676
www.hiltoncaribbean.com
The only casino on the island to offer a full Baccarat table. Open 24 hours.

Mayagüez Resort and Casino
Route 104, Km 0.3
Tel: 787-832-3030
www.mayaguez.com
Casino with lovely views of the Bay. 364 slot machines, open daily 8am–4am.

Sheraton Old San Juan Hotel
100 Brumbaugh Street, Old San Juan
Tel: 787-721-5100
www.sheratonoldsanjuan.com
Close to the cruise ship piers, this casino offers live music nearly every day and is open 10am–4am.

SHOPPING

Puerto Rico is a great shopping destination. Visitors will find everything from designer wear, jewelry, and local arts and crafts to spirits (rum), coffee, and tobacco.

Old San Juan

For a mix of sightseeing, art galleries, small antique shops and souvenirs, go to Old San Juan. Native handicrafts are good buys, as well as paintings and sculptures by Puerto Rican artists. Among these, the carved wooden religious idols known as *santos* (saints) have been called Puerto Rico's greatest contribution to the plastic arts and are sought by collectors. For the best selection of *santos*, head for Galería Botello, or Puerto Rican Arts and Crafts (204 Fortaleza Street; tel: 787-725-5596; www.puertoricanart-crafts.com).

There are a lot of T-shirt and souvenir shops, especially along Fortaleza Street and closer to the cruise ship ports, but the major shopping venues are on San Francisco and Cristo streets.

Factory stores for Ralph Lauren, Coach, and Gant are all on Cristo Street. And for something different, stop by El Galapón for beautiful masks.

Old San Juan is known as a premier destination for quality jewelry at discount prices, and there are many vendors lining Cristo and Fortaleza streets. Some shops worth entering are **Joyería Riviera** (1 San Geronimo Street; tel: 787-725-4000), **Club Jibarito & Hellenis** (202 Cristo Street; tel: 787-724-7797; www.clubjibarito.

com) and Bared (525 F.D Roosevelt Avenue; tel: 787-754-9393).

Condado

Condado is an oceanfront, pedestrian-oriented community. Famous for high-end shopping, Ashford Avenue features names such as Gucci, Dior, and Ferragamo. Other upscale businesses include Cartier, Louis Vuitton, Mont Blanc, and Zen Spa.

For high fashion, visit Hellmuth. Cristóbal Jewelry is also in the area and specializes in couture jewelry. Verovero represents Prada and Miu Miu bags and shoes, and Suola carries famous designer Valentino. Two other notable boutiques across from the landmark La Concha Hotel are Fashion Fitness and Mia.

Shopping Malls

San Juan boasts the largest shopping center in the Caribbean, **Plaza Las Américas**. (www.plazalasamericas. com). This shopping mecca of more than 300 stores features designer clothing, fine jewelry, pottery, a 13-theater multiplex, and more than 40 dining alternatives. Plaza's anchor stores include Macy's and Sears. It is easy to spend the day here.

Plaza Carolina (www.simon. com) in Isla Verde is a great spot to satisfy mall fever. It is the second-largest shopping center in Puerto Rico. Anchored by JC Penney and Sears, it features over 240 stores. Popular shops include Old Navy, The Children's Place, G by Guess, Aldo Shoes, and bebe.

Puerto Rico has two outlet malls, **the Route 66 Outlet Mall** in

Cigars

Cigars are a good purchase, and there are many shops in Old San Juan. **The Tobacco Shop** at Plaza Las Américas is well stocked, but a bit pricey. **Habana Cuba** (www.habanacubacigar.com) is on San Patricio Avenue in San Patricio, and **International House of Cigars** is on Avenida Miranda in Río Piedras. **El San Juan Resort and Casino** has a "cigar boutique," which sells fine cigars from the Dominican Republic, Honduras, and Jamaica.

Canóvanas and **Premium Outlets** in Barceloneta. The Route 66 Outlet Mall is close to Carolina and the metropolitan area, and minutes away from the hotels and beaches of Río Grande and Fajardo.

This outlet features more than 80 specialty stores and a food court with over a dozen restaurants. Stores such as Gap Outlet, Calvin Klein, Nike Factory Outlet, Tommy Hilfiger, and Skechers populate the 470,000-sq-ft (43,700-sq-meter) shopping mall.

West of San Juan is the other outlet shopping center – Premium Outlets. Located in Barceloneta and easy to reach via Highway 22, this recently expanded center attracts fashion-conscious locals and tourists alike. The village-style center has a retail mix ranging from discount clothing to electronics games stores. Some of the anchor stores are: Gap Outlet and Polo Ralph Lauren Factory Store.

Mall hours are standard: 9am to 9pm Monday to Saturday and 11am to 5pm on Sundays. Shopping centers with movie theaters have extended food court hours and stand-alone restaurants open later as well. Shops in Condado and Old San Juan tend to close earlier, between 6pm and 7pm.

What to Buy

Books

The following have a good selection of books in both English and Spanish:
Beta Book Café
Plaza Las Americas
Tel: 787-725-0592
Bookworm
1129 Ashford Avenue, Condado
Tel: 787-722-3344
Castle Books
San Patricio Shopping Center
Tel: 787-774-1790
La Tertulia
251 Cruz Street, Old San Juan
Tel: 787-724-8200

Souvenirs from El Yunque rainforest gift shop.

SPORTS

Participant Sports

Golf and Tennis

Golf courses and tennis courts are scattered throughout the island, though most of the better ones are in the large, more expensive resorts. A variety of hotels sometimes allow access to non-guests for a reasonable fee. For a list of courts at resorts and tennis clubs, see www.tennispoint.com. For the 26 golf courses, see www.worldgolf.com and www.carribean.golf.com.

Resorts with 18-hole championship golf courses include:
Embassy Suites Dorado del Mar
Dorado
Tel: 787-796-6125
www.embassysuitesdorado.com
Palmas del Mar
Humacao
Tel: 787-656-3015
www.palmaspac.com
Wyndham Río Mar
Río Grande
Tel: 800-474-6627
www.wyndhamriomar.com

Spectator Sports

Baseball and Basketball

Puerto Rico's national pastime is baseball (see page 87). The island has produced some of the great stars of the game.

The Puerto Rico Baseball League season runs from November to February, with teams in Caguas, Ponce, Mayagüez, and Carolina. The schedule can be found on http://mlb.mlb.com/mlb/events/winterleagues.

Many aspiring big-leaguers (and not a few has-beens) play in Puerto Rico. Games are almost daily, and tickets generally inexpensive. Those who want to keep abreast of American and National Leagues will find complete box scores in the local papers. Also, cable TV brings a variety of big-league games.

Basketball is another popular team sport. The Superior Basketball League has teams in almost all the larger cities.

Cockfighting

For a truly Puerto Rican sporting experience, cockfighting is hard to match. Although the sport is viewed as inhumane by many, its popularity on the island cannot be denied. In this sport, dozens of the proudest local cocks are matched one-on-one in a tiny ring, or *gallera*. The predominantly male crowds are almost as interesting as the fights themselves. These knowledgeable enthusiasts are familiar with a cock's pedigree through several generations. The shouts are deafening, the drinking is reckless, and the betting is heavy. Betting is done on a gentlemanly system of verbal agreement, and hundreds of dollars can change hands on a single fight.

Galleras are scattered all over, there are well over 100 and the fights in even the most rural areas can draw hundreds of people. Admission can be expensive, but the beer is cheap. For information on cockfighting in the San Juan area:
Club Gallístico de Puerto Rico
Isla Verde Avenue, Isla Verde
Tel: 787-791-1557
Club Gallístico Río Piedras
Route 844, Km 4.2, Trujillo Alto
Tel: 787-760-6815

Horse Racing

Horse racing in San Juan is at the **Camarero Racetrack** in Canóvanas, 10 miles (16km) east of the city. For more information on races, tel: 787-641-6060 or visit www.hipodromo-camarero.com.

Outdoor Activities

Adventure Sports

Acampa
1221 Ave Piñero
San Juan
Tel: 787-706-0695
www.acampapr.com
River hiking, waterfall climbing, and ziplines in a private reserve in Toro Negro Forest or Mucaro Reserve on the edge of the Carite Forest.
Aventuras Tierra Adentro
268A Avenida Jesús T. Piñero
Urb University Gardens
San Juan
Tel: 787-766-0470
www.aventuraspr.com
Canyoning and caving, including rappelling, climbing, swimming, free jumps, body rafting, and ziplines. Also rock climbing, and rope and rescue school.
Culebra Island Adventures
Tel: 787-529-3536
www.culebraislandadventures.com
Kayaking and snorkeling tours on Culebra island.
Rocaliza
Tel: 787-268-0101
www.rocaliza.com
Adventure tours including rock climbing, rappelling, ziplining, river trekking, and hiking.
Xtreme Divers
Tel: 787-852-5757
www.xtremedivers.com
Skydiving for beginners and experienced free-fallers, with tandem flights and courses using the airports at Arecibo and Humacao.

Birdwatching

Amateur and professional birdwatching guides can be contacted through Birdingpal, www.birdingpal.org/Puertorico.htm.
Birding Puerto Rico by Adventours
257 Aduana Street
Mayagüez
Tel: 787-530-8311
www.adventourspr.com
Half-, full-, or multiple-day trips and all-inclusive tours with accommodations covering east and west Puerto Rico.
Ornithological Society of Puerto Rico (Sociedad Ornitológica Puertorriqueña Inc – SOPI)
www.avesdepuertorico.org
Occasional birdwatching trips and the people to contact if you want to be involved with the Christmas bird count and other bird surveys.

Cycling/Mountain Biking

Club Cicloturismo de Puerto Rico
Tel: 787-755-7122
Contact for road and velodrome races, and non-competitive cycling meets. They organize varied routes of all distances and terrains to suit anyone.

For information on mountain bike trails, see www.singletracks.com or www.mtb-pr.com. Guided tours can be arranged with Puerto Rico Mountain Bike Tours, www.prmtbtour.blogspot.com.

Freshwater Fishing

Government fishing regulations require recreational fishing licenses for freshwater fishing (valid for one day, one week or one year) and establish size limits and daily quotas of several species. However, if you charter a boat with a captain, he will arrange the license. Reservoirs are managed by the Department of Natural and Environmental Resources (DNER). Some have facilities including boat ramps, information centers and restrooms. For reservoir fishing regulations or for directions to the facilities, call the DNER's Reserves and Refuges Division, tel: 787-999-2200, ext. 2713.

There are numerous clubs devoted to freshwater fishing in the island's

Saddled up ready to go.

man-made lakes and reservoirs. Bass, both large-mouth (*lobina*) and peacock (*tucunare*), are local favorites, though at least four other species like sunfish, tilapia, and catfish are sought after as well. The reservoirs are stocked with fish from the Maricao Fish Hatchery (Los Viveros).

Peacock Bass and Tarpon Tours
Tel: 787-364-6000
www.peacockbassandtarpontours.com
Freshwater fishing charters.

Saltwater Fishing

Saltwater fishing, in particular deep-sea fishing, is also popular, with several billfish tournaments held off the coast. Shallow-water fishing is also practiced on the island, and there's excellent tarpon fishing. For shallow-water fishing, take a skiff to the coastal mangroves. There is also good shallow-water fishing off Culebra.

For deep-sea fishing, boats can be chartered in San Juan, Fajardo, and Arecibo, which are close to the Atlantic's Puerto Rico Trench, dubbed Blue Marlin Alley. Today, most caught marlin are tagged and released. To fish wahoo, head to deep waters off Humacao. For tuna, head to the Mona Passage on boats departing from Rincón, Mayagüez, Cabjo Rojo, and La Parguera. The best months to catch blue marlin are August and September, while yellow and blackfin tuna, wahoo, and bonito have their own seasons.

If you are on a charter boat you do not need to buy a fishing permit as that will be handled by the captain or boat owner. Spear fishing is banned.

Deep-sea and shallow-water fishing charters are available from:

Adventures Tourmarine
Cabo Rojo
Tel: 787-255-2525
www.tourmarinepr.com

Caribbean Outfitters
Carolina
Tel: 787-501-3171
www.fishinginpuertorico.com

Castillo Tours and Watersports
San Juan
Tel: 787-791-6195
www.castillotours.com

Light Tackle Adventure Fishing
Cabo Rojo
Tel: 787-849-1430
www.lighttackleadventure.8k.com

Parguera Fishing Charters
La Parguera
Tel: 787-382-4698
www.puertoricofishingcharters.com

Tropical Fishing and Snorkeling Charters
Fajardo
Tel: 787-382-9012
www.tropicalfishingcharters.com

Hiking

There are several hiking trails in Puerto Rico and a great number afford spectacular vistas. There are particularly good hikes in the Caribbean National Forest at El Yunque, as well as in the Guánica State Forest and on Mona Island. Río Camuy Cave Park and Las Cabezas de San Juan Nature Reserve have what are considered walks rather than hikes, but are still enjoyable. The Puerto Rico Department of Natural Resources in San Juan (tel: 787-999-2200, ext. 5156) can provide more information on many of the country's trails. See *Adventure Sports*, above, for companies offering guided hiking tours.

Horse Riding

Hacienda Carabalí
Luquillo
Tel: 787-889-4954
www.carabalirainforestpark.com
With Paso Fino horses and an excellent reputation, this rainforest park also organizes ATV rides, mountain biking, and go-kart racing. Popular with cruise ship tours.

Rancho Buena Vista
Palmas del Mar Resort, Humacao
Tel: 787-479-7479
www.ranchobuenavistapr.com
Upscale ranch with beautiful Paso Fino horses. Rides designed for beginners, intermediate, and advanced; also pony rides for children.

Tropical Trail Rides
Isabela and Hacienda Campo Rico, San Juan
Tel: 787-872-9256
www.tropicaltrailrides.com
Horseback riding through countryside, forest, and on beaches. Thirty horses available. They also do ATV rides and dune buggy safaris.

Kayaking

Kayaks are an ecologically-friendly way of exploring the island's mangroves and its coast. They are also an excellent way to check out the stunning bioluminescent bays in Vieques and Fajardo. Companies that rent kayaks or offer tours include the following:

Kayaking Puerto Rico
Fajardo
Tel: 787-435-1665
www.kayakingpuertorico.com
Kayaking and snorkeling on the main island and on Culebra, bio-bay tours, beach tours, and hiking.

San Juan Waterfun
Isla Verde Beach, San Juan
Tel: 787-643-4510
Kayaks, catamarans, parasailing, and banana boat rides.

Las Tortugas Adventures
Tel: 787-809-0253
www.kayak-pr.com
River and coastal kayaking and Laguna Grande bio-bay tours for private groups.

Travesías Isleñas Yaureibo
Vieques
Tel: 939-630-1267
www.viequesoutdoors.com
Kayaking, biking, hiking, snorkeling, and tours.

Yokahú Kayak Trips
Fajardo
Tel: 787-604-7375
www.yokahukayaks.com
Bio-bay kayaking tour or reef and beach kayaking and snorkeling tour.

Sailing

There are some 20 marinas around the island, see www.caribya.com/puerto.rico/sailing.and.boating for a list. Most of Puerto Rico's sailors head to Fajardo or Ponce for weekends on the water. Try one of the charter companies below:

Ponce Yacht and Fishing Club
Tel: 787-842-9003
Puerto del Rey Marina
Fajardo
Tel: 787-860-1000
www.puertodelrey.com
Ventajero Sailing Charters
Fajardo
Tel: 787-645-9129
www.sailpuertorico.com
A 52ft (16-meter) charter sailing vessel

Scuba Diving and Snorkeling

Puerto Rico is prime scuba territory. Visibility around the main island can sometimes be affected by the outflow from rivers, particularly after heavy rain, but that does not apply around Vieques and Culebra, nor around Mona and Desecheo, where it is excellent. Vieques and Culebra are easily accessible, but Mona and Desecheo are isolated in the Mona Passage, reached only by charter boat or private yacht. Landing on Desecheo is forbidden because of unexploded ordnance. The flip side is that the estuaries of the main island attract a large number of fish and other creatures of the sea, including manatee. Humpback whales can be seen to the west of the island on their migrations. In the southwest, The Wall is 22 miles (35km) long stretching down over 2,000ft (610 meters) and is covered in healthy coral, home to a wide range of fish and other creatures.

There are many dive operators all round Puerto Rico, some attached to resorts or marinas, and all offer snorkeling. Those on the east coast offer safaris to Vieques and Culebra, but you should be prepared for a long boat ride and you may prefer to stay on the smaller islands and dive with a local company. Check the size of the party you will be diving with. Companies dealing with the cruise ship market take out dozens of divers and snorkelers at a time while others work with small groups. Note also that fish feeding is not recommended, as it encourages the aggressive species and upsets the balance of nature. Some operators offer sailing, snorkeling, and fishing in addition to scuba diving. Spear fishing is banned.

Culebra Divers
Dewey
Tel: 787-742-0803
www.culebradivers.com
Snorkeling and diving for small groups. Fifty dive sites within a 30- to 40-minute boat ride from the dock. Courses available.

Dive Copamarina
Copamarina Beach Resort & Spa
Guanica
Tel: 787-821-0505
www.copamarina.com
Boat dives in the southwest and along the south coast, a full service resort. The Wall here is 22 miles (35km) long stretching down over 2,000ft (610 meters) and is covered in healthy coral, home to a wide range of fish and other creatures.

Puerto Rico Technical Divers
Aguadilla
Tel: 787-997-3483
www.technicaldivingpr.com
Covers everything from recreational and technical diving courses to guided beach and boat dives.

Sea Ventures Fajardo Dive Center
Fajardo
Tel: 787-863-3483
www.divepuertorico.com
Snorkeling and diving off the east coast and off Culebra. A PADI five-star dive center.

Taíno Divers
Black Eagle Marina, Rincón
Tel: 787-823-6429
www.tainodivers.com
Daily diving and snorkeling trips to Desecheo Island. Whale-watching, fishing, and custom cruises. SUDS program for disabled soldiers.

Surfing

Puerto Rico has almost ideal conditions for surfing – warm water, brilliant sunshine, and heavy but even tubular surf. Many of the most popular spots are convenient to San Juan: Aviones, off Route 187 in Piñones, is probably the most renowned, and so named because of the airplanes that fly over from the nearby international airport. La Ocho, in Puerta de Tierra's Escambrón Beach, is also popular and crowded on weekends. The best surfing, however, is in the northwest, with surf spots stretching from Isabela to Rincón (see www.surfingpuertorico. com), convenient for the airport at Aguadilla. Punta Higüero, off Route 413 in Rincón, is famous, while Jobos Beach proves popular among Aguadilla and Isabela residents. The Rincón Surf Report, www.rinconsurfreport.com, gives daily reports and forecasts on surf and waves.

Swimming

Puerto Rico has sandy beaches, some crowded, others secluded and quiet. Many are *balnearios* with public bathing facilities that include lifeguards, refreshment stands, and dressing rooms. Around San Juan most popular are Luquillo and Vega Baja. All beach front, except the beach at the Caribe Hilton, is public, although some resorts make it difficult for non-residents to get to the beach through their property.

Swimmers are advised to be careful of strong surf and undertow at beaches, especially in the northwest. Only swim where you see other people swimming. Jobos Beach is notorious for drownings.

Windsurfing, Kiteboarding, and Paddleboarding

Windsurfing and kiteboarding are popular island-wide. Ocean Park in San Juan and La Parguera are ideal places to practice both sports. Rentals and lessons are available. And then there is paddleboarding...

GoodWinds
Dorado Beach Resort, San Juan
Tel: 787-233-7862
www.kitegoodwinds.com
Kiteboarding PR
Ocean Park, San Juan
Tel: 787-215-5667
www.kiteboardingpr.com
Vela Uno Paddleboarding
Punta las Marías, San Juan
Tel: 787-728-8716
www.velaunopaddleboarding.com

Health Clubs and Spas

Bodyderm Spa
Copamarina Beach Resort,
Guánica
Tel: 787-821-0505
www.copamarina.com
Golden Door Spa at Las Casitas Village
El Conquistador Resort, Fajardo
Tel: 787-863-1000, ext. 7300
www.elconresort.com
Mandara Spa
Wyndham Río Mar Beach, Golf and Resort Spa, Río Grande
Tel: 787-888-6000
www.wyndhamriomar.com
The Spa at Condado Vanderbilt Hotel
1055 Ashford Avenue, Condado
Tel: 787-977-6710
www.condadovanderbilt.com
The Ritz-Carlton Spa
Ritz-Carlton Hotel, Isla Verde
Tel: 787-253-1700
www.ritzcarlton.com
Zen Spa and Health Studio
1054 Ashford Avenue, Condado
Tel: 787-722-8433
www.zen-spa.com
Also in Plaza las Américas, Guaynabo, and Mayagüez

A – Z

A HANDY SUMMARY
OF PRACTICAL INFORMATION

A

Accommodations

Puerto Rico has a wide range of accommodations available. Parts of the coast are dominated by big resorts, but bed and breakfast places, guesthouses, beach houses, boutique hotels, and camping grounds, as well as a host of less conventional settings, complete the picture.

The island's large and splashy beach resorts come in two main varieties. The first comprises pricey beach front resorts with casinos, plenty of bars, and fine restaurants, as well as beautiful golf courses. Each is characterized by excellent sports facilities such as large swimming pools, well-maintained tennis courts, a gym, spa, and long stretches of beach. All the major US chains are represented here, including Hilton, Radisson, Ritz Carlton, Marriott, InterContinental, and Sheraton.

The second type is less lavish and tends to be only half as expensive. These include the white high-rises of San Juan's Condado and Isla Verde areas, which cater to a mix of holidaymakers and business people. They are likely to be less well maintained and the quality of service can be patchy.

Guesthouses tend to be less costly and more intimate than the big resorts, with around a dozen rooms. Many have beach front locations, about half have bars, and almost all have swimming pools. There may not be a restaurant on site, but there are always several within walking distance.

If you prefer to be independent, renting an apartment or condominium is a good self-catering option.

HomeAway (www.homeaway.com) and Vrbo (www.vrbo.com) vacation rentals have comprehensive listings of condominiums available in Puerto Rico.

Avoid shady hotels, and play it safe by sticking to the list endorsed by the Puerto Rico Tourism Company (www.seepuertorico.com).

The *parador* presents a unique lodging option in Puerto Rico. *Paradores* are small, privately owned hotels participating in a special government program that is supposed to assure a certain level of quality. Some of these family-run country inns are old coffee or sugar haciendas in scenic areas and offer the authentic ambience of Puerto Rican rural life. Beautiful old furniture and elegant dining facilities add to their appeal. Rates are mostly reasonable, often around $70–150 per night for a double room, and the food is usually much better than what you may find at nearby restaurants.

Be warned, however, many have declined drastically and some *paradores* have a distinctly utilitarian flavor with dormitory-style rooms. It pays to do a little research. Try to obtain photos of and recommendations for the establishment before making a reservation.

From the US mainland, *parador* reservations can be made through a central toll-free number: 800-866-7827. In Puerto Rico, call 800-981-7575 (toll-free). The Puerto Rico Tourism Company ((www.seepuertorico.com) has a list of certified *paradores*.

Admission Charges

The average museum admission is $5 for adults, but many museums and galleries in Puerto Rico are free of charge. Some nightclubs and pubs have admission fees, between $10 and $15, if there is a live band. Some nights women enter free. Public beaches administered by the National Parks Company also charge a small fee for parking ($2 for motorcycles, $3–4 for cars, and $4 for vans), but pedestrians can enter free of charge. Reduced or free admission is widely available for children and seniors (60 and up) at museums, movie theaters, and top attractions.

B

Budgeting for Your Trip

Food is one of the things people spend the most money on while on vacation. A typical meal at a moderately priced restaurant can average $20–25 per person for an appetizer, entrée, and dessert. A glass of wine will set you back between $6 and $9. Domestic and imported beers cost around $5 and desserts $6.

An evening at an all-inclusive resort is around $400 per person, but staying at a country inn or urban villa is between $70 and $120.

A taxi ride from Luis Muñoz Marín International Airport in Isla Verde to a hotel in zone 2 is $10, to zone 3 (Ocean Park, Condado, Miramar) $15, to zone 4 (Old San Juan and cruise ship piers) $19, and to zone 5 (Convention Center) $15, but there are extra charges for luggage, extra passengers, tolls, and at night. Bus admission is $0.75 or $0.50 and Urban Train rides are $1.50, $0.75 for seniors and children. Car rental rates average at $40 for the day.

Keeping Puerto Rico safe.

C

Children

Puerto Rico is a family-friendly destination, and many hotels offer family discounts and children's programs. These may include babysitting services and camp-like activities such as nature hikes, art workshops, and tennis lessons. For older kids, activities can include surfing and scuba-diving lessons, Spanish courses, and dance classes.

Most restaurants offer a children's menu, and some have special offers where children can eat for free.

Climate

Puerto Rico has one of the most pleasant and unvarying climates in the world, with daily highs almost invariably at 70–85°F (9–21°C). The island is at its wettest and hottest in August, with 7ins (18cm) the average monthly rainfall and 82°F (28°C) the average daily high. During the rainy season, sudden late-afternoon squalls are common.

Regional variations are noticeable: Ponce and the southern coast are warmer and drier than San Juan and the north. It is coldest in the higher altitudes of the Cordillera, where the lowest temperature in the island's history was recorded near Barranquitas: 39°F (4°C).

Average daily high temperatures for San Juan range from 75°F (24°C) in January and February to 82°F (28°C) from June through September.

High season in the Caribbean runs from Christmas to Easter, when the weather is at its most pleasant, warm, and dry. However, the north coast of Puerto Rico is sometimes affected by a cold front coming down from the eastern seaboard of the US, when it can feel quite chilly and windy, and the sea can be rough. This is, however, an advantage for surfers and windsurfers. The south coast is more protected, drier, and good at any time of year, although it gets very hot in the summer months. Some people avoid hurricane season, the worst months usually being September and October. Travelers who seek lower hotel rates and less crowded beaches prefer this time of year.

What to Wear/Bring

Puerto Rican dressing is casual yet mostly conservative: jeans, shorts, and long trousers are common. Only in a very small number of clubs are jackets and ties really required. However, shed the shorts and tennis shoes when you go out at night, as Puerto Ricans like to dress up. Colorful, medium-length dresses are versatile evening wear for women. Anything more than a light sweater is seldom necessary, even on winter nights in the Cordillera. An umbrella will come in handy, especially in rainy late summer on the island's northern coast.

However, a high-factor sunscreen and a hat are essential for those who plan to spend even a minimal amount of time outdoors.

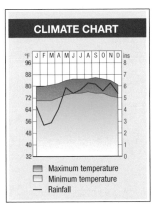

CLIMATE CHART

	Maximum temperature
	Minimum temperature
—	Rainfall

Crime and Safety

The serious crime rate in Puerto Rico is high, but this does not usually affect tourists. Nearly all crime is in San Juan and Ponce, big cities with busy ports where there is a substantial drug trade with consequent gang activity. Tourists are advised to stay away from poorer areas such as public housing complexes (*caseríos*) and slums (La Perla in San Juan). Tourist areas are patrolled by police and violent crime against tourists is very rare. However, travelers would be wise to take precautions, such as staying in well-lit and populated areas when walking at night.

Petty theft and confidence scams are more prevalent than violent crimes. Always lock your room, especially in smaller lodgings. Never leave luggage unattended or out of your sight. Most hotels will store bags at the front desk, as will many restaurants and shops. Never leave any valuables in your room. It is advisable to leave your room key at the front desk when you go out. Never leave your belongings unattended on the beach.

Always lock automobiles, regardless of whether you have left any valuables inside, as the radios that come with most rented vehicles are valuable, easily sellable and much coveted by thieves. If you do leave valuables in a vehicle, place them out of sight.

Travelers checks and credit cards are accepted, so there is no reason to carry more cash than you need.

Puerto Rico has an island-wide emergency number: 911. Most dispatchers understand some English. For a full list of emergency numbers, see page 260.

Customs Regulations

Customs regulations resemble those of the United States, and are carried out with similar thoroughness. Non-residents over the age of 21 may bring in 1 liter of alcohol and 200 cigarettes. Prohibited items for anyone entering the country include meat, whether fresh, dried or canned, narcotics, absinthe (or other alcohols containing *Artemisia absinthium*), plants, seeds, vegetables, fruit, soil, livestock, animal pests, fish and fish eggs, imports from embargoed countries (e.g. Cuba), leather souvenirs from Haiti, endangered wildlife species and products thereof, ancient cultural artifacts from pre-Columbian period and others, dog and cat fur, or items infringing trade and copyright regulations. Restricted items include firearms (advance clearance required), pets (cats and dogs must have a health certificate and a rabies vaccination certificate; birds must have a certificate stating they are free of psittcosis or ornithosis), medication (to be sufficient only for your visit, labeled and in original packaging, preferably with a prescription or letter from your physician). There are no restrictions on the export of tobacco or alcohol when you leave the country, although you should check your own country's allowances. Items which are prohibited or restricted on entry are also prohibited or restricted on departure.

These stipulations apply to those traveling to and from the United States as well. For more information: call the **Transportation Security Administration** (TSA), tel: 787-253-4591, or the **US Department of Agriculture**, tel: 787-253-4651; Puerto Rican Customs tel: 787-766-6050.

Duty-free shops are open for all international flights, and for flights to the United States and US possessions in the Caribbean.

D

Disabled Travelers

The Americans with Disabilities Act (ADA) applies to all public facilities in Puerto Rico. Most businesses can accommodate travelers with disabilities.

For general information or to file complaints, call the local Ombudsman for Persons with Disabilities, tel: 800-981-4125; 787-725-2333. The hearing-impaired can call 787-725-4012 or 787-725-0613. The central office of the Ombudsman for Persons with Disabilities is located at 670 Ponce de León Avenue, Caribbean Office Plaza, second floor, Miramar.

Regional offices are also in Aguada, Arecibo, Humacao, and Ponce.

The Office of the Ombudsman for Persons with Disabilities has a guide of locations and services that can accommodate handicapped travelers, including hotels, *paradores*, vacation centers, restaurants, sights, transportation, and medical services. The guide is available at the central office in Miramar, or it can be mailed if requested.

It is recommended that you call your accommodations ahead of time to verify that they accommodate handicapped travelers.

Parking for disabled travelers is available in most places, and many towns have ramps that accommodate wheelchairs. However, Old San Juan is known as a difficult place to navigate for travelers in wheelchairs. As of this writing, ferry services were also not accessible to those in wheelchairs.

The public beaches of Luquillo and Boquerón have wheelchair-accessible facilities.

Some of the trolleys in Old San Juan are wheelchair accessible, as are some of the AMA buses. There are no hire cars adapted to take wheelchairs. Special Needs At Sea rents out medical and other equipment for disabled travelers on cruises or staying at hotels, tel. 800-513-4515, www.specialneedsatsea.com.

E

Embassies and Consulates

Because Puerto Rico is not an independent nation, it cannot conduct diplomatic relations with anyone. Hence, there are no embassies in San Juan – but plenty of consulates and honorary consulates. These are listed in the yellow pages of the phone book under *Consulados* and in

Electricity

The voltage in Puerto Rico is the same as in the mainland United States (110 volts, 60 cycles AC).

the directory's "Newcomers' Guide," found between the yellow and white pages. You may also call the State Department's Service for the Foreign Citizen, tel: 787-723-2727.

Consulates include:
Canada, Hato Rey Center, 268 Ponce de León Avenue, Suite 1111, San Juan, tel: 787-759-6629. **UK**, (Virtual) Honorary Consulate, tel: 787-850-2400.

Emergency Numbers

San Juan

Emergency 911
Police 787-343-2020
Fire Department 787-343-2330
Medical Center of Puerto Rico 787-777-3535
Medical Emergencies 787-754-2550
US Coast Guard 787-729-6770
Rape Hotline 787-765-2285; 800-656-4673
Poison Control Center 787-726-5660; 800-222-1222
American Red Cross 787-759-7979
Operator/Information 411

Etiquette

Puerto Ricans are lively, friendly, and hospitable. Don't be surprised if a group of locals becomes noisy and boisterous while talking, particularly when discussing island politics; it is rarely as argumentative as foreigners assume. Puerto Ricans are also known for gesturing animatedly with their hands while they talk.

Upon meeting one another, Puerto Ricans like to shake hands, then give one kiss on the cheek, and they always greet each other with "*Buenos días*" ("Good morning"), "*Buenas tardes*" (Good afternoon), or "*Buenas noches*" (Good evening), also said upon parting company. It is common when walking to your table in a restaurant to greet fellow diners with "*buen provecho*," and waiters will probably say the same to you on serving your food. If visiting a church or other place of worship, women should cover their shoulders and dress appropriately, with long pants or a modest skirt, while men should also wear shirts and long pants. Beachwear is only for the beach.

El Capitolio, home of Puerto Rico's legislature.

Catching up on local news.

G

Gay and Lesbian Travelers

Attitudes towards gays and lesbians in Puerto Rico are similar to those in the States, though less accepting than in cities like New York City, Miami, and San Francisco.

San Juan is the more gay-friendly area of the island, with many bars, restaurants, and hotels in Condado, Ocean Park, and Old San Juan owned by gays and lesbians. Many have "gay nights." The beach at Ocean Park especially attracts gay travelers.

The first Sunday in June features a gay pride parade in Condado, as well as many activities in the week leading up to it.

Other areas that welcome gays and lesbians are Boquerón (southwest), Fajardo (northeast), and the small islands of Vieques and Culebra.

For listings of gay-friendly bars, accommodations, and places to go, visit www.puertorico.gaycities.com or www.babylonsanjuan.com where you will find a guide to gay bars and clubs.

H

Health and Medical Care

Puerto Rico's health care resembles that of the United States in that it has no national health service, and the sick and infirm are cared for on a pay-as-you-go basis. All travelers should take out health insurance to cover them for any eventuality while away from home.

Most hospitals have 24-hour emergency rooms but, if possible, check the yellow pages of the telephone book under *Hospitales*, or

search for *sala emergencia* in www.superpagespr.com. Pharmacies carry a full range of US prescription drugs and can offer advice on medical terms. The Spanish word for prescription is *receta*. In addition to independent pharmacies, the dozens of Walgreens around the island have pharmacy counters.

Puerto Rico is full of competent medical professionals. If you could choose where to fall ill, you would doubtless elect San Juan, as the number of universities and clinics there make it full of doctors and medical personnel. Still, facilities in other areas, though often old and disheartening, are generally run by capable physicians and nurses.

Listed below are some of the larger hospitals with emergency rooms and some 24-hour pharmacies. For listings in provincial cities, check the yellow pages in the phone book.

Hospitals

The island's major hospitals are located in and around San Juan.
Ashford Presbyterian Community Hospital
1451 Avenue Ashford, Condado
Tel: 787-721-2160
Hospital Auxilio Mutuo
Avenida Ponce de León, Hato Rey
Tel: 787-758-2000
Hospital Pavía
1462 Professor Augusto Rodriguez, Santurce
Tel: 787-727-6060
Hospital San Pablo
70 Santa Cruz Street, Bayamón
Tel: 787-620-4747
Río Piedras Medical Center Central Emergency Room
Américo Miranda Avenue, Río Piedras
Tel: 787-777-3535
San Jorge Children's Hospital
258 San Jorge Street, Santurce
Tel: 787-727-1000

Pharmacies

Walgreens
Mayagüez Mall, Mayagüez
Tel: 787-831-9251
Farmacias El Amal
Valle Real Shopping Center, Ponce
Tel: 787-844-5555
Walgreens
Fagot Avenue, Ponce
Tel: 787-841-2135
Walgreens
1130 Ashford Avenue, Condado, San Juan
Tel: 787-725-1510

Special Considerations

Puerto Rico has few dangerous bacteria and diseases, but one deserves a special mention. Almost all

of the island's rivers are infected with schistosomes, parasitic flatworms that cause the condition schistosomiasis (bilharzia), which can lead to severe damage to internal organs.

Some people say that river water is safe to drink and swim in on the upper altitudes of mountains, provided it is running swiftly, but this guide does not recommend it. Tap water is safe, however.

Dengue fever is also a risk. Use plenty of insect repellent, wear long sleeves and pants if you know there are mosquitoes around and use a mosquito net at night, as the only way to avoid dengue is to avoid being bitten by the *Aedes aegypti* mosquito.

No vaccinations are required, but Hepatitis A, polio and tetanus are recommended. See your doctor four to six weeks before traveling in case you need immunizations. For further information see the US government site: http://wwwnc.cdc.gov/travel/destinations/puerto-rico.

I

Internet

Most of the larger hotels provide guests with internet access either in their rooms or at least in a communal area. Shopping centers usually have free Wi-fi access, such as the food court of San Patricio Shopping Center in Guaynabo. Various restaurants and fast-food chains also offer free Wi-fi (Starbucks, Denny's, McDonald's, and Burger King). More downtown centers are making Wi-fi available, and the list is growing. In Old San Juan, all the plazas have Wi-fi.

Internet cafés are not very common on the island. Try **Internet@ctive**, between Pier 3 and Pier 4 in Covadonga Parking, Old San Juan, and on Isla Verde Avenue, in Cond. Los Corales, opposite KFC.

L

Lost Property

To contact the Luis Muñoz Marín International Airport police, call 787-791-0098.

For property left in taxis, call the Tourism Transportation booths in the Luis Muñoz Marín International Airport, tel: 787-253-0418, or email: lostandfound@prtourism.com or transportationclaims@prtourism.com.

To report lost or stolen credit cards and travelers checks, call:

Most stores stay open until 9pm.

American Express, tel: 800-327-1267
MasterCard, tel: 800-307-7309
Visa, tel: 800-847-2911

If you lose your US passport, call the State Department, tel: 787-722 2121; other nationalities should contact the relevant consulate (see page 260).

For property left on airplanes or in the airline area, call the airline directly.

M

Media

Print

Puerto Ricans are avid readers of periodical literature, and the national dailies, published in San Juan, cover the spectrum of political opinion.

Of the Spanish papers, *El Nuevo Día* publishes seven days a week and has the highest circulation on the island. Its sister publication, *Primera Hora* has a more populist slant and mass appeal. It publishes Monday through Saturday. A meaty tabloid with special features and arts excerpts, *El Vocero*, is a trim paper with more local news. Puerto Rico produces few magazines, but gets most of the weeklies from the United States and Spain. American newspapers are available here on the day of publication: in Spanish, *Diario Las Américas*, published in Miami; in English, *The New York Times*, *The New York Post*, *The Miami Herald*, and *The Wall Street Journal*.

Television and Radio

Puerto Rico has more than 100 radio stations, including the English-language WOSO (1030 on the AM dial), which is quite versatile, combining fine local coverage with network news. English-language WBMI is a religious station, and the St Thomas station may be picked up by some radios, particularly in the eastern part of Puerto Rico. Recommended Spanish music stations are Radio Uno and, on FM, Radio Fidelity.

The island has at least half a dozen Spanish-language TV stations of its own, but there are no English-language stations, save for the offerings on cable and satellite TV, which come from the United States and include all the American television networks. The government station, WIPR, broadcasts local programs in Spanish and some Public Broadcasting Service (PBS) programs in English.

Money

All business in Puerto Rico is transacted in US dollars, and visitors are advised to buy travelers checks in that currency if you prefer not to carry cash or withdraw money from cash machines. Travelers checks are accepted all over the island.

Most restaurants, hotels, and stores in well-traveled areas accept the following cards: American Express, MasterCard, Visa, Carte Blanche, Discovery, and Diners Club.

The Banco Popular at the Luis Muñoz Marín International Airport provides currency exchange, tel: 787-791-0326.

Banking

Puerto Rico is the banking center of the Caribbean Basin and as such has branches of almost all of the leading North American banks, as well as many European and Puerto Rican institutions. ATMs (called ATH – *aa-teh-acheh* – in Puerto Rico) are installed in most towns around the island.

Tipping

Puerto Rico has a service economy resembling that of the United States, and this means tipping for most services received.

Some hotels and hotel restaurants include a 15–17 percent service charge to the bill, so always check your bill.

Otherwise, follow the American rules of thumb: 15 percent in restaurants, including *fondas* and *colmados* but not fast-food joints; 10 percent in bars; 10–15 percent for cab drivers, hairdressers, and other services.

One dollar per bag is a good rule for hotel porters, and a few bucks should keep the person who cleans your room happy.

O

Opening Hours

Business hours follow the US rather than the Latin tradition, and the afternoon siesta is generally not practiced. Most stores are open Monday to Saturday 9am–9pm, banks Monday to Friday 8.30am–4.30pm; certain branches of each bank may open on Saturday and evenings. Most post offices are open from Monday to Friday 8am–5pm and on Saturday 8am–noon. Some selected stores of major supermarket chains are open 24 hours a day, seven days a week.

P

Postal Services

Puerto Rican postal services are administered by the US Postal Service. Regulations and tariffs are the same as those on the mainland. Stamps may be purchased at any post office. They may also be bought from vending machines in hotels, stores, and airports.

The US Postal Service Authorized Abbreviation for Puerto Rico is PR. Visit www.usps.com.

United Parcel Service (UPS) and Federal Express (FedEx) also provide services in Puerto Rico, as do some private mail-service centers.

Phone numbers for the main mail carriers are:
Federal Express, tel: 800-463-3339
General US Postal Office (information), tel: 787-622-1756
UPS, tel: 800-742-5877

Public Toilets

Restrooms are identified as such in English or in Spanish as *baños*. If identified in Spanish, the ladies' room is marked with *Damas* and the men's room with *Caballeros*.

Some public restrooms are better maintained than others, but a general rule of thumb is not to sit on the toilet seat. Many times you will not find toilet paper in public restrooms, except in good restaurants and larger hotels, so it's always a good idea to carry tissue paper or napkins with you just in case.

All of the public beaches administered by the country's National Parks Company have public restrooms.

R

Religious Services

Puerto Rican history is steeped in religion, particularly the Roman Catholic tradition, as the Spanish monarchs at the time of colonization sent *conquistadores* along with priests to convert their new territories.

Roman Catholics still make up the majority of the population, approximately 85 percent, while Protestant churches and other groups represent about 15 percent of the population. Most religious denominations on the island offer services in English. For more information, check the listings on the yellow pages under *Iglesias* or in the English-language blue pages under Churches. Some services in English that are close to the San Juan tourist areas follow. Call to verify service times, as they may be subject to change.

S

Smoking

Smoking is banned in virtually all public areas. The law doesn't allow

Public Holidays

New Year's Day January 1
Three Kings Day January 6
Eugenio María de Hostos Birthday Second Monday in January
Martin Luther King, Jr Day Third Monday in January
Presidents' Day Third Monday in February
Emancipation Day March 22
Good Friday March/April
José de Diego Day Third Monday in April
Memorial Day Last Monday in May
US Independence Day July 4

Luis Muñoz Rivera Day Third Monday in July
Puerto Rico's Constitution Day July 25
José Celso Barbosa Day July 27
Labor Day First Monday in September
Columbus Day Second Monday in October
Veterans' Day November 11
Discovery of Puerto Rico Day November 19
Thanksgiving Day Fourth Thursday in November
Christmas Day 25 December

businesses to designate areas for smokers. Smoking is prohibited in restaurants, bars, casinos, clubs, pubs, and liquor stores. It is also not permitted in businesses dedicated to the sale of food, public buildings and transportation vehicles, convention centers, shopping malls, and outdoor cafés (if an employee takes an order there), among other places.

People may smoke in areas that are in the open air, out of work areas, in private homes, in vehicles when a child under the age of 13 is not present, and in freestanding tobacco shops. Fines for violating the law start at $250 for individuals for the first offence and even $2,000 for a repeated offence.

Smoking is also prohibited in hotel common areas. Check with your hotel for individual smoking policy in rooms.

T

Tax

Puerto Rico has a 6 percent commonwealth sales and use tax and municipalities also charge

an additional sales tax of up to 1 percent (together: 7 percent). The sales tax is applicable to jewelry, electronics, rental vehicles, and most goods and services. Medical services, prescription medicine, products derived from petroleum, and non-processed foods are exempt from the tax. Other groceries are subject to the sales tax. There are additional taxes on alcohol and cigarettes, though these are included in marked prices and do not appear as surcharges. An excise tax applies to incoming automobiles.

There is also a room tax in Puerto Rico, which varies according to type of accommodation and facilities. Hotels with casinos charge 11 percent, hotels without casinos, guesthouses and motels 9 percent, small inns such as *paradores* and short-term apartment or villa rentals 7 percent. Anything in excess of this has been levied by the hotel, there is no additional sales tax on hotel occupancy. San Juan hotels are especially notorious for adding on "taxes" that are actually service charges.

Telephones

International area codes for Puerto Rico are **787** and **939**. There are no regional dialing codes in Puerto Rico. International dialing codes:
Australia +61
Canada +1
Ireland +353
New Zealand +64
South Africa +27
UK +44
US +1

Coin-operated telephones are common and cost about 50¢ for local calls, depending on the particular pay phone. For calls to the US and Canada, dial 1, then the area code, then the number. An operator will tell

Puerto Ricans are predominantly Roman Catholics.

Time Zone

Atlantic Time Zone, four hours behind GMT and one hour ahead of Eastern Standard Time.

you how much money to deposit.

Puerto Rico's links with the US mean that there is a high rate of phone ownership and nearly everybody has a mobile/cellular phone. The island does not have the same concentration of fixed lines and broadband uptake as in the US, but mobile phones continue to proliferate. The Puerto Rico Telephone Company (PRTC) dominates local calls but the long-distance and mobile markets are more diverse. AT&T Mobility has the largest number of subscribers, followed by Claro.

If you wish to place a call through an operator, dial "0." Directions are usually printed on the phone, and are always printed in the first pages of the phone directory.

The phone directories in Puerto Rico are in Spanish, with a special wine-and-blue-colored section in English providing commercial and government telephone numbers and giving translations of the Spanish headings under which information can be found.

Telegraph facilities are available through Western Union or Telex. Western Union telegraphs (tel: 800-325-4045) and cash transfers arrive at food stores of the Pueblo chain.

Tourist Information

Visitors may pick up free publications that provide useful information on places to go, sights to see, history, and general information about the island. Most readily available are ¡Qué Pasa! (www.quepasa.pr), the official magazine of the Puerto Rico Tourism Company, the Puerto Rico Hotel and Tourism Association's Bienvenidos (www.bienvenidospuertorico.net) and Places to Go. These are usually found at the larger hotels and tourist offices.

The Puerto Rico Tourism Company has its main office at:
La Puntilla Building, 2 Paseo de La Princesa, Old San Juan
Tel: 787-721-2400
Toll free: 1-800-866-7827

Tourists may also get information at:
Ochoa Building, 500 Tanca Street, Old San Juan
Tel: 787-721-2400, ext. 3901

There is a Tourism Company Information Center at the Luis Muñoz Marín International Airport, on the first level of concourse C (tel: 787-721-2400, ext. 5216).

Tourist Offices Abroad

On the US mainland, call the Puerto Rico Tourism Company at 800-223-6530 (toll-free). Offices are located in Florida, tel: 800-815-7391, ext 10, and Los Angeles, tel: 800-874-1230, ext 10.
Outside the United States:
Canada
230 Richmond Street West, Suite 902, Toronto ON M5V 1V6
Tel: 416-368-2680
Email: sunny@prtourismcanada.com
UK
c/o Hills Balfour, 58 Southwark Bridge Road, London SE1 0AS
Tel: 020-7593 1700
Email: puertorico@hillsbalfour.com

Websites

www.seepuertorico.com
This is the official website of the Puerto Rico Tourism Company giving a brief overview of sights and things to do while in Puerto Rico.
www.meetpuertorico.com
The Puerto Rico Convention Bureau's website for anyone planning or attending a conference at the Convention Center.
www.prhta.org
Puerto Rico Hotel and Tourism Association has lots of tourist information and related issues such as "green" developments in hotels.
www.puertoricosmallhotels.com
Information on small, out of the way places to stay.
www.topuertorico.org
A broad-ranging website with island information and city guides.
www.puertorico.com
Lots of information on the island and businesses involved in tourism and hospitality.
www.touroldsanjuan.com
All the necessary information about Old San Juan.
www.enchanted-isle.com, www.viequesisland.com
Everything you need to know about Vieques.
www.culebra-island.com, www.culebra.org
Two sites with information on where to stay, eat, and play on Culebra.

Tour Operators

Tour Operators
Ecoquest Adventures and Tours
Tel: 787-616-7543
www.ecoquestpr.com
Specializes in organizing adventures

and tours that include ziplining, rappeling, hiking, and kayaking. Exciting action tours include pristine river hikes, rapplling, and ziplining across canyons with scenic views of rivers and waterfalls.
Pure Adventure Puerto Rico
Tel: 787-202-6551
www.pureadventurepr.com
This company offers a crash course in scuba diving, kayak adventures, bird watching expeditions, and more.

For certified divers, discover the excellent diving waters off Puerto Rico's eastern coast.
Travesías Isleñas Yaureibo, Inc.
Tel: 939-630-1267; 787-447-4104
www.viequesoutdoors.com
This company is owned and operated by bilingual Vieques natives, who guide visitors to explore the best Vieques has to offer: includes historical attractions, Bio Bay kayaking, and snorkeling.

Visas and Passports

No visa or passport is required for US citizens entering Puerto Rico from the United States.

Visitors and cruise passengers planning to go to other Caribbean islands, excluding the US Virgin Islands, must have a valid passport to return to US territory. Those with permanent residence, however, are advised to bring their green cards.

Foreign nationals must present the same documentation and papers required for entry into the continental US. The Visa Waiver Program (VWP) enables nationals of 37 participating countries (including Australia, Ireland, New Zealand, and the UK) to travel to the US for stays of 90 days or less without obtaining a visa. VWP travelers are required to have a valid authorization through the online Electronic System for Travel Authorization (ESTA) prior to travel and are screened at the port of entry into the US. See http://travel.state.gov for more details.

Weights and Measures

Throughout the island of Puerto Rico distances are measured in kilometers, but speed limits are indicated in miles.

Weight is measured in pounds and gas is sold in liters; most other things use the British imperial system.

LANGUAGE

UNDERSTANDING THE LANGUAGE

GENERAL

The language of Puerto Rico is Spanish. While it is by no means true that "everyone there speaks English," a majority of Puerto Ricans certainly do, especially in San Juan. Almost everyone in a public-service occupation will be able to help in either language.

The Puerto Rican dialect of Spanish resembles that of other Antillean islands, and differs from the Iberian dialect in its rapidity, phoneme quality, and elisions. For a more detailed look at this rich tongue, see page 81.

There are many excellent Spanish-English dictionaries for sale, but Barron's, edited at the University of Chicago, is particularly recommended for its sensitivity to the vocabulary and syntax of the Latin American idiom. Cristine Gallo's *The Language of the Puerto Rican Street* is an exhaustive lexicon of the kind of Puerto Rican slang that most dictionaries would blanch at printing.

BASIC RULES

Spanish is a phonetic language; words are pronounced exactly as they are spelled. Spanish distinguishes between the two genders, masculine and feminine, and the subjunctive verb form is an endless source of headaches for students.

Generally, the accent falls on the second-to-last syllable, unless it is otherwise marked with an accent (´) or the word ends in d, l, r, or z. Accents are also used in questions, so that *cuando*, when, becomes ¿*cuándo?* when?

Vowels in Spanish are always pronounced the same way.

Vowels

a as in bat
e as in bed
i as in feet
o as in cot
u as in rude
ai,ay as in write
ei,ey as in eight
oi,oy as in toy

Consonants

Consonants are almost like those in English, the main exceptions being:
b and **v** are almost interchangeable and are pronounced as a cross between the English sounds except at the beginning of a word when they are pronounced 'b.'
c is hard before a, o, or u (as in English), and is soft before e or i, when it sounds like s. Thus, *censo* (census) sounds like senso.
g is hard before a, o, or u (as in English), but where English g sounds like j – before e or i – Spanish **g** sounds like a guttural h (similar to the Scottish loch); g before ua is often soft or silent, so that *agua* sounds more like awa, and Guadalajara like Wadalajara.
h is silent.
j sounds like the English h.
ll sounds like y, as in yellow, or the lli in million, but sometimes as the g in the English beige.
ñ sounds like the ni in onion, as in the familiar Spanish word *señor*.
q is followed by u as in English, but the combination sounds like k instead of like kw.
rr is rolled or trilled more than in English.
x between vowels sounds like a guttural h, as in México or Oaxaca, but in other locations can sound like x, s, sh, or j.

y alone, as the word meaning "and," is pronounced ee.
z as in the English sip.

Note that **ch, ll, and ñ** are separate letters of the Spanish alphabet; if looking in a phone book or dictionary for a word beginning with ch, you will find it after the final c entry. A name or word beginning with ll will be listed after the l entry and ñ after the final n entry.

When addressing someone you are not familiar with, use the more formal *usted*. The informal *tú* is reserved for relatives, children, and friends.

WORDS AND PHRASES

Hello Hola
How are you? ¿Cómo está usted?
How much is it? ¿Cuánto es?
What is your name? ¿Cómo se llama usted?
My name is... Yo me llamo...
Do you speak English? ¿Habla inglés?
I am British/American Yo soy británico/norteamericano
I don't understand No entiendo
Please speak more slowly Hable más despacio, por favor
Can you help me? ¿Me puede ayudar?
I am looking for... Estoy buscando...
Where is...? ¿Dónde está...?
I'm sorry Lo siento/Perdón
I don't know No sé
No problem No hay problema
Have a good day Que tenga un buen día
That's it Eso es
Here it is Aquí está
There it is Allí está
Let's go Vámonos
See you tomorrow Hasta mañana
See you soon Hasta pronto
See you later Hasta luego
Show me the word in the book Muéstreme la palabra en el libro
At what time? ¿A qué hora?

TRANSPORTATION

EATING OUT

ACTIVITIES

A – Z

LANGUAGE

When? ¿Cuándo?
yes sí
no no
please por favor
thank you (very much) (muchas) gracias
you're welcome de nada
excuse me con su permiso
OK bien
goodbye adiós
good evening/night buenas tardes/ noches
here aquí
there allí
today hoy
yesterday ayer
tomorrow mañana (note: mañana also means "morning")
now ahora
later después
right away ahora mismo
this morning esta mañana
this afternoon esta tarde
this evening esta tarde
tonight esta noche

ON ARRIVAL

I want to get off at... Quiero bajarme en...
Is there a bus to the museum? ¿Hay un autobus (una guagua) al museo?
What street is this? ¿Qué calle es esta?
How far is...? ¿A qué distancia está...?
airport aeropuerto
customs aduana
baggage claim reclamo de equipaje
suitcase maleta
train station estación de tren
bus station estación de autobuses/ guaguas
metro station estación de tren urbano
bus autobus/guagua
bus stop parada de guaguas
ticket boleto/taquilla
round-trip ticket boleto de ida y vuelta
hitchhiking auto-stop/pon
toilets servicios/baños
This is the hotel address Esta es la dirección del hotel
I'd like a (single/double) room Quiero una habitación (sencilla/doble)
... with shower con ducha
... with bath con baño
... with a view con vista
Does that include breakfast? ¿Incluye desayuno?
May I see the room? ¿Puedo ver la habitación?
washbasin lavabo
bed cama
key llave
elevator/lift ascensor/elevador
wheelchair silla de ruedas

stairs escaleras
wheelchair ramp rampa de impedidos
air conditioning aire acondicionado
internet connection conección a la red cibernética
trip viaje
business negocio
pleasure placer
vacation vacación

EMERGENCIES

Help! ¡Socorro!/¡Auxilio!
Stop! ¡Alto!/¡Pare!
Call a doctor Llame a un médico
Call an ambulance Llame a una ambulancia
Call the police Llame a la policía
Call the fire brigade Llame a los bomberos
Where is the nearest telephone? ¿Dónde está el teléfono más cercano?
Where is the nearest hospital? ¿Dónde está el hospital más cercano?
I am sick Estoy enfermo/a (male/ female)
I have lost my passport/purse (bag) He perdido mi pasaporte/cartera

ON THE ROAD

Where is the spare wheel? ¿Dónde está la rueda de repuesta?
Where is the nearest garage? ¿Dónde está el taller más cercano?
Our car has broken down Nuestro carro se ha dañado
I want to have my car repaired Quiero que reparen mi carro
It's not your right of way Usted no tiene prioridad/derecho de paso
I think I must have put diesel in my car by mistake Me parece haber echado combustible de motor diesel por error
the road to... la carretera a...
left izquierda
right derecha
straight on derecho
far lejos
near cerca
opposite frente a
beside al lado de
parking lot estacionamiento
over there por allí
at the end al final
town map mapa de la ciudad
road map mapa de carreteras
street calle
square plaza
give way ceda el paso
exit salida
dead end calle sin salida
wrong way va contra el tránsito

no parking prohibido estacionar/no estacione
expressway autopista
toll highway autopista/expreso
toll peaje
tire goma/llanta
speed limit límite de velocidad
gasoline station gasolinera
gasoline gasolina
unleaded sin plomo
diesel diesel
water/oil agua/aceite
air aire
puncture pinchazo
bulb bombilla
lights luces
breaks freno

ON THE TELEPHONE

How do I make an outside call? ¿Cómo hago una llamada al exterior?
What is the area code? ¿Cuál es el código de área?
I want to make an international (local) call Quiero hacer una llamada internacional (local)
I'd like a wake-up call for 8 tomorrow morning Quiero que me despierten a las ocho de la mañana
Hello? ¿Díga?/¡Aló!
Who's calling? ¿Quién llama?
Hold on, please Un momento, por favor
I can't hear you No le oigo
Can you hear me? ¿Me oye?
He/she is not here Él/ella no está aquí
The line is busy La línea está ocupada
I must have dialed the wrong number Debo haber marcado un número equivocado

SHOPPING

Where is the nearest bank? ¿Dónde está el banco más cercano?
I'd like to buy Quiero comprar
How much is it? ¿Cuánto es?
Do you accept credit cards? ¿Aceptan tarjetas de crédito?
Can I pay with a check/cheque? ¿Puedo pagar con cheque?
I'm just looking Sólo estoy mirando
Have you got...? ¿Tiene...?
I'll take it Me lo llevo
I'll take this one/that one Me llevo este/ese
What size is it? ¿Que talla es?
size (clothes) talla
small pequeño
large grande
cheap barato
expensive caro
enough suficiente
too much demasiado

a piece una pieza
each cada uno/la pieza/la unidad
bill la factura (shop), la cuenta (restaurant)
bank banco
bookshop librería
pharmacy farmacia
hairdressers peluquería
post office correo
department store tienda por departamentos
closed cerrado
open abierto
on holiday feriado
business hours horas de oficina

Market Shopping

Supermarkets (supermercados) are self-service, but often the best and freshest produce is to be had at the town market (mercado) or the street market (mercadillo).
Prices are usually by the pound (por libra) or by the unit (por unidad).
fresh fresco
frozen congelado
organic orgánico
basket cesta/canasta
bag bolsa
bakery panadería
butcher's carnicería
cake shop repostería/pastelería
fishmonger's pescadería
grocer's verdurería
tobacconist tabaquero/estanquero
thriftshop tienda de segunda mano

SIGHTSEEING

mountain montaña
hill colina
valley valle
river río
lake lago
lookout mirador
old town casco antiguo
monastery monasterio
convent convento
cathedral catedral
church iglesia
palace palacio
hospital hospital
town hall alcaldía
nave nave
statue estatua
fountain fuente
tower torre
castle castillo
Iberian ibérico
Phoenician fenicio
Roman romano
Moorish moro
Romanesque románico
Gothic gótico
museum museo
art gallery galería de arte

exhibition exposición
tourist information office oficina de turismo
free gratis
admission/admission fee entrada/precio de entrada
every day diario/todos los días
all day todo el día
swimming pool piscina
to book reservar

DINING OUT

breakfast desayuno
lunch comida/almuerzo
dinner cena
meal comida
snack merienda
appetizer aperitivo
first course primer plato
main course plato principal, entrada
dessert postre
drink included bebida incluída
wine list carta de vinos
the bill la cuenta
fork tenedor
knife cuchillo
spoon cuchara
plate plato
glass vaso
wine glass copa
napkin servilleta
ashtray cenicero
straw sorbeto
Waiter, please! ¡Camarero, por favor!
coffee café
...black negro
...with milk con leche
...decaffeinated descafeinado
sugar azúcar
tea té
herbal tea infusión
milk leche
mineral water agua mineral
...fizzy con gas
...non-fizzy sin gas
juice (fresh) jugo (natural)
beer cerveza
soft drink refresco
with ice con hielo
wine vino
red wine vino tinto
white blanco
rosé rosado
dry seco
sweet dulce
house wine vino de la casa
sparkling wine vino espumoso
Where is this wine from? ¿De dónde es este vino?
Cheers! ¡Salud!

TABLE TALK

I am a vegetarian Soy vegetariano
I am on a diet Estoy a dieta

What do you recommend? ¿Qué recomienda?
Do you have local specialties? ¿Hay especialidades locales?
I'd like to order Quiero pedir
That is not what I ordered Ésto no es lo que pedí
May I have more wine? ¿Me da más vino?
Enjoy your meal Buen provecho
That was delicious Eso estuvo delicioso/sabroso/rico

MENU DECODER

Breakfast and Snacks

azúcar sugar
bocadillo sandwich in a bread roll
bollo bun/roll
jalea/mermelada/confitura jam
huevos eggs
...cocidos boiled, cooked
...fritos fried
...revueltos scrambled
tocineta bacon
mantequilla butter
pan bread
integral whole wheat/wholemeal
avena oatmeal
pimienta black pepper
sal salt
sandwich sandwich in square slices of bread
tostada toast
yogúr yoghurt

Main Courses

Carne/Meat

cabrito kid
carne picada ground meat
cerdo pork
chorizo paprika-seasoned sausage
chuleta chop
conejo rabbit
cordero lamb
costilla rib
cuerito roast suckling pig's skin
entrecot beef rib steak
filete steak
jamón ham
jamón cocido cooked ham
jamón serrano cured ham
lechón asado roast suckling pig
lengua tongue
lomo loin
morcilla black pudding
rez beef
riñones kidneys
salchichón sausage
sesos brains
solomillo fillet steak
ternera veal or young beef
a la brasa/parilla charcoal-grilled
a la plancha grilled

al horno/asado **roast**
bien cocido **well done**
en salsa **in sauce**
frito **fried**
guisado **stew**
parrillada **mixed grill**
pincho **skewer**
poco cocido **rare**
relleno **stuffed**
término medio **medium**

Pollo/Poultry

codorniz **quail**
faisán **pheasant**
pato **duck**
pavo **turkey**
perdiz **partridge**
pintada **guinea fowl**
pollo **chicken**

Pescado/Fish

almeja **clam**
anchoas **anchovies**
anguila **eel**
atún **tuna**
bacalao **cod**
besugo **sea bream**
boquerones **fresh anchovies**
caballa **mackerel**
calamar **squid**
camarones **shrimp**
cangrejo **crab**
caracol **sea snail**
carrucho **queen conch**
cazón **dogfish**
centollo **spider crab**
cigala **Dublin Bay prawn/scampi**
dorado **dolphin fish, mahi mahi**
fritura **mixed fry**
gamba **prawn**
jibia/chopito **cuttlefish**
jueyes **land crab**
langosta **spiny lobster**
langostino **large prawn**
lenguado **sole**
lubina/róbalo **sea bass**
mariscada **mixed shellfish**
mariscos **shellfish**
mejillón **mussel**
merluza **hake**
mero **grouper**
ostión **large oyster**
ostra **oyster**
pescadilla/pijota **small hake**
pez espada **swordfish**
pulpo **octopus**
rape monkfishrodaballo **turbot**
salmón **salmon**
salmonete **red mullet**
sardina **sardine**
trucha **trout**
tiburón **shark**
viera **scallop**

Vegetables/Cereals

ajo **garlic**
alcachofa **artichoke**
apio **celery**

arroz **rice**
berenjena **eggplant/aubergine**
cebolla **onion**
cereal **cereal**
champiñón/seta **mushroom**
coliflor **cauliflower**
crudo **raw**
ensalada **salad**
espárrago **asparagus**
espinaca **spinach**
garbanzo **chick pea**
guisante **pea**
haba **broad bean**
habichuela **bean**
habichuela colorada/roja **red bean**
judía **green bean**
lechuga **lettuce**
lenteja **lentil**
maíz **corn/maize**
papa **potato**
pepino **cucumber**
pimiento **pepper/capsicum**
puerro **leek**
rábano **radish**
repollo **cabbage**
tomate **tomato**
verduras **vegetables**
zanahoria **carrot**

Fruit and Desserts

aguacate **avocado**
albaricoque **apricot**
cereza **cherry**
china **orange**
ciruela **plum**
frambuesa **raspberry**
fresa **strawberry**
fruta **fruit**
granada **pomegranate**
guineo **banana**
higo **fig**
limón **lemon**
limón verde **lime**
mandarina **tangerine**
manzana **apple**
melocotón **peach**
melón **melon**
pasa **raisin**
pera **pear**
piña **pineapple**
plátano **plantain**
sandía **watermelon**
toronja **grapefruit**
uva **grape**
flan **caramel custard**
helado/mantecado **ice cream**
natilla **custard**
pastel **pie**
postre **dessert**
queso **cheese**
tarta/torta/bizcocho **cake**

NUMBERS, DAYS, AND DATES

0 cero
1 uno

2 dos
3 tres
4 cuatro
5 cinco
6 seis
7 siete
8 ocho
9 nueve
10 diez
11 once
12 doce
13 trece
14 catorce
15 quince
16 dieciséis
17 diecisiete
18 dieciocho
19 diecinueve
20 veinte
21 veintiuno
30 treinta
40 cuarenta
50 cincuenta
60 sesenta
70 setenta
80 ochenta
90 noventa
100 cien
200 doscientos
500 quinientos
1,000 mil
10,000 diez mil
1,000,000 un millón
week semana
weekday día de semana
weekend fin de semana
Monday lunes
Tuesday martes
Wednesday miércoles
Thursday jueves
Friday viernes
Saturday sábado
Sunday domingo
January enero
February febrero
March marzo
April abril
May mayo
June junio
July julio
August agosto
September septiembre
October octubre
November noviembre
December diciembre

WEATHER

sunny soleado
cloudy nublado
rain/rainy lluvia/lluvioso
humid húmedo
umbrella paraguas/sombrilla
storm tormenta
hurricane huracán
wind viento
waves olas

FURTHER READING

GENERAL

Emotional Bridges to Puerto Rico: Migration, Return Migration, and the Struggles of Incorporation (Perspectives on a Multiracial America), by Elizabeth M. Aranda.
None of the Above: Puerto Ricans in the Global Era (New Directions in Latino American Culture), edited by Frances Negrón Muntaner.
The Puerto Ricans: A Documentary History, by Kal Wagenheim and Olga Jiménez de Wagenheim.
Puerto Rico in the American Century: A History since 1898, by César J. Ayala and Rafael Bernabé
Puerto Rico: Island in the Sun, by Roger A. LaBrucherie.
Puerto Rico Mio, Four Decades of Change, photographs by Jack Delano.
Taíno Revival: Critical Perspectives on Puerto Rican Identity and Cultural Politics, by Gabriel Haslip-Viera.
The Taínos: Rise and Decline of the People Who Greeted Columbus, by Irving Rouse.
When I was Puerto Rican, by Esmeralda Santiago.
Witchcraft and Welfare: Spiritual Capital and the Business of Magic in Modern Puerto Rico, by Raquel Romberg.

FICTION

Eccentric Neighborhoods, by Rosario Ferré.
Macho Camacho's Beat, by Luis Rafael Sánchez.
The Meaning of Consuelo, by Judith Ortiz Cofer.

Ojos de Luna, by Yolanda Arroyo Pizarro.
Reclaiming Medusa: Short Stories by Contemporary Puerto Rican Women, edited by Diana Vélez.
True and False Romances, by Anna Lydia Vega.

CUISINE

Puerto Rican Cookery, by Carmen Aboy Valldejuli.
Puerto Rican Cuisine in America, by Oswald Rivera.
Puerto Rican Dishes, by Berta Cabanillas and Carmen Ginorio.
Puerto Rico True Flavors, by Wilo Benet.
Rice and Beans and Tasty Things: A Puerto Rican Cookbook, by Dora Pomano.
The Spirit of Puerto Rican Rum: Recipes and Recollections, by Blanche Gelabert.

ARTS, CUSTOMS, AND SOCIAL

Contemporary Puerto Rican Installation Art: The Guagua Aerea, the Trojan Horse, and the Termite, by Laura Roulet.
Divided Borders: Essays on Puerto Rican Identity, by Juan Flores.
Taíno: Pre-Columbian Art and Culture from the Caribbean, by Ricardo Alegría and José Arrom.

OTHER INSIGHT GUIDES

Insight Guides cover nearly 200 destinations, providing information on culture and all the top sights, as well as superb photography. *Insight Guide Caribbean* covers the Lesser Antilles, while *Insight Guide Caribbean Cruises* covers ports of call throughout the region. Other guides to the region include Insight Guides *Belize; Costa Rica; Cuba;* and *Guatemala, Belize and the Yucatán;* and *Mexico.*

Send Us Your Thoughts

We do our best to ensure the information in our books is as accurate and up-to-date as possible. The books are updated on a regular basis using local contacts, who painstakingly add, amend and correct as required. However, some details (such as telephone numbers and opening times) are liable to change, and we are ultimately reliant on our readers to put us in the picture.

We welcome your feedback, especially your experience of using the book "on the road". Maybe we recommended a hotel that you liked (or another that you didn't), or you came across a great bar or new attraction we missed.

We will acknowledge all contributions, and we'll offer an Insight Guide to the best letters received.

Please write to us at:
Insight Guides
PO Box 7910
London SE1 1WE
Or email us at:
hello@insightguides.com

CREDITS

Photo Credits

akg images 36
Alamy 5MR, 27, 66, 70/71T, 71BL, 72, 73, 75, 78/79T, 79TR, 106B, 186, 222, 231, 234, 236
AWL Images 26, 138, 178
Bigstock 5ML
Bill Wassman/Apa Publications 111T, 134BR, 135ML, 161, 169, 189T, 201T, 220, 224T
Camera Press 76
Corbis 6BL, 10/11, 16, 20, 21, 46, 47, 54, 61, 71BR, 146/147
Dreamstime 5TR
Fotolia 135BR, 192BL, 193TR
Getty Images 7BR, 7MR, 22/23, 25, 28L, 49, 52, 64, 78BR, 83, 85, 86, 87, 88, 108, 117, 119, 120/121, 125, 127, 129, 133, 145, 150/151, 166T, 168, 170, 209, 230B, 261
Glyn Genin/Apa Publications 4MR, 4BL, 4BR, 5BR, 5ML, 14, 15T, 15B,

17, 19, 30, 34, 42, 56/57, 59, 62, 65, 67, 68, 69, 70BL, 71ML, 71TR, 74, 77, 78BL, 81, 82, 84, 90/91, 96, 97T, 97B, 104, 105, 106T, 107, 111B, 114, 115, 116, 118, 128, 130, 131T, 131B, 132, 134BL, 134MR, 136/137, 139, 140, 141T, 143T, 143B, 148, 149, 152, 153, 156, 157, 158/159, 160, 162, 163, 164, 165, 166B, 167, 171T, 171B, 173T, 173B, 174, 175, 176/177, 179, 181, 184, 185, 187, 188, 189B, 190, 192/193T, 192BR, 193ML, 193BL, 194/195, 196, 197, 199, 200T, 200B, 201B, 203, 204, 205, 206, 208, 211, 212/213, 214, 215, 219, 221B, 221T, 223, 225, 226/227, 228, 229, 230T, 233, 235, 237, 238, 239, 240, 241, 243, 245, 246, 247, 248, 249, 250T, 251, 252, 254, 256, 258, 259, 260, 262, 263, 265

Hilton Hotels & Resorts 126
iStock 1, 2/3, 4ML, 5TL, 6M, 7T, 53, 55, 58, 60, 63, 92/93, 94/95, 102, 103, 109, 110, 122, 123, 134/135T, 141B, 193BR, 210, 253, 269
Jorge Collazo 89
Jose Oquendo 70BR
Library of Congress 51
NOAA 191
Pictures Colour Library 28R, 29
Private archive 135TR
Public domain 24, 33, 35, 37, 38, 39, 40, 41, 43, 44
Reuteurs 79BR
Robert Harding 48, 79BL, 79ML, 112, 144, 155, 172, 224B
Scala Archives 31
Shutterstock 6BL
SuperStock 8/9, 12/13, 183, 207
The Art Archive 32

Cover Credits

Front cover: San Juan street *Getty Images*
Back cover: (top) Playa Flamenco *iStock*; (middle) mask *Glyn Genin/ Apa Publications*

Front flap: (from top) Luquillo *Glyn Genin/Apa Publications*; Ponce firestation *Glyn Genin/Apa Publications*; folk art *Glyn Genin/ Apa*; Arroz Con Gandules *iStock*

Back flap: La Mina Falls *Glyn Genin/ Apa Publications*
Spine: colonial door *iStock*

Insight Guide Credits

Distribution

UK
Dorling Kindersley Ltd
A Penguin Group company
80 Strand, London, WC2R 0RL
sales@uk.dk.com

United States
Ingram Publisher Services
1 Ingram Boulevard, PO Box 3006,
La Vergne, TN 37086-1986
ips@ingramcontent.com

Australia and New Zealand
Woodslane
10 Apollo St, Warriewood,
NSW 2102, Australia
info@woodslane.com.au

Worldwide
Apa Publications GmbH & Co. Verlag
KG (Singapore branch)
7030 Ang Mo Kio Avenue 5
08-65 Northstar @ AMK
Singapore 569880
apasin@singnet.com.sg

Printing
CTPS-China
First Edition 1987
Sixth Edition 2015

www.insightguides.com

Project Editor
Rachel Lawrence
Author
Magdalena Helsztyńska
Update Production
AM Services
Picture Editor
Tom Smyth
Map Production
Original cartography Berndtson &
Berndtson, updated by Carte
Production
Rebeka Davies and Aga Bylica

Legend

City maps
Freeway/Highway/Motorway
Divided Highway
Main Roads
Minor Roads
Pedestrian Roads
Steps
Footpath
Railway
Funicular Railway
Cable Car
Tunnel
City Wall
Important Building
Built Up Area
Other Land
Transport Hub
Park
Pedestrian Area
Bus Station
Tourist Information
Main Post Office
Cathedral/Church
Mosque
Synagogue
Statue/Monument
Beach
Airport

Regional maps
Freeway/Highway/Motorway (with junction)
Freeway/Highway/Motorway (under construction)
Divided Highway
Main Road
Secondary Road
Minor Road
Track
Footpath
International Boundary
State/Province Boundary
National Park/Reserve
Marine Park
Ferry Route
Marshland/Swamp
Glacier   Salt Lake
Airport/Airfield
Ancient Site
Border Control
Cable Car
Castle/Castle Ruins
Cave
Chateau/Stately Home
Church/Church Ruins
Crater
Lighthouse
Mountain Peak
Place of Interest
Viewpoint

Contributors

This new edition was commissioned
and edited by **Rachel Lawrence**,
Insight's Americas editor. It was
thoroughly updated by **Magdalena
Helsztyńska** and builds on earlier
editions produced by **Eleonora
Abreau-Jiménez**, **Tad Ames**, **Barbara
Balletto**, **Christopher Caldwell**,
Susan Charneco, **Adam Cherson**,
Natalia de Cuba Romero, **Sarah

Ellison Caldwell, **Susan Hambleton**,
Angelo López, **Larry Luxner**, **Hanne-
Maria Maijala**, **Ebedet Negrón**,
Kathleen O'Connell, **Gabrielle
Paese**, **Webster** and **Robert Stone**,
and **Gerry Tobin**.
  Many of the photographs were
taken by Insight regular **Glyn Genin**,
who captured the beauty of the
island and its people.

About Insight Guides

Insight Guides have more than
40 years' experience of publishing
high-quality, visual travel guides. We
produce 400 full-colour titles, in both
print and digital form, covering more
than 200 destinations across the
globe, in a variety of formats to meet
your different needs.
  Insight Guides are written by
local authors, whose expertise is
evident in the extensive historical
and cultural background features.

Each destination is carefully
researched by regional experts to
ensure our guides provide the very
latest information. All the reviews
in **Insight Guides** are independent;
we strive to maintain an impartial
view. Our reviews are carefully
selected to guide you to the best
places to eat, go out and shop, so
you can be confident that when
we say a place is special, we really
mean it.

INDEX

Main references are in bold type

INSIGHT GUIDES

INSPIRING YOUR NEXT ADVENTURE

Insight Guides offers you a range of travel guides
to match your needs. Whether you are looking for
inspiration for planning a trip, cultural information,
walks and tours, great listings, or practical advice, we
have a product to suit you.